Diving & Snorkeling Philippines

Heneage Mitchell

LONELY PLANET PUBLICATIONS
Melbourne • Oakland • London • Paris

Diving & Snorkeling Philippines
- A Lonely Planet Pisces Book

1st Edition – January 2002

Published by
Lonely Planet Publications Pty Ltd, ABN 36 005 607 983
90 Maribyrnong St., Footscray, Victoria 3011, Australia

Other offices
150 Linden Street, Oakland, California 94607, USA
10a Spring Place, London NW5 3BH, UK
1 rue du Dahomey, 75011 Paris, France

Photographs
by photographers as indicated

Front cover photograph
Diver approaches sea fans at Canyons
(Puerto Galera, Mindoro), by Tim Rock

Back cover photographs
Cuttlefish, by Tim Rock
Diver peers through the *Tristar B* wreck
(Basterra Reef, Sulu Sea), by Robert Yin
Boracay, by Mark Daffey

Most of the images in this guide are available for licensing from **Lonely Planet Images**
www.lonelyplanetimages.com

ISBN 1 86450 364 5

dive site maps are Transverse Mercator projection

Printed by H&Y Printing Ltd., Hong Kong

Contents

Introduction 9

Overview 11

History 11
Geography 13

Practicalities 15

Climate 15
Language 15
Getting There 16
Gateway City – Manila 16
Getting Around 17
Entry 19
Money 19
Time 20
Electricity 20
Weights & Measures 20
What to Bring 20
Underwater Photography 21
Business Hours 22
Accommodations 22
Dining & Food 22
Shopping 23

Activities & Attractions 24

Luzon 24
Mindoro 25
The Visayas 26
Mindanao 29
Palawan 29

Diving Health & Safety 31

Pre-Trip Preparation 31
Recompression Facilities 32
DAN 33

Diving in the Philippines 34

Snorkeling 35
Dive Training & Certification 36
Live-Aboard Diving 36

Luzon Dive Sites 40

La Union 40

1 Fagg Reef 42
2 Red Buoy 43
3 Black Buoy 44
4 VOA Reef 45
5 Research Reef 45

Subic Bay 46

6 *Oryoku Maru* (The Hell Ship) 48
7 USS *New York* 49

8 *El Capitan* 50
9 *San Quintin* 51

Anilao **51**

10 Cathedral Rock 53
11 Sombrero Island 54
12 Bajura 55
13 Sepok Wall 56
14 Mapating 56
15 Caban Cove 57
16 Mainit 57
17 Hot Springs 58

Mindoro Dive Sites **60**

18 Talipanan Reef 63
19 Manila Channel (Northwest Channel) 64
20 Coral Gardens (The Hill) 65
21 Big La Laguna Beach 65
22 Monkey Beach 66
23 Ernie's Cave 67
24 West Escarceo 67
25 Hole in the Wall 68
26 Shark Cave 69
27 Pink Wall & Canyons 69
28 Sinandigan Wall 70
29 Washing Machine 70
30 Verde Island Wall 71

Sibuyan Sea Dive Sites **72**

31 MV *Mactan* 73
32 Banton Big Rock Coral Garden 74
33 Banton Northwest Wall 74
34 Banton Southeast Wall 75

The Visayas Dive Sites **76**

Boracay **76**

35 Cathedral Cave 78
36 Yapak 78
37 Punta Bonga 1 & 2 79
38 Friday's Rock 80
39 Crocodile Island 80
40 Laurel Island 81
41 Nasog Point 83
42 Dog Drift 83

Malapascua Island **84**

43 Wreck of the *Doña Marilyn* 85
44 Gato Island 86
45 Monad Shoal 87
46 Capitancillo Island 89

Mactan Island & Cebu City **89**

47 Tambuli Fish-Feeding Station 91
48 Kon Tiki House Reef 92
49 Marigondon Cave 93

Moalboal **93**
50 Copton Point 95
51 Panagsama Beach (House Reef) 95
52 Pescador Island 96
53 Tongo Point 97
54 Sunken Island 98
Dumaguete **98**
55 Sumilon Island 100
56 Liloan 101
57 Tacot 101
58 Calong Calong 102
59 Apo Island 103
Bohol **104**
60 Cabilao Island 105
61 Napaling 107
62 Tangnan Wall 108
63 Balicasag 108
64 Kalipayan (Happy Wall) 110
65 Arco Point (Hole in the Wall) 110
66 Cervera Shoal 111
67 Pamilacan Island 111
Southern Leyte **112**
68 Max Climax Wall & Baluarte 113
69 Tangkaan Point 113
70 Napantaw Fish Sanctuary 114
71 Peter's Mound 114
Mindanao Dive Sites **115**
Camiguin **116**
72 Agutaya Reef 117
73 Medina Underwater Springs 118
74 Jigdup Shoal 118
75 Punta Diwata 119
76 Cabuan Point 119
77 Sipaka Point 120
78 Constancia Reef 120
Davao **121**
79 Ligid Caves 123
80 Pinnacle Point 124
81 Pindawon Wall 124
82 Mushroom Rock 125
83 Marissa 1, 2 & 3 125
84 Malipano Japanese Wrecks 126
85 Linosutan Coral Gardens 126
General Santos City **127**
86 Maharlika Beach Resort 128
87 Tampuan (Tinoto Wall) 128
Sulu Sea Dive Sites **130**
88 *Jessie Beazley* 132
89 Tubbataha North 132

90 Tubbataha South . . . 134
91 Basterra North Reef . . . 135
92 Basterra South Wall . . . 136

Palawan Dive Sites 137

Coron 137
93 Apo Reef . . . 139
94 Hunter's Rock . . . 140
95 *Tae Maru* (Concepcion Wreck) . . . 141
96 *Akitsushima* (Flying Boat Tender) . . . 141
97 Lusong Gunboat . . . 142
98 *Olympia Maru* . . . 142
99 *Mamiya Maru* . . . 142
100 *Kogyu Maru* . . . 143
101 Tangat Wreck . . . 143
102 *Irako* . . . 144
103 Tangat Gunboat . . . 144
104 Black Island Wreck . . . 145
105 Dimakya Island . . . 145
106 Barracuda Lake . . . 146

El Nido 147
107 Dilumacad . . . 148
108 Inambuyod Boulders . . . 148
109 Tres Marias . . . 149
110 Miniloc Island . . . 149
111 Banayan Point . . . 150

Port Barton 150
112 Shark Point . . . 152
113 Middle Rock . . . 152
114 Royalist Shoal . . . 153
115 Ten Fathoms . . . 153
116 Wilson Head . . . 154
117 Black Coral . . . 154

Puerto Princesa & Environs 154
118 Verano Rocks (Twin Rocks) . . . 156
119 East Pandan . . . 156
120 Helen's Garden . . . 157
121 Henry's Reef . . . 157

Marine Life 158
Hazardous Marine Life . . . 161

Diving Conservation & Awareness 163
Responsible Diving . . . 164

Listings 166
Telephone Calls . . . 166
Diving Services . . . 166
Live-Aboards . . . 172
Tourist Offices . . . 173

Index 174

Author

Heneage Mitchell

Heneage Mitchell, a British national, has lived and dived in the Philippines for more than 20 years. In 1982, he became the first foreigner to own and operate a dive center in the Philippines (Aqua Tamyo Tropical Sports Center in Bauang, La Union). He has been a diving instructor since 1983 and is the vice president of CMAS-Philippines.

H, as he prefers to be called, has authored several books on diving in the Philippines and regularly contributes to various international magazines. He also edits and publishes *The Philippine Diver*—Asia's first English-language dive magazine, published three times a year since 1986 and now on the web at www.diver.com.ph.

H and his wife, Waree, recently launched the *Thai Diver and Resort Guide*, Thailand's first and only magazine dedicated to scuba diving. They now divide their time between Manila and Bangkok.

From the Author

As you leaf through this book you will quickly see that the Philippines, Southeast Asia's oldest dive destination, can also lay claim to being the region's most diverse, prolific and well-organized dive destination. If you've dived throughout the region, you already know that. If you haven't yet discovered the fabulous underwater world beneath the Philippines' seas, then a truly memorable experience awaits you.

Many people contributed to the creation of this guide. I'd like to take the opportunity to thank several of them. Apologies to those I may have inadvertently left out.

First, thanks are due to PADI Instructor and Course Director Bill "Bubbles" Burbridge of Seafari in Pattaya, Thailand, who taught me how to dive more years ago than either of us would probably care to remember. To PADI Course Director Tim Aukshun of Ocean Deep in Bauang, La Union. To the staff of *The Philippine Diver* magazine, particularly Ana Santos and Garry Chua. To Ralph Espino of Dive Buddies, Betty Sarmiento of Aquaventure, Frank Doyle of La Laguna Beach Club, Allan Nash of Asia Divers, Rio Cahambing of Southern Leyte, Karl Heinz-Epp of Savedra Divers and marine biologist Jay Maclean for their valuable input and review of the text. To Tim Rock for his fabulous photos and support. To my loving wife, Waree, for all the tea and hugs. And lastly but most sincerely, to the wonderful, warm-hearted Filipino people who, more than 22 years ago, generously welcomed me into their country, patiently put up with my grumpy foreign ways and made me feel so at home. *Mabuhay, at maraming salamat po sa inyo lahat!* (Aloha, and thanks very much to everyone!)

Contributing Photographers

Many photographers have captured the spirit of the Philippines and its colorful and vibrant marine world. Thanks to Gavin Anderson, Sammy L. Ang, John Borthwick, Mark Daffey, Veronica Garbutt, Sarah J. H. Hubbard, Richard I'Anson, John Pennock, Steve Rosenberg, Tim Rock, David Ryan, Grant Somers, Ted Streshinsky, Scott D. Tuason, Graham Tween, Eric L. Wheater and Robert Yin for supplying photos for this book.

From the Publisher

This first edition was published in Lonely Planet's U.S. office under the guidance of Roslyn Bullas, the Pisces Books publishing manager. Sarah J. H. Hubbard edited the text and photos with buddy checks from David Lauterborn and Pelin Ariner. Emily Douglas designed the cover and the book's interior. Navigating the nautical charts were cartographers Sara Nelson, Rachel Driver and Brad Lodge. U.S. cartography manager Alex Guilbert supervised map production. Lindsay Brown reviewed the Marine Life section for scientific accuracy. Portions of the text were adapted from Lonely Planet's *Philippines, Read This First: Asia* and www.lonelyplanet.com.

Pisces Pre-Dive Safety Guidelines

Before embarking on a scuba diving, skin diving or snorkeling trip, carefully consider the following to help ensure a safe and enjoyable experience:

- Possess a current diving certification card from a recognized scuba diving instructional agency (if scuba diving)
- Be sure you are healthy and feel comfortable diving
- Obtain reliable information about physical and environmental conditions at the dive site (e.g., from a reputable local dive operation)
- Be aware of local laws, regulations and etiquette about marine life and environment
- Dive at sites within your experience level; if possible, engage the services of a competent, professionally trained dive instructor or divemaster

Underwater conditions vary significantly from one region, or even site, to another. Seasonal changes can significantly alter site and dive conditions. These differences influence the way divers dress for a dive and what diving techniques they use.

There are special requirements for diving in any area, regardless of location. Before your dive, ask about environmental characteristics that can affect your diving and how trained local divers deal with these considerations.

Warning & Request

Things change—dive site conditions, regulations, topside information. Nothing stays the same for long. Your feedback on this book will be used to help update and improve the next edition. Excerpts from your correspondence may appear in *Planet Talk,* our quarterly newsletter, or *Comet,* our monthly email newsletter. Please let us know if you do not want your letter published or your name acknowledged.

Correspondence can be addressed to:
Lonely Planet Publications
Pisces Books
150 Linden Street
Oakland, CA 94607
email: pisces@lonelyplanet.com

Introduction

ERIC L. WHEATER

The Philippines—a tropical nation of 7,107 islands (at high tide)—lies north of Indonesia and southeast of China, bounded by the South China Sea to the west and the Pacific Ocean to the east. Within the boundaries of the Philippines are several smaller bodies of water, including the Sibuyan Sea, the Sulu Sea and the Visayan Sea. Each of these has unique characteristics and biospheres, making for a vast diversity of attractions both underwater and topside.

Despite decades of ambivalent press, notoriously unpredictable political spasms, natural disasters and a less-well-developed infrastructure than many of its Southeast Asian neighbors, the Philippines has much to offer travelers. The country's amazingly varied people and cultures reflect its diverse landscape, which encompasses verdant rice terraces, active volcanoes, underground rivers, startling hills, tropical rainforests and, of course, spectacular coral-fringed islands.

The Philippines' sport-diving industry is among the earliest founded. Since the nation's first dive center, Aquatropical, opened its doors for business in Anilao in

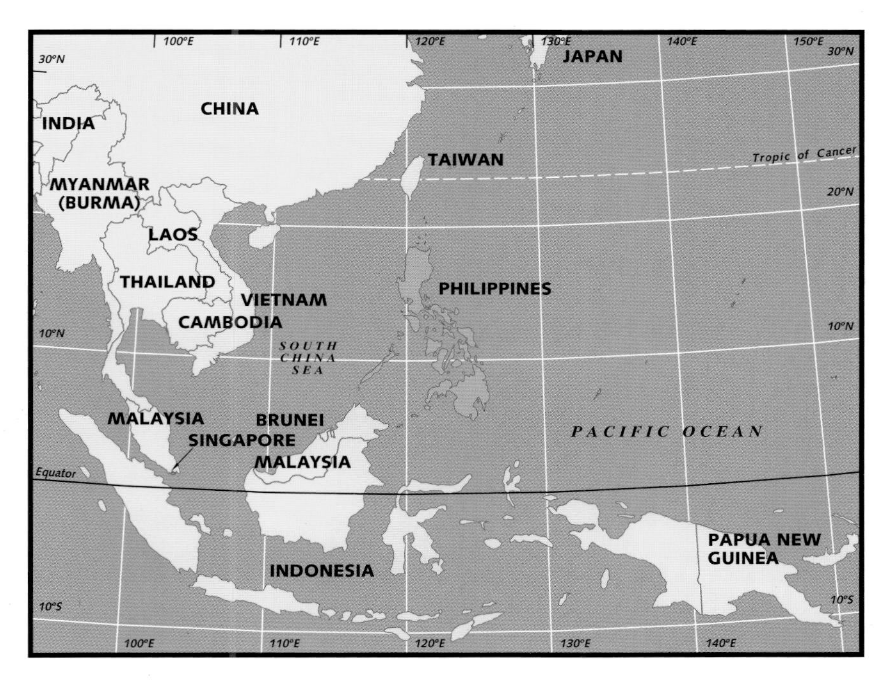

1966, the Philippines has attracted divers from around the world. Today, hundreds of dive centers scattered throughout the islands enable divers to access countless fantastic dive sites.

From shallow shore dives to remote seamounts accessed only by live-aboards, the Philippines offers varied diving conditions. Marine life ranges from tiny colorful nudibranchs to giant whale sharks, with thousands of species of vertebrates and invertebrates decorating the country's reefs, wrecks and walls. At some sites, brisk currents sweep divers over lush soft corals, while at others you can snorkel lazily at the surface as tropical fish flit amid the shallow hard corals below you. No matter what your interests or budget, the wide variety of resorts, hotels, live-aboard boats and dive centers around the country will help you find what you're looking for both above and below the waterline.

This book includes general descriptions of many popular dive sites, as well as some that are not as well known. Each site is described in terms of outstanding features and typical marine life, as well as depth, currents and other practical considerations. To help you make the most of your topside hours, this book also provides practical information about climate, language and culture, entry formalities, getting around, what to bring and more.

GRANT SOMERS

Boaters congregate as the sun sets over Negros Island, the Visayas.

Overview

JOHN BORTHWICK

The Philippines greeted the 21st century with a population estimated at more than 77 million people. About 60% of the populace lives in rural areas, though this figure is steadily falling as rural residents head for urban centers, such as Manila and Cebu City, and urban sprawl eats up formerly rural areas.

Ethnologically, the vast majority of Filipinos are related to Malaysians and Indonesians. Culturally, they are an amalgam of East and West, having long associations with China, Vietnam, Japan, the United States, Europe and India. When Spain took hold of the country in the 16th century, it introduced Catholicism into the culture. Today, with more than 90% of the population identifying themselves as Christian, the Philippines is the only predominantly Christian country in Asia. Muslim communities are thought to encompass about 5% of the population, predominantly in Mindanao and the Sulu Islands.

Travel Advisories

Safety can be an issue for travelers to the Philippines, with kidnappings of foreigners, bombing incidents and violence during political demonstrations making recent headlines. Though the security situation has generally improved in recent years and most of the country is hospitable to travel, rebel activity and armed banditry in certain areas of the Philippines (such as Mindanao) still pose potential security concerns. You can get up-to-date information and travel advisories from the U.S. Department of State (www.state.gov) and the Philippine Department of Tourism (www.tourism.gov.ph).

History

The first inhabitants of the Philippines arrived up to 300,000 years ago, probably migrating over a land bridge from the Asian mainland. The Negrito, or Aeta, arrived 25,000 years ago, but they were driven back by several waves of immigrants from Indonesia, followed by maritime immigrations of Malayan people. In AD 1380 the Arab-taught Makdum arrived in the Sulu archipelago and began to establish what became a powerful Islamic sphere of influence over the next hundred years.

Ferdinand Magellan arrived in 1521 and claimed the archipelago for Spain. Magellan was killed by local chiefs who quite naturally disapproved of this notion. Ruy Lopez de Villalobos followed in 1543 and named the territory Filipinas after

Philip II of Spain. Permanent Spanish occupation began in 1565, and by 1571 the entire country, except for the strictly Islamic Sulu archipelago, was under Spanish control.

JOHN BORTHWICK

Lapu-Lapu poised to deliver the fatal blow to Magellan, as depicted on a mural in Cebu.

A Filipino independence movement grew in the 19th century, and Filipinos fought on the side of the Americans in 1898 during the Spanish-American War. When the Spanish were defeated, General Aguinaldo declared the Philippines independent. The U.S., however, had other plans and promptly purchased the islands from the Spanish for US$20 million. The U.S. eventually recognized the Filipinos' desire for independence, and Manuel L. Quezon was sworn in as president of the Philippine Commonwealth in 1935 as part of a transitional phase pending full independence. Japan invaded the Philippines in 1942, brutally interrupting this process, and ruled until the U.S. reinvaded two years later. The Philippines received full independence in 1946.

Ferdinand Marcos was elected president in 1965, declared martial law in 1972 and ruled virtually as a dictator until 1986. His regime was attacked by both communist and Muslim guerrillas, and he was accused of ballot rigging and fraud. The assassination of prominent opposition figure Benigno Aquino in 1983 sparked massive antigovernment protests. A snap election in 1986 saw the opposition parties rally around Aquino's widow, Cory. Both parties claimed victory, but Aquino was widely believed to have polled the most votes. She initiated a program of nonviolent civil unrest, which resulted in Marcos fleeing the country.

Aquino reestablished the democratic institutions of the country, but failed to tackle economic problems or win over the military and the powerful Filipino elite. U.S. strategic influence in the country diminished following the 1991 Mt. Pinatubo eruption that destroyed the U.S. Clark Air Base and after the Philippine Senate refused to ratify the lease on the Subic Bay Naval Station. Aquino survived seven coups in six years and was succeeded by her defense minister, Fidel Ramos, in 1992. Ramos attempted to revitalize the economy, attract foreign investment, cleanse corruption and expand provision of utilities.

The Philippines government and the Moro National Liberation Front signed a peace accord in September 1996, ending, formally at least, the MNLF's 24-year struggle for autonomy in Mindanao. The peace agreement foresaw the MNLF being granted considerable autonomy in many of island's provinces. Peace in the area remains elusive, however, following the rise of a splinter group, the militant Moro Islamic Liberation Front (MILF), which opposes the agreement. The government continues to conduct military operations in MILF-held areas in Basilan and Sulu.

In 1998, Ramos was replaced as president by the Philippines' answer to Bruce Willis, Joseph Estrada. Estrada, a former movie star, promised a lot economically and delivered it—not to the general population, however, but into his own pocket. He was impeached and brought to trial in late 2000 on charges of taking bribes from gambling syndicates and using the proceeds to line his own dens and to build extravagant houses for his mistresses. When Estrada and his political allies tried to derail the trial by blocking prosecutors' access to his financial accounts, the people decided they'd had enough and staged mass demonstrations in the streets of Manila.

Estrada finally threw in the towel on January 19, 2001, and the next day his former vice president, Gloria Arroyo, was sworn in as the new president of the Philippines. In an inauguration speech that must have sounded eerily familiar to the people of the Philippines, Arroyo promised to wipe out poverty and corruption; she refused to grant Estrada amnesty for his crimes, instead intending to let the courts decide his fate.

Geography

The Philippines has a total landmass of more than 300,000 sq km (nearly 120,000 sq miles). Only about 1,000 islands are larger than 1 sq km (0.4 sq mile), only 2,000 of its islands are inhabited, and 2,500 aren't even named. Luzon and Mindanao are by far the largest islands and comprise roughly 66% of the country's area.

Many of the islands of the Philippines were formed though volcanic and tectonic activities. Seismic pressure and ancient volcanic eruptions have contributed to the extremely fertile nature of much of the country's soil. About half the country is under cultivation, and about a third remains forested, despite tree felling and slash-and-burn agriculture. The mountainous regions of northern Luzon are major producers of fruits and vegetables, and the flat, fertile, volcanic-ash-rich plains north of the capital, Manila, are known as the "rice bowl of the Philippines" for the abundant harvests gleaned from the region's ubiquitous rice paddies.

JOHN PENNOCK

The rice terraces of Banaue Valley were carved more than 2000 years ago.

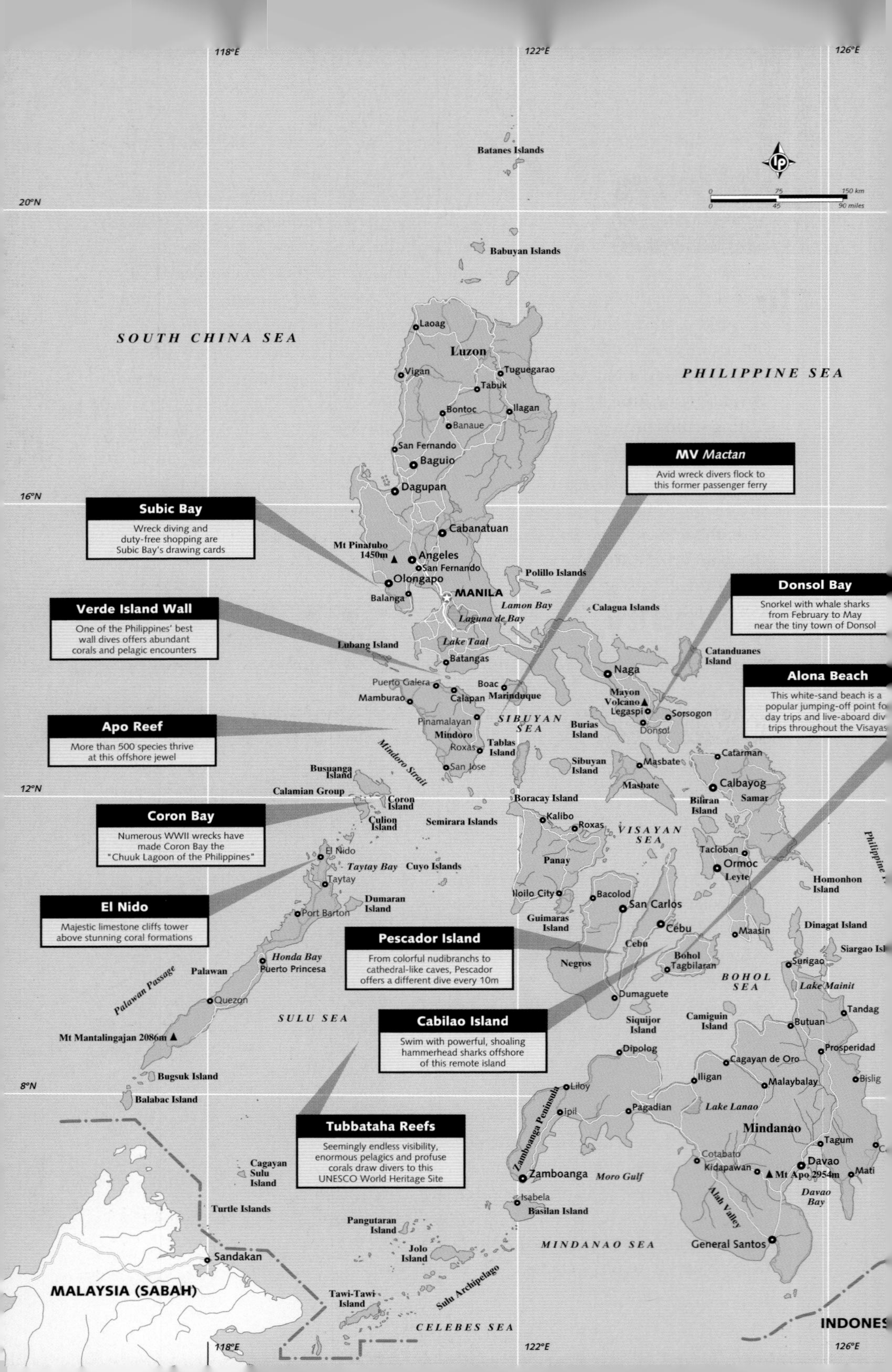

118°E
122°E
126°E
20°N
16°N
12°N
8°N
0
75
150 km
45
90 miles
SOUTH CHINA SEA
PHILIPPINE SEA
SULU SEA
SIBUYAN SEA
VISAYAN SEA
BOHOL SEA
MINDANAO SEA
CELEBES SEA
Subic Bay
Wreck diving and duty-free shopping are Subic Bay's drawing cards
MV Mactan
Avid wreck divers flock to this former passenger ferry
Verde Island Wall
One of the Philippines' best wall dives offers abundant corals and pelagic encounters
Donsol Bay
Snorkel with whale sharks from February to May near the tiny town of Donsol
Alona Beach
This white-sand beach is a popular jumping-off point fo day trips and live-aboard div trips throughout the Visayas
Apo Reef
More than 500 species thrive at this offshore jewel
Coron Bay
Numerous WWII wrecks have made Coron Bay the "Chuuk Lagoon of the Philippines"
El Nido
Majestic limestone cliffs tower above stunning coral formations
Pescador Island
From colorful nudibranchs to cathedral-like caves, Pescador offers a different dive every 10m
Cabilao Island
Swim with powerful, shoaling hammerhead sharks offshore of this remote island
Tubbataha Reefs
Seemingly endless visibility, enormous pelagics and profuse corals draw divers to this UNESCO World Heritage Site
Batanes Islands
Babuyan Islands
Laoag
Luzon
Vigan
Tuguegarao
Tabuk
Bontoc
Ilagan
Banaue
San Fernando
Baguio
Dagupan
Cabanatuan
Mt Pinatubo 1450m
Angeles
San Fernando
Olongapo
Balanga
MANILA
Polillo Islands
Lamon Bay
Calagua Islands
Laguna de Bay
Lake Taal
Lubang Island
Batangas
Catanduanes Island
Naga
Mayon Volcano
Legaspi
Sorsogon
Donsol
Puerto Galera
Boac
Marinduque
Mamburao
Calapan
Pinamalayan
Mindoro
Roxas
San Jose
Tablas Island
Burias Island
Sibuyan Island
Masbate
Masbate
Catarman
Calbayog
Samar
Biliran Island
Mindoro Strait
Busuanga Island
Calamian Group
Coron Island
Culion Island
Semirara Islands
Boracay Island
Kalibo
Roxas
Panay
Tacloban
Ormoc
Leyte
Philippine
Homonhon Island
El Nido
Taytay Bay
Cuyo Islands
Taytay
Dumaran Island
Iloilo City
Bacolod
San Carlos
Cebu
Cebu
Guimaras Island
Maasin
Dinagat Island
Port Barton
Siargao Isl
Honda Bay
Puerto Princesa
Palawan
Palawan Passage
Negros
Bohol
Tagbilaran
Surigao
Lake Mainit
Quezon
Dumaguete
Tandag
Siquijor Island
Camiguin Island
Butuan
Mt Mantalingajan 2086m
Dipolog
Prosperidad
Cagayan de Oro
Bugsuk Island
Iligan
Malaybalay
Bislig
Balabac Island
Liloy
Ipil
Pagadian
Lake Lanao
Zamboanga Peninsula
Mindanao
Tagum
Cotabato
Davao
Kidapawan
Mt Apo 2954m
Mati
Zamboanga
Moro Gulf
Davao Bay
Cagayan Sulu Island
Isabela
Basilan Island
Allah Valley
Turtle Islands
Pangutaran Island
General Santos
Jolo Island
Sandakan
MALAYSIA (SABAH)
Tawi-Tawi Island
Sulu Archipelago
INDONES

Practicalities

DAVID RYAN

Climate

The Philippines enjoys two seasons annually—the dry season (from November to May) and the rainy season (from June to October)—dictated by the shifting winds brought about by the *amihan* (northeast monsoon) and *hagabat* (southwest monsoon), respectively. Temperatures average 22°C (70°F), with the hottest months from March to May, when the temperature can soar to 34°C (95°F) or more. Humidity is usually around 70%. The coolest months are from December to February.

Sea conditions are affected by winds during either season, but are at their best between late February and early June throughout the archipelago. Though the protection afforded by mountain ranges and landmasses creates local weather patterns exclusive to specific areas, most dive regions have accessible dive sites year-round.

Avoid a Whirlwind Dive Trip

Typhoons—cyclones that are spawned as tropical storms in the Pacific Ocean—hit the Philippines an average of 18 times a year. The "typhoon belt," the region most severely affected by passing typhoons, encompasses the middle of the country (southern Luzon to the Visayas). Typhoons typically occur here between July and October, with long periods of relatively calm and balmy weather between storm systems.

These storms bring torrents of rain and devastating winds often in excess of 200km/hr (125mph), then usually blow out into the South China Sea and over to Vietnam or in the direction of Taiwan. In general, the later in the rainy season a typhoon appears, the stronger it is.

Obviously, diving in affected areas immediately before, during or in the immediate aftermath of a typhoon is neither practical nor recommended. Dangerous sea conditions, heavy rains, unpredictable tidal flows and limited visibility result from the passage of a typhoon. Usually the rains decrease and seas subside within a few days, but heavy flooding and infrastructural damage often impact travel to and from affected provinces.

Language

The geography and history of the Philippines have conspired to produce a multiplicity of languages. Though approximately 120 languages are officially recognized, more than 7,000 dialects are spoken throughout the country. The concept of a national language developed after the Spanish-American War in 1898, and Tagalog was declared the national language in 1936. Several other contenders for this role included Cebuano, Hiligaynon and Ilocano. A compromise reached in 1973 confirmed Pilipino as the national language, which is now spoken or understood by more than 40% of the population. Pilipino is based on Tagalog, but has linguistic elements of other Philippine languages. Despite this, English is the most widely spoken and understood language and remains the language of commerce and politics in the Philippines.

Getting There

Most visitors to the Philippines arrive by air. The most likely arrival point is Ninoy Aquino International Airport (NAIA) in Manila. A relatively small airport by international standards, NAIA is nonetheless a reasonably efficient facility served by most major international airlines. When departing the country, you'll need to pay the departure tax in cash, so keep a few hundred pesos handy.

Mactan-Cebu International Airport in Cebu is the country's second largest airport and is served by several airlines with flights from Malaysia, Singapore and Japan, as well as some international charter flights. Most domestic flights to the Visayas arrive here. Cebu is the jumping-off point for all central-Visayas destinations, with fast ferry connections or bus lines to almost anywhere in the region.

Gateway City – Manila

Most divers will not want to stay in Manila—the smog, appalling traffic, litter, anarchic shantytowns and armed guards everywhere can put off those unfamiliar with such scenes. If you prefer to pass on Manila's unobvious charms, many dive centers can arrange immediate transfers from the airport to your final destination. But Manila isn't such a bad place to spend a few days, once you get to know it.

GRAHAM TWEEN

You can see the ruins of General MacArthur's headquarters on Corregidor.

This city of some 8 million souls has a wide range of hotels and pension houses to suit all budgets, as well as some interesting shopping and entertainment options. You can play golf day or night near the old city wall at the centrally located Club Intramuros Golf Course, dine at a huge variety of restaurants featuring cuisine from around the world, visit Christian churches, Chinese temples and Moslem mosques and enjoy modern shopping malls with every amenity. You can even sail or cruise on Manila Bay, perhaps to the historic island of Corregidor, or just enjoy the famous sunset, spectacular in part because of the light refracting off the omnipresent clouds of pollution.

Play It Safe

In general, the Philippines is a safe place to travel. Crimes against foreigners usually target the unwary and the unprepared. Travelers are advised to exercise good judgment and remain aware of their surroundings. To avoid problems, follow a few general rules:

- Keep your bags with you and in view at all times.
- Never accept a drink from a stranger, a favorite ploy of drug-and-rob gangs.
- Never accept an invitation to join any form of gambling game—you *will* lose.
- If you're offered a very good exchange rate, you're probably being set up. Change money at banks or accredited exchange facilities.
- If you feel a taxi driver is overcharging you, and you want to dispute the fare, get out of the taxi and remove all your belongings before bringing the matter to the driver's attention.
- If it seems too good to be true, it is.

It is unusual for foreigners to be accosted by officials of the Philippine government, police or armed forces unless the foreigner is obviously behaving badly. If anyone claims to be an official, demands to see your ID or harasses you in any way (especially if they are not wearing a uniform), politely insist on seeing their ID.

Around Manila and in some other parts of the country, Tourist Police Stations are set up to help resolve visitors' complaints—in some cases they can and actually will help.

Getting Around

Traveling in the Philippines can be a nightmare if you don't take into consideration some of the annoying details that can end up ruining your vacation. For example, a passing typhoon can wreak havoc on a tight schedule, especially if you are trying to connect with international flights. Likewise, ferry schedules, although somewhat reliable, are prone to delays and even last-minute cancellations, even when the weather is perfect. If you are planning a provincial trip, allow time for the unexpected—in the rainy season, this may mean planning to leave an idyllic location for a somewhat less appealing but infinitely more practical location (such as Manila) a day or more in advance of your connecting flight.

Fortunately, when you want to go somewhere in the Philippines, you generally have more than one way of getting there. Although Manila has the country's only urban buses, an efficient network of inexpensive jeepneys, tricycles and minibuses service most islands, and taxis and rental cars are available at many destinations. Interisland travel options include planes, ferries, *banca* boats (outriggers) and even seaplanes and helicopters.

Bus prices are generally reasonable, but buses are not always air-conditioned, and legroom is at a premium. Stations are cacophonous, confusing and potentially dangerous places for the unwary—keep your bags with you at all times and treat with suitable cynicism anyone offering to guide you or carry your bags.

Jeepneys, the pride and joy of the Philippines, are still the main transport preference for many urban dwellers. They were originally fashioned out of reclaimed U.S. Army jeeps, but now come in a variety of shapes and sizes. These colorful vehicles follow prescribed routes for a fixed price (usually a few pesos), but stop to pick up and drop off passengers wherever they want—in the middle of the road, at traffic lights, on pedestrian crossings. These "kings of the road" are apparently exempt from traffic laws, despite featuring in most accidents and incidents throughout Metro Manila. They are noisy, spew great clouds of noxious diesel fumes, are crowded, cheap, utterly inefficient and totally Filipino.

RICHARD I'ANSON

As the popular joke goes: "How many people can you get on a jeepney?" "One more, sir!"

Tricycles, jeepneys' poor cousins, are also endemic throughout the Philippines. Typically, a "trike" is a motorcycle with a sidecar, but you'll see many different variations on this theme. Some cities, most *barangays* (neighborhoods) and many towns rely on the tricycle for basic transportation. Unlike travel by jeepney, it's often necessary to negotiate your fare.

Avis, Hertz, Budget and many other car rental companies supply rental cars with or without drivers. When driving in the Philippines, be warned that discipline on the roads is virtually nonexistent. The roads themselves are often in poor repair, congested and poorly signed.

A wide variety of domestic air carriers operate throughout the islands. These airlines fly a bewildering assortment of planes—from small aircraft operating from primitive grass strips to sophisticated A-300 Airbuses and everything in between. Overall, odds are good that you'll arrive at your destination safely and with your baggage. Most airlines have baggage weight restrictions, which can be a problem for divers traveling with gear. Philippine Airlines does manage a Flying Sportsman's Club, allowing registered members to carry up to 30kg (66lbs) of baggage on domestic flights. Unfortunately, not every Philippine Airlines office seems to have heard of this arrangement, so it's best to apply at the PAL main office (Legaspi Street, Makati City, Metro Manila).

Many domestic airports charge a terminal, or departure, fee ranging from a few pesos to 50 pesos or more. Note that Manila has several domestic terminals, so be sure to check which terminal your flight leaves from and allow time for Manila's notorious rush-hour traffic.

As one would expect in a country with more than 7,000 islands, ferries are a popular and functional way to get around. For those who are not in a hurry, traveling on budget, have more baggage than airlines allow or who just can't get enough of the sea, getting from one island to another by ferry is a very attractive option. In some cases, it's the only option. In general, the most luxurious accommodation on a ferry is still cheaper than the equivalent plane fare, meals are usually supplied, and the trip is often relaxing and exhilarating. Cebu is a hub for the Visayas, and plenty of fast Super Cat catamarans ply the sea-lanes to locations throughout the Visayas. Be forewarned that ferry schedules are often upset by inclement weather.

Entry

Visitors must hold a valid passport and tickets for onward journey. Citizens of nearly all countries do not need a visa to enter the Philippines for stays of less than 21 days. Visa extensions for stays of up to 6 months are generally available in the Philippines through the main immigration office at Intramuros and some travel agencies, though moratoriums on extensions are sometimes in effect. A certificate of vaccination against yellow fever is required for those coming from infected areas. Before departure, visitors should check with their travel agent, as regulations may change without notice.

Money

The Philippine peso (P, also spelled piso) is the official currency. Exchange rates are quite volatile, usually changing to a rate more favorable for the hard-currency holder. Hard currency can be exchanged almost everywhere. Cash is exchanged at a higher rate than traveler's checks. When changing traveler's checks, you'll usually be asked to show a passport and the original receipt for the checks, so keep them handy.

Moneychangers operate semi-legally in the Philippines. They often offer a higher rate than the banks, but you should be wary of any unusually high offers, as they are likely to involve some sort of scam.

Visa, MasterCard and, to a lesser extent, Diners Club, American Express and JCB credit cards are widely accepted. Credit card cash advances are available at some ATMs throughout the country.

Time

The Philippines is eight hours ahead of Greenwich mean time; no adjustment is made for daylight saving time. During standard time, when it's noon in Manila, it's 8pm the previous day in Los Angeles, 11pm the previous evening in New York, 4am the same day in London and 2pm the same day in Sydney.

Electricity

Despite decades of intermittent power shortages, these days most major cities have reasonably reliable power. However, in the provinces it's a different matter—you can expect to be without power for long periods in some areas. Choose a resort with a generator if this could be a problem for you.

Power supplied on the national grid is supposed to be 220v/50hz, but be warned that it frequently fluctuates between 190v and 250v, which can wreak havoc on sensitive equipment. Outlets accommodating two flat pins are standard throughout the country. Bring adapters and converters as needed.

Weights & Measures

The Philippines officially uses the metric system, but old habits die hard, and many measurements and distances are expressed using the imperial system. Many dive operators still refer to dive depths in feet and tank pressure in pounds per square inch. In this book, both metric and imperial measurements are given, except for specific measurements in dive site descriptions, which are given in metric units only. See the conversion chart on the inside back cover for conversion information.

What to Bring

General Supplies

Most items you may want or need are available at reasonable prices throughout the country. However, the more remote the location, the fewer products are available and the higher their cost. Sunscreen, insect repellent and most common medications are widely available at pharmacies across the land. One caveat is that Sudafed, the congested diver's best friend, is banned in the Philippines, so be sure to bring your own supply if needed.

The Philippines enjoys a balmy if not outright hot climate year-round. Many visitors consequently dress as scantily as possible. While it's fine to roam around the beach in a pair of shorts, a bikini or a swimsuit, bear in mind that Filipinos are quite judgmental about people who dress this way in town. It's wise for men to wear long pants and for women to wear a modest dress. In fact, government offices have a strict dress code: Shorts, undershirts and sandals are not allowed.

Dive-Related Equipment

Although most of the time the water is warm enough to dive in just a bathing suit, given the many opportunities to come into contact with scraping, burning and stinging organisms, it's a good idea to wear some protective clothing. Most divers choose to wear a 3mm wetsuit, which can be rented at most local dive shops. A lycra dive skin is also a good option.

You can rent a wide range of equipment and accessories at most major dive centers. In almost all cases, equipment standards are high: Established dive centers replace their equipment every year or eighteen months. Most live-aboards can supply rental equipment, but may charge an additional fee if they sourced the equipment through a third party.

Snorkelers should consider bringing their own mask, fins and snorkel if visiting remote locations: Sometimes rental equipment is decidedly substandard, although if there are dive centers around, you'll likely be able to rent suitable gear. You can also buy most well-known brands at many locations throughout the country.

For those who choose to bring their own gear, almost every major equipment manufacturer and many smaller ones have a distributor with repair facilities in the Philippines, and prices are quite competitive.

Reputable dive centers—and that encompasses 99% of the operators—will require a C-card and possibly a logbook before renting scuba equipment, and most will insist that you dive with a supervised group.

Underwater Photography

The Philippines is one of the best places in the world for underwater photography. From Anilao's unique and plentiful nudibranchs to the whale sharks of Donsol, the mantas of Tubataha, the corals of the Visayas and Malapascua's thresher sharks, the Philippines is a great place to capture your favorite marine subjects on film.

Fuji, Kodak and other brands of print film are readily available, but you may have to search for color slide film anywhere outside of Manila or Cebu, so either bring your own or stock up in town. One-hour print processing is common throughout the country, but some remote areas may not use the freshest chemicals or photographic paper, so you may not be happy with the outcome. If you

TIM ROCK

You'll find varied underwater photo ops.

are a professional photographer or are especially concerned about quality, Fuji's main lab in Quezon City is by far the best place to develop both slide and print film. Slides can also be processed at some outlets in Manila and Cebu, and some live-aboard boats offer onboard E6 processing.

A few dive shops have a good selection of underwater cameras and housings. Dive Buddies (in Makati City, Metro Manila) carries a fairly comprehensive range of Ikelite housings and accessories, but in general the underwater camera market is quite small. You should bring o-rings for housings, batteries for your camera and strobe, and whatever spare parts your equipment may need.

Business Hours

No matter what you want to buy, if it's sold in the Philippines, it can be bought at almost any hour of the day or night. *Sari-Sari* stores (literally "everything" in Tagalog) are found everywhere, are open around the clock and sell everything from bottled water to mosquito coils. Many Filipinos do all their shopping at these efficient, family-run enterprises, and the prices are usually not much higher than those at the local supermarket are.

That said, most shopping malls don't open until after 10am and remain open until 8 or 9pm, depending on the day. Despite the fact that the Philippines is a Catholic country, Sundays are no impediment to retailers—stores are open seven days a week, except on major holidays (Christmas, New Year's, Easter and the annual pilgrimage to ancestors' tombs on October 30).

Banks are open from 9:30am to 3 or 4pm. Government offices are usually open from 8am to 5pm, with a lunch break from about noon to 1 or 2pm. Other break times, whether officially sanctioned or not, may interrupt the work schedule.

Accommodations

Most beach destinations and major cities offer travelers a range of accommodation options. Most dive destinations have budget cottages and rooms starting at US$10 a night, as well as comfortable boutique resorts with private rooms or cottages from US$20. An air-conditioned room in a Manila pension (guesthouse) can cost less than US$10 per night. Three-star hotels, found in many larger cities, start as low as US$18. Most high-end local hotels offer services and amenities similar to the popular international chains, typically at a cost of more than US$100 per night. Many resorts on private islands often include diving and meals and cost from US$50 to $100 a night. At the extreme high-end of the scale, exclusive resorts, such as Amanpulo, charge upward of US$900 a night.

Dining & Food

Dining in the Philippines can be a treat. In most major cities, a wide range of international cuisine competes with local fare for the diner's attention. European cuisine is very popular throughout the islands. Chinese cuisine with a Filipino twist is widely available, reasonably priced and delicious. You'll find no shortage of seafood restaurants in most places you'll visit, and many regions offer seasonal delicacies, such as coconut crabs, panga (tuna jaw), endemic clams and fruit (Davao's delicious durian, described on page 122, is one interesting example).

Local Filipino food borrows heavily from a mélange of cultures, especially Chinese and Malay. Filipinos tend to avoid vegetables in their diet, preferring to eat meat and fish whenever possible, but a meal is not complete (or even regarded as a meal) unless copious quantities of rice are consumed. (Poorer families in the Visayas may substitute cheaper corn for rice.) MSG is also widely used, but if you don't want it in your food, you can tell the waiter *walang vegin* or *walang ajinomoto tak tak tak.*

Somewhat alarmingly for many foreign visitors, Filipinos often deep-fry their meat and fish and also love to eat pork fat, again preferably deep-fried. Though some dishes may not appeal to you, don't pass up the chance to try *lechon baboy,* a spit-roasted pig served with a rich liver sauce. It's often jokingly referred to as "my heart attack" or "young man's food." (If you eat too much of it, you'll certainly die young.) Another popular food to try is *kilawin*, called *kinilaw* in Cebu. It's made of raw fish, usually Spanish mackerel or tuna, marinated in local cane vinegar and coconut milk and spiced with small chilies, ginger and shallots. It's delicious, especially when eaten with an ice-cold San Miguel beer, one of the Philippine's most successful products.

RICHARD I'ANSON

Chilies and limes season local cuisine.

Shopping

Shopping in the Philippines can be a blast for both mallers and market crawlers alike. Whether it's the latest Gucci loafer or an intricately woven basket you're looking for, the Philippines has it. While this is probably not the best place to shop for an expensive watch or a high-end electronic product, you'll find a huge range of competitively priced international and local goods, some of which are cheaper here than at more obvious shopping capitals such as Hong Kong.

Local handicrafts can be a good buy, but be warned that many shell and animal items cannot be legally imported into some countries. Baskets, woven goods and woodcarvings are among the many popular Filipino crafts available at stores and stalls across the land. Locally produced clothes and fashion accessories are real bargains. Filipinos make some very appealing intricate silverware, and Filipino costume jewelry is exported around the world. T'boli and other tribal weaving is also much in demand.

SCOTT TUASON

Activities & Attractions

For a country as culturally diverse and ecologically profuse as the Philippines, it's hard to cover in a few pages the vast scope of activities available to travelers. Below you'll find an array of noteworthy activities and attractions found within the regions that divers frequent.

Luzon

Nearly all visitors will spend a bit of time in **Manila**, the capital of the Philippines. Though this sprawling metropolis is rough around the edges, it does contain a few gems of cultural and touristic importance.

Sightseeing tours are widely available. Perhaps the most intriguing is a half- or full-day trip to the island of **Corregidor** at the mouth of Manila Bay. This was the last bastion of U.S. armed forces under siege by Japanese forces in 1942 and from where Gen. Douglas MacArthur unwillingly retreated to Australia, uttering the now-famous words, "I shall return." **Intramuros**—the old walled Spanish city with churches, cathedrals and authentically restored period buildings—is worth an afternoon walk.

Nearly every city has a memorial to national hero Dr. José Rizal, but the one in Manila's **Rizal Park** is particularly noteworthy: It's at the site where the Spanish executed Rizal in the late 19th century. The memorial is the de facto geographical center of the city and is the point all road signs refer to when expressing distances to Manila. Also within the park are statues, monuments, historical markers, government offices and the **National Museum**.

Nightlife in Manila is about as good as it gets anywhere in Asia. Filipinos are gifted **musicians**, and there is no shortage of venues for outstanding **performances** covering the entire musical spectrum, from Dixieland to rock and roll. After dark, check out the restaurants and clubs around J. Nakpil Street in Malate to see what Manila's trendy youth are up to. In the dry season, there are frequent **street parties** here and at adjacent Remedios Circle, one block farther along Adriatico Street, with live music and alfresco wining and dining.

Golfers can take advantage of the many world-class **golf courses** both within the Metro Manila area and in the adjacent provinces. **Shoppers** will want to check out the Makati and Ortigas malls and stores, such as SM, Glorietta, Rustans and Robinsons. **Duty-free stores** are in Manila, Subic, San Fernando and Clark (the former U.S. air base adjacent to Angeles City), as well as in Cebu. (Visitors can avail themselves of duty-free shopping at authorized stores up to 48 hours after arrival.)

Not far from Manila is the city of **Olongapo**, home to Subic Bay, the former U.S. naval base. It can be visited in a long daytrip but is certainly worth spending a day or two exploring. Aside from duty-free shopping, Subic Bay has several other enticing activities, such as a **casino** for the frivolous and **jungle trekking** and **survival courses** for outdoorsy types, as well as a wide range of marine activities such as **windsurfing, sailing, waterskiing, deep-sea fishing** and, of course, some excellent **diving**. Along the coast, **Barrio Baretto** is a popular beach resort area with good restaurants and some seedy bars left over from the U.S. Navy R and R (rest and relaxation) days.

Angeles City, a few hours north of Manila, is another holdover from the Vietnam R&R circuit and is starting to show its age. The former air base has been converted into a **duty-free** zone with countless shops and is home to a 36-hole **golf course** (Mimosa) and a Holiday Inn.

Although many divers will head for Anilao and Balayan Bay to sample some of Luzon's best diving, **Batangas** also has its share of worthwhile attractions. Batangas is famous for its coffee and fan knives, or *balisongs*, which are sold at numerous roadside stalls. But its star attraction is picturesque **Taal Lake**, with Taal Volcano's crater protruding from its center. **Tagaytay Ridge** affords a fantastic view of this still-active volcano, whose last major eruption was in 1965. At the ridge's highest point (Mt. Sungay at 750m/2,460ft) is the **People's Park in the Sky**. It's now open to the public for a paltry US10¢ entrance fee, well worth the money and time if only for the stunning views.

JOHN PENNOCK

The pre-dawn sky over Taal Lake, home of the Taal Volcano.

Mindoro

The majority of visitors to Mindoro will undoubtedly arrive in **Puerto Galera**, one of the world's most picturesque tropical harbors. Almost all of the bays along the coastline, from Sabang in the east to Tamaraw Beach west of Puerto Galera, have good **swimming** and **snorkeling** right off the beach. Corals are quite healthy, but beware of currents, which can be treacherous if you stray too far out. **Kayaking** is fast becoming a popular pastime and is an ideal way to explore the many secluded bays and beaches along the coast.

Though Puerto Galera is a relatively small town, it has ample traveler's amenities, such as **restaurants, nightlife** and **entertainment**. There is a nine-hole **golf**

course up in the hills overlooking the town—a pleasant way to spend an afternoon, but don't expect to be amazed by the greens and roughs, only the views. **Trekking** and **mountain biking** are sensible options for the fit and active.

If you are into **spelunking**, you'll find some interesting caves just 45km (28 miles) southeast of Puerto Galera in Mindoro's capital city, Calapan. Check out the amazing waterfall along the coastal road on your way out to them. Calapan is also a popular jumping-off point for **trekking** the 2,505m (8,215ft) Mt. Halcon. The high peaks of the Mindoro interior are home to endemic **wildlife** such as the Mindoro *tamaraw* (a pygmy carabao), sea eagles and other exotic flora and fauna.

The Mindoro highlands are also home to the **Mangyan Tribe**. Though their settlements are remote, and they generally avoid contact with strangers, they're a friendly and hospitable people. Because they can be elusive, it's best to travel with a knowledgeable guide if you seek contact with them. Mangyans make **baskets** and other native products, which they trade with lowlanders for rice and other staples. Mangyan baskets command a high price with collectors, perhaps because Mangyans are selective about who they'll trade with.

The Visayas

The Visayas is a generic term that encompasses a vast swathe of central Philippine territory, including Boracay, Cebu, Negros, Bohol, Leyte, Iloilo and many other islands. Each has its own unique culture, ecosystem, character and charm.

Boracay

With one of the finest **beaches** in Asia, if not the world, Boracay's fame rests upon its talcum-powder shores. Though the island is little more than a speck off the northwest tip of Panay, it's easily the best-known Philippine tourist spot—and often the most crowded. The gorgeous beach offers a tremendous choice of cafés, restaurants, bars, hotels, resorts, cottages, golfing, crafts, clothing, souvenirs, windsurfing, sailing, banana boats, inner tubes, snorkeling, island hopping and, of course, dive centers. The *amihan*, a strong westerly wind, blows from November to March—much of the sand and many of the tourists disappear during the rainy season as a consequence, but the winds do make for exciting **windsurfing** and **sailing**.

MARK DAFFEY

Boracay is famous for its white-sand beaches and warm shallow waters.

Cebu

Although not the largest of the Visayan Islands, Cebu is the most developed and has been the region's hub for hundreds of years. Portuguese explorer **Ferdinand Magellan** came to Cebu on April 8, 1521. Unfortunately, Magellan failed to keep his nose out of local politics and was subsequently killed by a local chieftain, Lapu-Lapu, at the Battle of Mactan. A **shrine** between the airport and Punta Engaño on Mactan now marks the place where Magellan was slain. Other Magellan **relics** include a statue of the infant Jesus that was given by Magellan to the wife of Cebu's King Jumabon. The statue is now housed on Cebu in the only basilica in East Asia. Across the road is a shrine housing **Magellan's Cross.** Nearby **Fort San Pedro,** the first fort constructed by the Spanish on Philippine soil, houses the regional office of the **National Museum.**

Negros

Negros, the sugarcane capital of the Philippines, is divided into two provinces, Negros Occidental and Negros Oriental. Ancient **steam engines** still chug up and down some of the old rusty tracks at harvest time, carrying groaning loads of the sweet plant.

The capital of Negros Occidental is **Bacolod,** famous for its colorful ***Masskara* fiesta,** held each October. Bacolod's **regional cuisine** includes exceptionally fine barbecued and roasted chicken and the delicious shellfish that are seasonally available at seafood restaurants throughout town. You can see the unique **Mural of Birhen Sang Barangay,** a large mosaic made up of 95,000 pieces of natural seashells, at the Chapel of Santa Clara in Bacolod. There is also a **casino,** a modern **convention center** and **restaurants, nightclubs** and **hotels** to suit most budgets.

Dumaguete, the capital of Negros Oriental, is very much a student town. The **Siliman University** campus has some buildings of interest, such as the library. **Nightlife** revolves around the Music Box, a popular disco and hangout for students and locals alike. There are several **beach resorts** along the coast in either direction from Dumaguete.

Bohol

Though seldom explored by visitors, Bohol is a fascinating island with a treasure trove of natural and man-made wonders. One of the cleanest islands in the country, Bohol is a poor but proud province and a safe place to travel.

Alone among the islands of the Philippines, Bohol mounted a successful rebellion against the oppressive Spanish friars in 1744 and remained free of colonial domination for the next 85 years. The first recorded pact between a Spaniard and a Filipino was undertaken here on March 28, 1521, and a second was entered into in 1565. This second **historic treaty** is commemorated by a **marker** in the small barangay of Bool, 3km (2 miles) from the capital, Tagbilaran.

Bohol has several other distinguishing facets to it, the most famous being the **Chocolate Hills** in Carmen, about 55km (35 miles) from Tagbilaran. This bizarre range of 1,268 cone-shaped mounds reaches elevations between 60 and 120m (195 and 395ft). The hills are green in the rainy season and brown in the dry. Despite many excavations and years of scientific research, no one knows how or why they acquired their distinctive form.

JOHN PENNOC

A rainbow adds a touch of magic over the Chocolate Hills.

Lush **forests, rivers, hills** and **valleys** are open for **hikers** to explore. Although the **tarsier**, a tiny, wide-eyed monkey (the smallest on earth), is a nocturnal animal, you might get lucky and see one in the hills of Corella, about 16km (10miles) from Tagbilaran.

Other sites of interest include the **Baclayon Church**, 6km (4 miles) east of Tagbilaran, the oldest stone church in the country and home to a **museum** containing locally produced religious artifacts. At **Hinagdanan Cave** in Dauis, about 6km (4 miles) from Tagbilaran, freshwater pours out of the rock into a bathing pool surrounded by stalagmites and stalactites.

Leyte

After several years' absence, General MacArthur first set foot upon Philippine soil here in Leyte, just south of the capital, Tacloban. His historic return is commemorated with a life-size **bronze statue** of the famous corncob-pipe smoking general together with his entourage, including the late small-statured but giant-hearted Filipino elder statesman Gen. Carlos Romulo. Romulo was a signatory of the United Nations and in 1949 became the first Asian president of the United Nations General Assembly.

Mindanao

Mindanao comprises a vast tract of land that has both stunning scenery and abject poverty. It's home to the majority of Filipino Muslims, as well as unique ethnic groups such as the Badjao Sea Gypsies (who spend their lives aboard native outriggers ranging across the Philippines' southern waters), the Tausog and the T'boli. Conflict between the Muslims and Christians has been going on for decades and shows no sign of abatement despite government efforts to promote peace treaties. Although Mindanao historically is not the safest place to travel, it's unusual for foreigners to find themselves in harm's way here—of those that do, it's often partly of their own doing.

Davao City is famous for its delicious but rank **durian fruit**, which no airline or ferry will knowingly allow onboard. From Davao you can hike or climb the Philippines' highest mountain, 2,954m (9,689ft) **Mt. Apo**, via several different routes. You may catch a glimpse of an endangered **Philippine eagle**, the world's second largest species of eagle and the national bird of the Philippines, from the mountain's slopes. Visitors may tour an **eagle breeding station** for a small fee.

General Santos, home to an amazing number of dive sites, is also the nation's tuna fishing and canning capital. Several tribal groups live near Gen San, as it's known, and trips to the villages are recommended for cultural enthusiasts.

Cagayan de Oro, a rather subdued city, is a gateway of sorts to the region. Off the coast and a few miles to the northwest is the delightful island of **Camiguin**, one of the area's best-kept secrets. Aside from some excellent **beaches** and **diving** and **snorkeling** sites, Camiguin has many other attractions, such as a **sunken cemetery**, several volcanoes—including the active **Hibok-Hibok Volcano** (1,250m/4,100ft)—**hot springs**, **cold springs**, **waterfalls** and the remains of the **Catarman Church**, constructed in 1697 and demolished in a cataclysmic volcanic eruption in 1871.

Palawan

This long sliver of an island is one of the Philippines' last frontiers. Its stunning natural beauty puts it at risk of getting too much attention, but a passionate local environmental movement may help curtail the negative impacts of tourism.

At Palawan's northern end, **Coron Bay** is where many divers visiting Palawan will arrive. The **shipwrecks** littering the bottom of this pristine bay are only a part of its appeal. **Kayaking** around the towering **limestone cliffs** and **saltwater lakes** is a fantastic opportunity to discover some of this area's hidden natural wealth. Keep your eyes peeled—you may even chance across an endangered **Philippine dugong**, a close relative of the manatee, as you glide across Coron Bay's usually calm waters. Certainly you will see Palawan **nidos**, or swiflets, whose nests are used to make **bird's nest soup**.

Another stunning **kayaking** destination as well as a great **diving** area, **El Nido** has towering limestone and marble **cliffs** to explore. Relatively undeveloped except for some upmarket island **resorts**, El Nido has retained its laid-back atmosphere. Visitors can opt to take a long banca boat ride to **St. Paul's Subterranean River**, which can be navigated by boat for more than a kilometer.

St. Paul's Subterranean River

JOHN BORTHWICK

Jacques Cousteau, the doyen of divers, made this stunning underground river world famous in the early '80s when he filmed a remarkable documentary here. He and his crew penetrated the system for more than 2km (1¼ miles) and recorded the life and structures along its length.

If you're planning to dive here, use the services of an experienced local divemaster with intimate knowledge of the cave. To enter the park, visitors must have a permit, available through authorized tour agencies and the St. Paul Subterranean National Park superintendent (146 Manalo Street, Puerto Princesa, ☎ (48) 433 2409).

The capital of Palawan and jumping-off point for Tubataha Reef and other Sulu Sea dive spots, **Puerto Princesa** has a charm and spirit all of its own. The city limits spread almost 100km (60 miles) from coast to coast, but the city center is in reality quite small. **Taytay Bay**, on the east coast north of Puerto Princesa, is home to several **resorts** and is a **tropical beach** lover's delight with reasonable **snorkeling**, though the diving is somewhat overrated. **Honda Bay**, just north of Puerto Princesa, has some fair **diving**, some very good **snorkeling** and a secret not many locals are willing to share. Juvenile **whale sharks** often cruise through the bay, but their exact whereabouts is kept secret by local conservationists to prevent the disruption of their sensitive environment.

Diving Health & Safety

TIM ROCK

The Philippines is a relatively safe country to visit with regard to infectious diseases and general health. Malaria exists in rural areas, but is not usually a risk to travelers. There have been recent large outbreaks of dengue fever, so take appropriate precautions to avoid mosquito bites. Food and waterborne diseases, including dysentery, hepatitis and liver flukes, are a risk. Bottled water is widely available. You should be particularly careful of eating shellfish, which are periodically affected by algae, causing diarrhea and vomiting, visual disturbances and even breathing problems. The U.S. Centers for Disease Control & Prevention regularly posts updates on health-related concerns around the world specifically for travelers. For up-to-date regional health information visit their website (www.cdc.gov), or call (toll-free from the U.S.) ☎ 888-232-3299 and request Document 000005 to receive a list of documents available by fax.

All major cities have medical facilities. Medical practitioners generally have high standards and the charges are relatively low. There are exceptions however—before you seek medical treatment you should get referrals from local residents to avoid ending up with an incompetent doctor and/or a grossly inflated bill.

General precautions you should take include preventing and taking care of coral scrapes and insect bites, which can become infected very quickly. Also stay out of the sun, which can burn you even on a cloudy day, drink plenty of water and try not to overindulge in the local beers and spirits.

Pre-Trip Preparation

At least a month before your trip, inspect your dive gear. Remember, your regulator should be serviced annually, whether you've used it or not. If you use a dive computer and can replace the battery yourself, change it before the trip or buy a spare one to take along. Otherwise, send the computer to the manufacturer for a battery replacement. If possible, find out if the dive center rents or services the type of gear that you own. If not, you might want to take spare parts or even spare gear. Purchase any additional equipment you may need, such as a dive light and tank marker light for night diving, a line reel for wreck diving, etc. Make sure you have at least a whistle attached to your BC, and be sure to pack a surface marker tube (also known as a safety sausage or come-to-me).

About a week before your departure, do a final check of your gear, grease o-rings, check batteries and assemble a save-a-dive kit. Don't forget to pack a first-aid kit and medications such as decongestants, ear drops, antihistamines, antibiotic ointment, insect repellent and motion sickness tablets.

The Philippines does not require visitors to show any specific immunizations. However, if arriving from an area that has had a recent cholera outbreak or has a risk of yellow fever, you should acquire the necessary immunizations before arriving and be prepared to show proof of treatment if requested. If planning to travel extensively around Palawan, which does have some areas prone to malaria, you should start taking antimalarial treatments several weeks before arriving and continue with the treatment per the manufacturer's recommendations. Many drugs are available over the counter throughout the Philippines, but it's wise to fill any necessary prescriptions before you leave your own country.

Diving & Flying

Most divers visiting the Philippines arrive by plane. While it's fine to dive soon after flying, it's important to remember that your last dive should be completed at least 24 hours *before* your flight to minimize the risk of decompression sickness, caused by residual nitrogen in the blood.

Recompression Facilities

While the Philippines has four reliable recompression chambers (in Manila, Cavite, Subic and Cebu), air evacuation options to them are limited, and transport time can be lengthy. Considering this, diving conservatively goes without saying.

You should expect your dive operator to do his best to make the necessary arrangements in the case of a diving emergency. Depending on the symptoms and location of the victim, the dive operator will arrange evacuation to the nearest chamber or medical facility, as appropriate. Both the Philippine Air Force and private operators such as Subic Seaplanes assist with evacuations. However, their range is relatively limited: Don't expect them to miraculously appear in the middle of the Sulu Sea, for example.

If you find yourself dealing with a diving emergency without the help of local divers, the following numbers should be useful.

Evacuation Services

Philippine Air Force Search & Rescue
Villamor Air Base, Pasay City, Metro Manila
☎ (63-2) 854 6701, 853 5013 or 853 5008

Subic Seaplanes
☎ (63-47) 252 2230 or 0919-325 1106 (cell)

Recompression Chambers

Never arrive at a chamber without calling first. You can save valuable time if the chamber staff can assist with transportation or refer you to another facility when their chamber is in use.

Manila

Armed Forces of the Philippines Medical Center
V. Luna Rd., Quezon City
Contact: Jojo Bernado, M.D., or Fred C. Martinez
☎ (63-2) 920 7183 or 921 1801, local 8991 or 6445

Cavite

Sangley Recompression Chamber
Philippine Fleet, Naval Base Cavite
Sangley Point, Cavite City
Contact: Capt. Pablo Acacio
☎ (63-46) 524 2061 (ask to be connected to the Sangley operator), local 4490, 4191 or 4193

Subic

Subic Bay Freeport Zone
SBMA, Olongapo City, Zambales
Contact: Lito Roque
☎ (63-47) 252 7052 or 252 7566

Cebu

VISCOM Station Hospital
Camp Lapu Lapu, Lahug, Cebu City
Contact: Mamerto Ortega or Macario Mercado
☎ (63-32) 232 2464 through 2468, local 3369

DAN

Divers Alert Network (DAN) is an international membership association of individuals and organizations sharing a common interest in diving and safety. It operates a 24-hour diving emergency hotline in the U.S.: ☎ **919-684-8111 or 919-684-4DAN (-4326)**. The latter accepts collect calls in a dive emergency.

The Philippines falls under the responsibility of DAN South East Asia (www.danseap.org). It also operates a 24-hour hot line that can be called from within the Philippines: ☎ **02 855 9911**. Dr. Ben G. Luna staffs the SEAP Philippines office (Makati Medical Center, Suite 123, 2 Amorsolo Street, Makati City, ☎ (63-2) 817 5601, danphil@cnl.net).

Though DAN does not directly provide medical care, it does provide advice on early treatment, evacuation and hyperbaric treatment of diving-related injuries. Divers should contact DAN for assistance as soon as a diving emergency is suspected.

DAN membership is reasonably priced and includes DAN TravelAssist, a membership benefit that covers medical air evacuation from anywhere in the world for any illness or injury. For a small additional fee, divers can get secondary insurance coverage for decompression illness. For membership details contact DAN at ☎ 800-446-2671 in the U.S. or ☎ 919-684-2948 elsewhere. DAN can also be reached at www.diversalertnetwork.org.

TIM ROCK

Diving in the Philippines

With more than 7,000 islands and countless miles of coral reefs, the Philippines offers a wealth of varied diving opportunities. Whether it's swimming with whale sharks, cruising with mantas, exploring caves and wrecks or simply hanging out near the awesome walls and reefs, this tropical paradise will fascinate divers of all skill levels and interests. Divers can choose from a morning of beach diving to days or even weeks of live-aboard cruising enjoying remote diving at some the best dive sites in the world.

Philippines dive sites are varied, but they do share some common characteristics. Water temperatures throughout the Philippines fall between 25 and 28°C (77 and 82°F), the warmest months being March through June. Though conditions are best between late February and early June, most regions have some diving available year-round.

Some areas have swift, unpredictable currents, while other areas, such as Subic Bay, have negligible currents at many sites. Tidal ranges are generally not more than 1m (3ft) and are usually only a factor with regard to visibility and current—most divers prefer to dive as close as possible to high tide, as the detritus from coastal settlements tends to be at its farthest point from shore and visibility is generally at its best. Obviously, it pays to check with local dive professionals for advice on currents and other factors before you plan your dive.

While most dive sites offer abundant and colorful marine life, the Philippines is not without its share of environmental challenges. Despite education and regulation efforts, destructive dynamite fishing is still a problem in many areas, and coral bleaching from the 1998-99 El Niño conditions is widespread along the country's shallow reefs. Dive operators generally take divers to the best sites the regions offer, and divers should make every effort to minimize their impact on the reef.

Literally hundreds of dive sites dot the length and breadth of the country—it would be impossible to include them all in a book light enough to pack in your dive bag. In this book you'll find selections that are representative of the vast diversity of sites throughout the Philippines. Many are personal favorites, some are included because they are well known and others may be rarely dived but are just too good to leave out. The depth ranges included with each dive site description indicate where the site's best features are, and a "+" after the range means deeper dives are possible. Be sure to plan your dives and dive your plans—keep an eye on your depth gauge, especially along wall sites.

Banca Boats

Generations ago, sailors figured out that a paddle and a hollowed-out palm tree with two bamboo outriggers attached to it makes for a relatively stable and navigable craft. Later, the addition of a sail and rudder made it a more efficient vessel. More recently, someone dropped a lawn-mower engine onto the back and presto—the modern banca boat was born.

Bancas come in all sizes, but their shape remains basically the same: long and slender, sometimes with a cabin or awning at the stern, with bamboo outriggers lashed to cross struts with lavishly applied fishing line.

Although some dive centers boast modern fiberglass speedboats, the majority of diving and most island hopping is still done by banca—you might say they are the jeepneys of the sea.

For divers, a few words of advice:

Despite the outriggers, bancas (especially the smaller ones) are not particularly stable, and less so in high seas. They require a skilled driver who knows how to pilot them through the waves. The larger bancas used by many dive operators are more stable, but when getting on or off a smaller banca (six persons or fewer), you should always ask the driver, or *bancero*, where he wants you to sit—the balance can be critical. Likewise, let the bancero know when you are ready to enter the water or hoist yourself aboard so he can counterbalance the boat.

Although bancas are required by law to carry life vests, they seldom do. If you have your dive equipment with you, you may want to secure the mask, fins and weight belt around the belt of the BC, then inflate the BC so everything will float if there is an accident. Some divers do this and then secure the rig to a crosspiece so it won't float away. Others simply gear up before leaving.

Getting into the water from a banca is usually accomplished by doing a backward roll. Getting back on board is not always so easy. The preferred procedure is to remove your weight belt, BC, tank and fins and pass them up to the bancero before climbing aboard. Usually, there is a ladder to help you climb back in the boat, but if not, you can easily fabricate one out a piece of rope. Simply secure the rope to the hull and then tie a loop at sea level. With your fins off, step into the loop, grab onto the side of the hull and stand up.

Finally, if hiring your own banca, always negotiate the price first—and don't pay until you are safely back on land where you want to be!

TIM ROCK

Snorkeling

In the Philippines, snorkeling (also known as skin diving) is a rich and rewarding experience. Rental snorkeling gear of varying quality is widely available, or for a reasonable price you can buy what you need. All dive regions have at least a few good snorkeling sites. In many resort areas you can simply put on your mask and fins and paddle from the beach into pleasant shallow reef areas with lots to see.

Excellent snorkeling is rarely more than a short boat ride away from any coastal area. Snorkelers can often join dive boats on suitable trips to shallow reefs for a reasonable price, and many dive operators are happy to arrange a custom snorkeling trip. Another option is to hire a motorized outrigger, or banca boat, from the beach, but be warned that you may not get the quality of service and equipment or get taken to the most appropriate location for your skill level.

TIM ROCK

Explore the shallow reefs.

Dive Training & Certification

The Philippines is one of the world's best places to learn to dive. You can choose among literally hundreds of dive centers, most affiliated with PADI, with thousands of qualified instructors eager to advance you to the next level of training. Prices are reasonable and equipment standards are often very high. The Philippine Commission on Sport Scuba Diving registers and accredits dive establishments, providing some assurance that registered shops offer quality services.

Philippine waters are likewise well suited to training requirements, with warm clear water and shallow coral reefs ideal for beginners, as well as rewarding deep dives, wrecks and caves perfect for advanced and technical training.

Technical diving courses are widely available. Leading agencies include PADI, IANTD and ANDI. For divemaster training and instructor development, few places can beat the Philippines—dive courses are run year-round in popular resort areas, so you'll find ample opportunities to guide divers, assist with courses and learn how to maintain and repair equipment.

Live-Aboard Diving

The Philippines has an abundance of world-class sites too far from land to be easily visited by conventional dive boats. Live-aboards, or safari dive boats, offer divers the chance to visit some truly spectacular locations and to enjoy the company of like-minded souls. Luxurious vessels—as well as a host of large banca boats, converted fishing boats, yachts, junks and assorted marine anomalies—visit sites such as Tubbataha, Semirara, the Sibuyan Sea, the Visayas and even the Spratleys (more properly referred to as the Kalayaan Group).

The Sulu Sea season runs from mid-February to mid-June. Throughout the rest of the year, the larger live-aboards have some really good deals for transition trips (when the vessel is moving from one location to another, such as from Luzon to Puerto Princesa) and weekend trips, and many of the larger resorts plan trips on their own boats to all sorts of exotic locations.

Some of the larger vessels offer onboard E6 processing, tech-diving equipment, chase boats and even gourmet meals. Smaller boats' amenities can vary greatly. Though most small-vessel operators are reputable, some aren't insured, don't follow safety regulations, lack basic navigational aids and have inexperienced crews. It's very much a case of "buyer beware" when selecting a live-aboard boat.

Dive Site Icons

The symbols at the beginning of each dive site description provide a quick summary of some of the following characteristics present at each site:

Good snorkeling or free-diving site.

Remains or partial remains of a wreck can be seen at this site.

Sheer wall or drop-off.

Deep dive. Features of this dive occur in water deeper than 27m (90ft).

Strong currents may be encountered at this site.

Strong surge (the horizontal movement of water caused by waves) may be encountered at this site.

Drift dive. Because of strong currents and/or difficulty in anchoring, a drift dive is recommended at this site.

Beach/shore dive. This site can be accessed from shore.

Poor visibility. The site often has visibility of less than 12m (40ft).

Caves are a prominent feature of this site. Only experienced cave divers should explore inner cave areas.

Marine preserve. Special regulations apply in this area.

Pisces Rating System for Dives & Divers

The dive sites in this book are rated according to the following diver skill-level rating system. These are not absolute ratings but apply to divers at a particular time, diving at a particular place. For instance, someone unfamiliar with prevailing conditions might be considered a novice diver at one dive area, but an intermediate diver at another, more familiar location.

Novice: A novice diver should be accompanied by an instructor, divemaster or advanced diver on all dives. A novice diver generally fits the following profile:

- ◆ basic scuba certification from an internationally recognized certifying agency
- ◆ dives infrequently (less than one trip a year)
- ◆ logged fewer than 25 total dives
- ◆ little or no experience diving in similar waters and conditions
- ◆ dives no deeper than 18m (60ft)

Intermediate: An intermediate diver generally fits the following profile:

- ◆ may have participated in some form of continuing diver education
- ◆ logged between 25 and 100 dives
- ◆ dives no deeper than 40m (130ft)
- ◆ has been diving in similar waters and conditions within the last six months

Advanced: An advanced diver generally fits the following profile:

- ◆ advanced certification
- ◆ has been diving for more than two years and logged over 100 dives
- ◆ has been diving in similar waters and conditions within the last six months

Regardless of your skill level, you should be in good physical condition and know your limitations. If you are uncertain of your own level of expertise for a particular site, ask the advice of a local dive instructor. He or she is best qualified to assess your abilities based on the site's prevailing dive conditions. Ultimately, however, you must decide if you are capable of making a particular dive, a decision that should take into account your level of training, recent experience and physical condition, as well as the conditions at the site. Remember that conditions can change at any time, even during a dive.

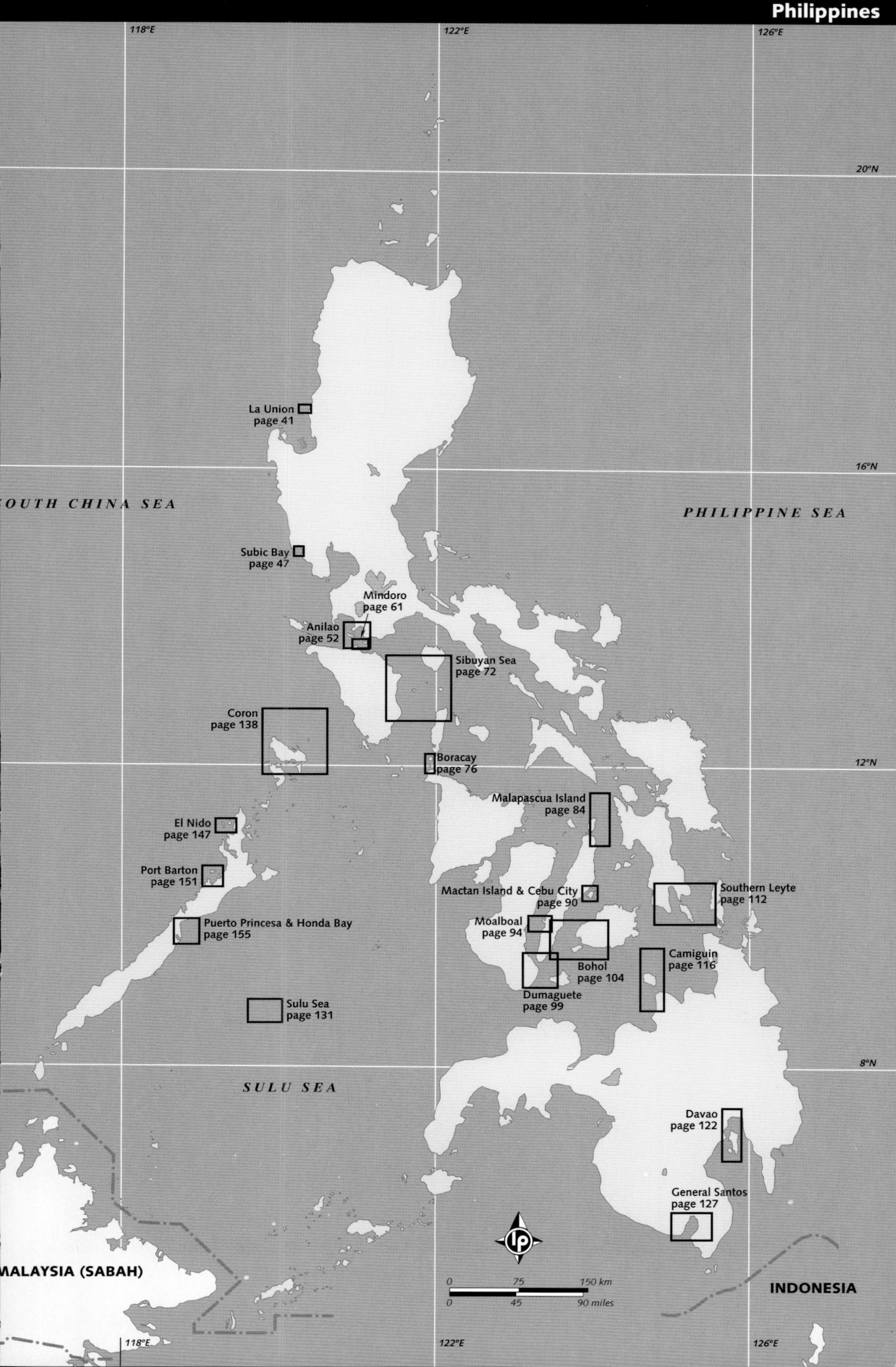
118°E
122°E
126°E
20°N
16°N
12°N
8°N
SOUTH CHINA SEA
PHILIPPINE SEA
SULU SEA
La Union
page 41
Subic Bay
page 47
Mindoro
page 61
Anilao
page 52
Sibuyan Sea
page 72
Coron
page 138
Boracay
page 76
Malapascua Island
page 84
El Nido
page 147
Port Barton
page 151
Mactan Island & Cebu City
page 90
Southern Leyte
page 112
Puerto Princesa & Honda Bay
page 155
Moalboal
page 94
Bohol
page 104
Camiguin
page 116
Dumaguete
page 99
Sulu Sea
page 131
Davao
page 122
General Santos
page 127
MALAYSIA (SABAH)
INDONESIA
0 75 150 km
0 45 90 miles
lp
118°E
122°E
126°E

Luzon Dive Sites

The largest island of the Philippine archipelago, Luzon is home to the capital, Manila. Manila Bay, famous for its sunsets, is not a desirable place to dive, given the tons of noxious effluent that finds its way daily into its murky waters. However, the Metro Manila area has a number of dive centers that sell and service equipment, arrange daytrips to nearby dive sites and book live-aboard trips to destinations throughout the country. Luzon itself has several great diving areas just off its coast, including San Fernando (La Union), Subic Bay, Anilao and Bicol (Donsol).

La Union

It's a five-hour drive from Manila to San Fernando, the provincial capital of La Union, where a 3km (2 mile) stretch of sand aptly called Long Beach is home to a number of resorts and hotels, as well as the region's sole dive center, Ocean Deep.

Shallow Research Reef runs the length of Long Beach, and several deeper reefs are nearby. La Union is an excellent year-round dive destination and a great place to learn diving, as it's well north of the typhoon belt, and the waters of the Lingayen Gulf are well protected from prevailing winds throughout most of the year.

TED STRESHINSKY

The sun sets over Manila Bay, one of the finest harbors in Southeast Asia.

Unfortunately, years of blast fishing have seriously damaged many of the reef structures around La Union, and the practice continues unabated. Nonetheless, some spots are still relatively healthy.

Visibility can easily exceed 50m (160ft) in the peak season (between March and June), but drops to as low as 10m (33ft) after heavy rains. Diving is done off small two-diver bancas, which can be a bit cramped for longer journeys. These bancas offer no shade, so wear a hat and splash on the sunscreen.

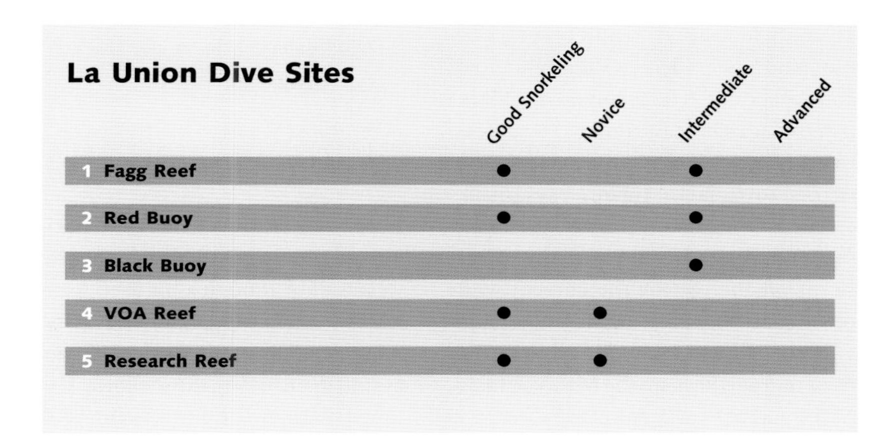

La Union Dive Sites

	Good Snorkeling	Novice	Intermediate	Advanced
1 Fagg Reef	●		●	
2 Red Buoy	●		●	
3 Black Buoy			●	
4 VOA Reef	●	●		
5 Research Reef	●	●		

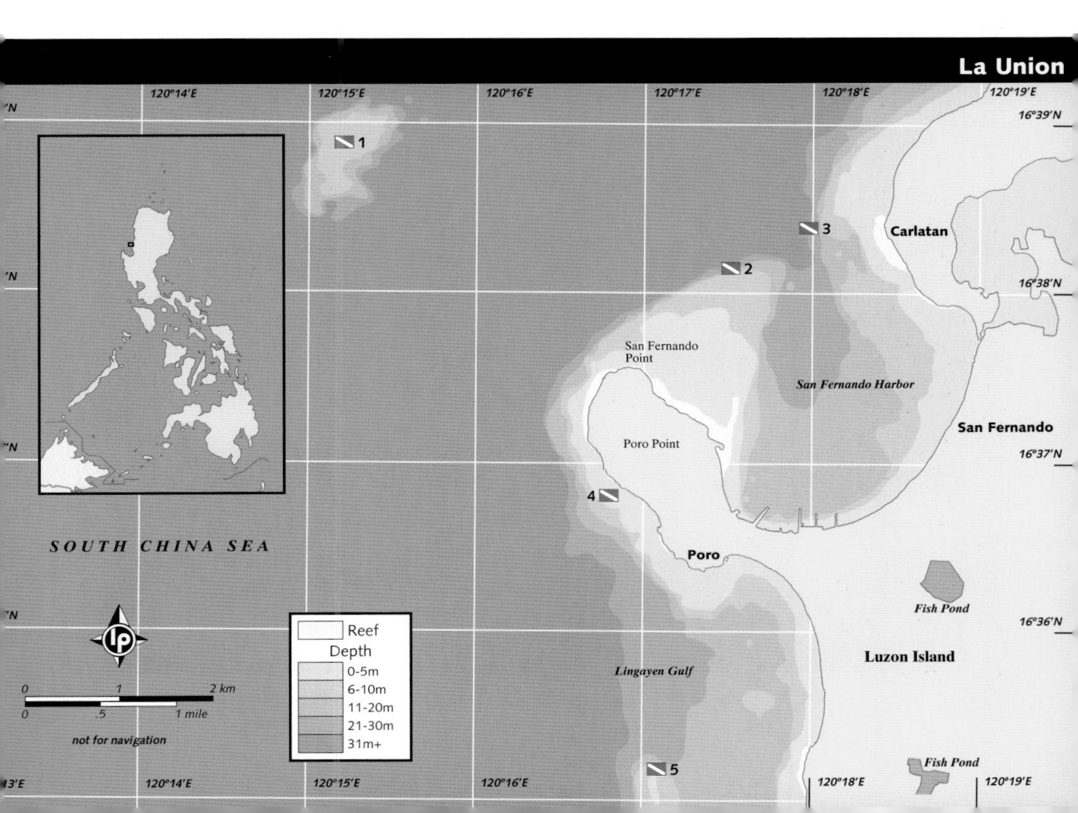

1 Fagg Reef

Location: 3km (2miles) offshore of San Fernando

Depth Range: 4-40m+ (13-130ft+)

Access: Boat

Expertise Rating: Intermediate

On this large reef, a massive wall slopes down to the extremely deep continental shelf, which skirts the shore before sweeping west around Cape Bolinao across the Lingayen Gulf. The reeftop has some interesting bommies, as well as sandy lanes that run between rocky outcrops covered in a variety of hard and soft corals. The assortment of large fish includes king barracuda, Napoleon wrasses, pelagic whitetip and blacktip sharks, tuna, jacks, turtles, rays, mackerel and wahoos. Whale sharks have been seen cruising off the wall by divers swept off the reef by the current while making a safety stop.

Perhaps the most interesting attractions on Fagg Reef are the M10A1E tanks. At the end of WWII, U.S. forces scrapped these tanks and dropped them off a barge. Luckily for us, three came to rest between 40 and 44m on a small ledge off Fagg's west wall. Although a bit deep for recreational scuba divers (you have about 3 minutes bottom time before you need to ascend to off-gas on the shallower reef sections), these are excellent technical diving sites. Two other tanks lie deeper still.

STEVE ROSENBERG

Napoleon wrasses cruise the west coast of Luzon.

Don't Get Swept Away

Virtually all coral reefs with healthy, diverse marine life are subject to currents, at least some of the time. This relationship between rich marine life and currents is no coincidence: Most reef creatures rely on them in one way or another. But strong currents don't have to mean difficult diving, provided you utilize proper techniques.

SARAH J H HUBBARD

A safety sausage helps a diver be seen at the surface.

- Know your skill level. If you are unsure of your ability to undertake any given dive, consult your divemaster.
- Divers should always carry sufficient signaling devices. You should have a marker tube (see photo), a signal light and a whistle. The best marker tubes are brightly colored and about 3m (10ft) high. They roll up and can easily fit into a BC pocket or be clipped onto a D-ring. They're inflated orally or with a regulator.
- Stay with the group. Resist the temptation to dive on your own, as to do so may take you out of sight of the dive boat and cause you to become lost.
- Currents can push you downward as they rush over a reef. To avoid diving too deep, swim away from the wall to where the current is likely to diminish. Also, use your BC to increase positive buoyancy, remembering to closely monitor your rate of ascent to avoid rising too fast.
- Don't do drift dives at night or during twilight. If you get swept away from your group, the darkness will make it much harder for the dive boat to find you.
- Finally, dive with an experienced local dive guide who knows what conditions to expect, as well as how to deal with them.

2 Red Buoy

Location: San Fernando Harbor

Depth Range: 3-38m (10-125ft)

Access: Boat

Expertise Rating: Intermediate

At times there actually *is* a red buoy to mark this site, although storms may wash it away during the rainy season—the harbor mouth is quite exposed. A strong current sometimes washes out of the harbor, attracting pelagics such as dogtooth tuna, mackerel, jacks and, very occasionally, some sharks and leopard rays.

A short wall drops from 5 to 30m. Southwest of the wall the reef is quite shallow and largely bombed out, but some pronounced ravines and crevices provide shelter for the large fish that find their way into them. About 200m from the wall is an impressive depression known as **The Fishbowl,** which looks like a large amphitheater. Although the reef lacks many healthy corals, The Fishbowl's great visibility attracts lots of fish. Pelagics seem to like swimming around the bowl's circumference looking for a snack, which could include a grouper, snapper, parrotfish, wrasses, blennies, squirrelfish or any one of the number of other smaller species that divers often see here.

SAMMY ANG

A silver curtain of jacks schools in the current.

3 Black Buoy

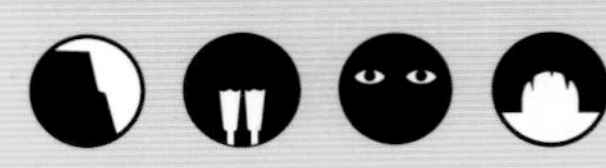

Location: San Fernando Harbor

Depth Range: 3-30m (10-100ft)

Access: Boat

Expertise Rating: Intermediate

OK, so there really isn't a black buoy here, but years ago one marked the channel into the harbor, and the name has been used ever since. Most banceros can find the site easily enough—it's just south of where the reef breaks the surface at low tide.

Visibility can be quite poor, as the water is usually turbid. When the tide ebbs and flows from the nearby muddy harbor, a lot of sediment washes over the broken-up reeftop.

There usually isn't much of a current once you start down the precipitous wall. The deeper section of the wall is pocked by more than 20 caves—some have big lobsters in them, while others are favored by sleeping whitetips and, occasionally, nurse sharks.

4 VOA Reef

Location: Off Poro Point

Depth Range: 4-23m (13-75ft)

Access: Boat

Expertise Rating: Novice

VOA (Voice of America) Reef, named for the U.S. radio station's massive antenna that dominates the Poro Point cliffs, is another good training site, night dive and an excellent snorkeling area. The reef tops out at 4m and reaches down to 23m. Unlike Long Beach, the sea bottom here is covered in coral sand. The visibility tends to be better because coral sand, which is heavier than the sediment prevalent at many sites, sinks rapidly back to the bottom after bad weather.

The inshore side of the reef has lots of sandy areas with healthy coral bommies growing all over the place. Lots of brain, table and boulder corals and a few basket sponges predominate. The sand is dotted with many anemones, some sea whips and lots of shells (including green turbans, several species of cowries, augers and cone shells). The seaward reef wall is also quite good, with a few gorgonians and plenty of hard corals, as well as some really bright orange and red soft corals at the southern end, which is a good 10m deeper than the northern end.

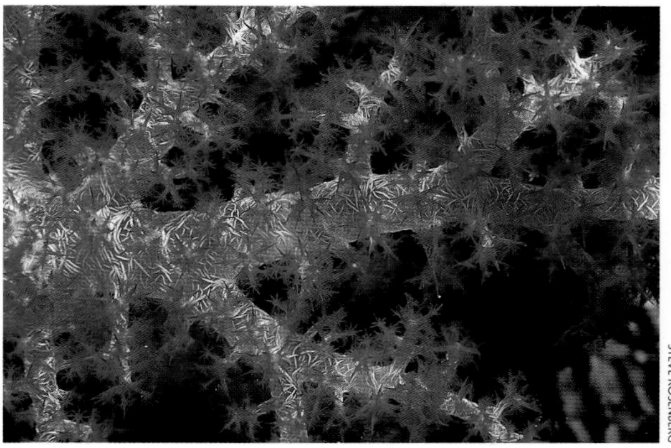

STEVE ROSENBERG

Bright soft corals dot the southern end of VOA Reef.

5 Research Reef

Location: Off Long Beach

Depth Range: 2-28m (7-92ft)

Access: Boat

Expertise Rating: Novice

Research Reef has many sites worth visiting along both the shallower beach side and the deeper small wall on its seaward side. The reeftop is at about 5m, and the reef slopes to a sandy bottom at about 28m.

From shore you can swim out to some pretty coral gardens between 2m and 10m—good for training dives and snorkeling. The seafloor is a mixture of sand and silt dotted with coral bommies all the way out to the reef.

The most popular area of Research Reef is **The Caves**, where several small cave-like passageways cut through the reef—even novice divers can swim through these. The largest passage is on the reef's west face. Lobsters are usually seen here, especially at night.

From here a knowledgeable dive guide may take you a few dozen meters over the sandy bottom to some large coral bommies that rise to within 10m of the surface. One of these has a 20m passageway going into its center (the entrance is at 25m).

Hawksbill turtles were once common in this area, but few are seen these days. Fish life is quite varied, including small groupers, jacks, snappers, sweetlips, parrotfish, many anemones with clownfish, a few leatherjackets and some octopuses. Lots of smaller reef fish and fry dart about between the few healthy hard and soft corals and the skeletons of the reef's former glory. Bluespotted rays and copious map and tiger cowries rest in the sand. You might catch a glimpse of a pelagic or two, especially away from the wall, where the visibility often drops considerably.

Research is also a good night diving spot, shallow and full of life, albeit mostly smaller fish, the larger ones being easy prey for local fishermen.

STEVE ROSENBERG

Look for painted crays amid Research Reef's corals.

Subic Bay

Olongapo, on Subic Bay, is a 2½ to 3½ hour drive northwest of Manila, depending on the traffic. Victory Liners (a commercial bus line) runs air-conditioned buses direct from Manila from early morning to late at night. You can also take a 20-minute flight from Manila. The former U.S. naval base at Olongapo is now a free port (duty-free) zone with a number of relatively pricey hotels on offer. Nearby you'll find several fair beaches with basic infrastructure, as well as accommodations ranging from modest to luxurious.

Most of Subic Bay's best diving is in the harbor, on the wrecks of varying antiquity and structural integrity. Coral enthusiasts will enjoy the diving off Grande Island, which is also a good spot for snorkelers to explore. You can also arrange trips to the Capones Islands, a couple of hours north of Subic, through a few local dive centers.

Subic also has a fully-functional recompression chamber staffed by experienced professionals. You are welcome to visit and tour the facility, but try to do so as a guest, not as a customer.

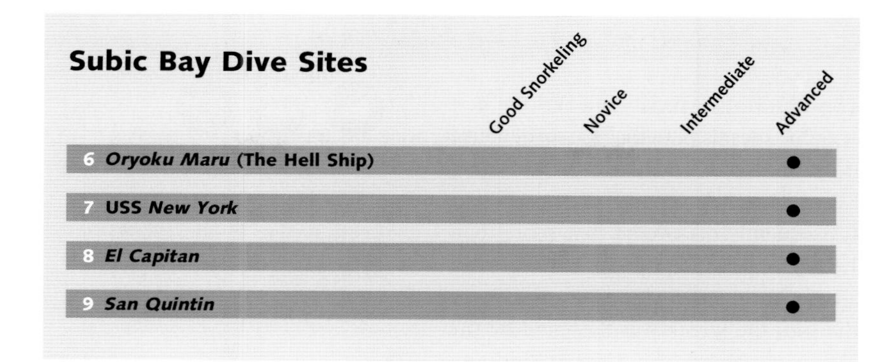

Subic Bay Dive Sites

	Good Snorkeling	Novice	Intermediate	Advanced
6 *Oryoku Maru* (The Hell Ship)				●
7 USS *New York*				●
8 *El Capitan*				●
9 *San Quintin*				●

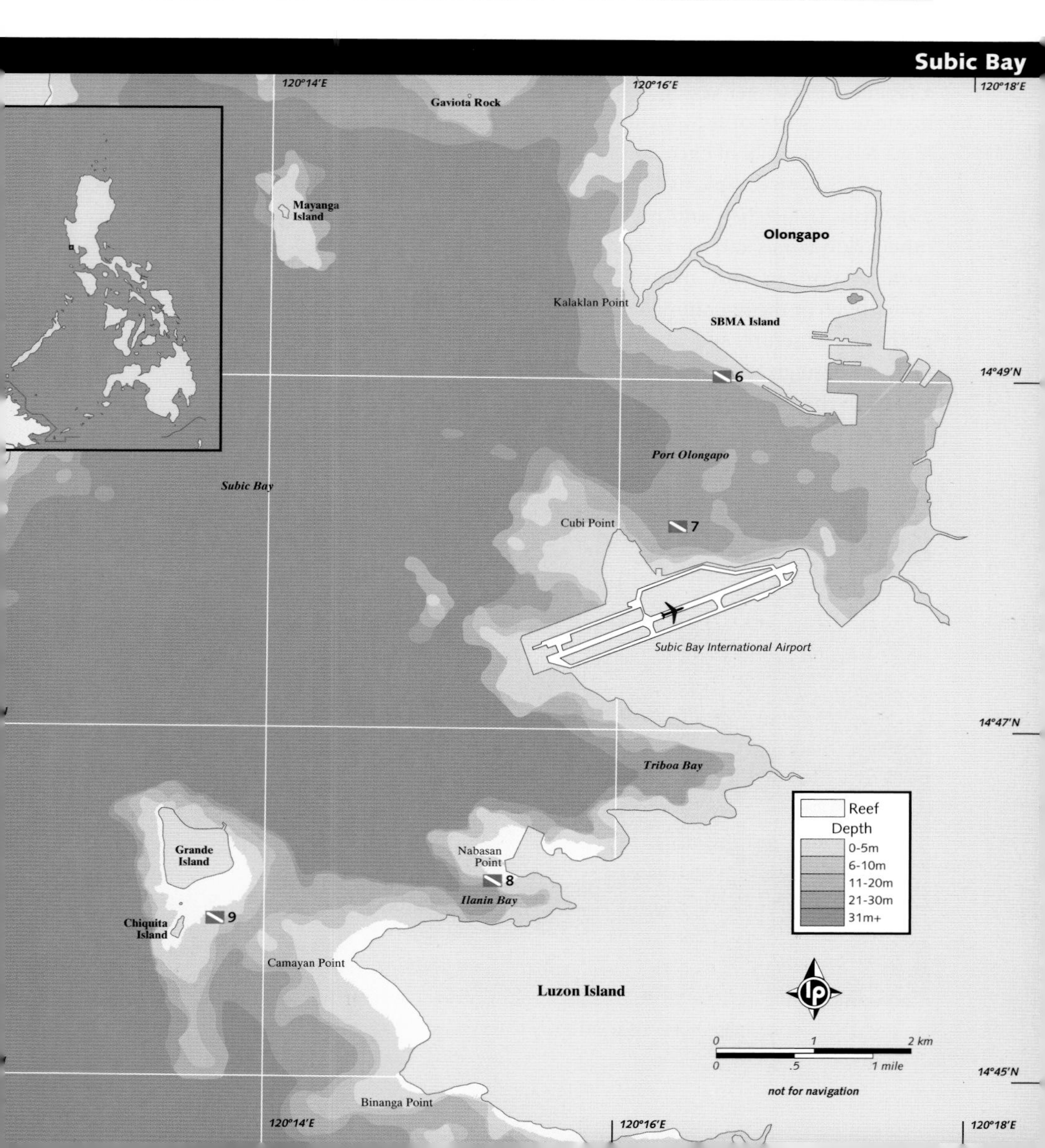

6 *Oryoku Maru* (The Hell Ship)

Location: 400m (1,300ft) from Alava Pier

Depth Range: 15-20m (50-65ft)

Access: Boat

Expertise Rating: Advanced

This notorious wreck, while not the best of Subic sites, is nonetheless worth a dive if only for its bloody history. Sunk in a U.S. air attack during WWII, it was subsequently discovered that more than 1,600 U.S. prisoners of war were onboard, all of whom perished in the attack. After the war, the wreck was flattened by the U.S. Navy, as it lay in a major shipping channel.

Not much is left to suggest it was once a Japanese passenger vessel, but it's now home to a variety of fish, including a resident shoal of barracuda, butterflyfish, sweetlips, fusiliers, angelfish, triggerfish and many others. Soft corals and some hard corals, sponges and hydroids cover much of the remaining tangled superstructure, and you may be lucky enough to spot a lobster or two in the debris. The current can pick up here, and the visibility, which can vary from 3 to 15m, is usually better just after high tide.

Wreck Diving

Wreck diving can be safe and fascinating. Penetration of shipwrecks, however, is a skilled specialty and should not be attempted without proper training. Wrecks are often unstable; they can be silty, deep and disorienting. Use an experienced guide to view wrecks and the amazing coral communities that have developed on them.

STEVE ROSENBERG

Sweetlips hover near shadowy ledges amid the Hell Ship's rubble.

7 USS *New York*

Location: 15-minute boat ride from Alava Pier

Depth Range: 15-28m (50-92ft)

Access: Boat

Expertise Rating: Advanced

This battleship is the most impressive wreck site in Subic Bay and a dive that any wreck enthusiast would not want to miss. Commissioned in 1899 as the USS *Rochester* and subsequently renamed *New York*, this vessel saw action in Manila Bay during the Spanish American War, in China during the Chinese Revolution and throughout the Pacific during WWI. Decommissioned in 1932, she was stripped of most of her fittings and lay at anchor for 10 years off the Alava Pier before retreating U.S. forces scuttled her to prevent the massive guns from falling into the hands of the advancing Japanese army.

She now rests on her port side in 28m, relatively intact save for the enormous holes the demolition experts blasted to sink her. The bow of the *New York* is distinctive, as it slopes forward rather than astern from the deck, and innumerable gun ports are mounted along the sides of the vessel.

The most prominent features of this wreck—one of only a few diveable battleships in the world—are of course the guns, but the battleship is easily penetrable. Most of the potential diver hazards were removed during her decommissioning. Make sure you go with an experienced guide and are qualified to penetrate a wreck, as the vessel is massive, and it's easy to get lost in the maze of corridors and passageways.

The *New York* is now liberally festooned with sponges, hydroids and a

ROBERT YIN

A diver takes a closer look at one of the *New York's* cannons.

variety of soft corals. Watch out for lionfish, which are all over the place. Other fish life includes some large triggerfish, sweetlips, fusiliers and batfish. Look inside the main interior passageway for a colony of groupers. A few spiny lobsters still survive in the many nooks and crannies, and you may find yourself being circled by a fairly impressive shoal of barracuda cruising around the wreck. Divers sometimes see bluespotted rays, especially along the muddy bottom of the bay.

Visibility on the wreck varies from 3 to 15m—diving at neap tide usually provides a chance for better vis and great photo opportunities. Currents within the bay are usually negligible.

8 *El Capitan*

Location: Ilanin Bay

Depth Range: 5-20m (16-65ft)

Access: Boat

Expertise Rating: Advanced

Regarded by many as one of the best wreck dives in the Philippines, *El Capitan* is certainly one of the better wrecks for photography. Visibility, as with most sites in Subic Bay, ranges from 5 to 15m. Try to hit it just after high tide for the best chance at good vis, and watch out for currents, which can be a factor here.

You come upon the wreck in only 5m of water and, despite some serious damage to the structure, will immediately recognize this as a small freighter (130m long, 3,000 tons). This penetrable wreck lies on its port side with the bow at 20m. It's covered in clams, lots of soft corals and sponges, hydroids and clouds of small tropical fish, and some hard coral is dotted about the surrounding seafloor. Around the wreck resides a wide assortment of tropical fish, including lionfish, glasseyes, wrasses, tangs, gobies, batfish, damselfish, spotted sweetlips, crabs, clownfish and the occasional lobster.

TIM ROCK

Juvenile wrasses are among *El Capitan's* varied resident fish.

9 *San Quintin*

Location: Close to Grande Island

Depth Range: 12-16m (40-53ft)

Access: Boat

Expertise Rating: Advanced

To obstruct American warships, the Spanish scuttled the *San Quintin* in 1898 at the mouth of Subic Bay. Though the wreck is now little more than rubble, it's surrounded by a variety of marine life, much of it larger than you will find within the bay itself. Look for wrasses, gobies, glasseyes, tangs, spotted sweetlips, lobsters and crabs.

Currents can be a little awkward—plan your dive carefully to avoid getting swept off the wreck into open water and away from the dive boat. As the site is somewhat exposed, the sea conditions can pick up quite quickly, making this a potentially uncomfortable ride to a rough entry and exit. However, because of the currents, visibility tends to be better here than in the bay.

Anilao

Just south of Manila, the province of Batangas has some of the best dive sites off the coast of Luzon. These include Fortune Island, sites near Matabungkay and, most famous, Balayan Bay, home to the sleepy little town of Anilao, the birthplace of diving in the Philippines.

The rugged, bamboo- and jungle-covered coastline of this region is almost as dramatic as the underwater scenery. Anilao, world famous for its macrophotography opportunities, is home to many nudibranch species, some of which exist only here. Currents can be a factor at most of the inshore sites, and more so at offshore sites such as Maricaban Island. Visibility ranges between 3 to 24m (10 to 80ft), depending on the tide and the time of year.

TIM ROCK

Banca boats take divers to Anilao sites year-round.

A portion of a long-awaited highway from Manila to Batangas was opened in 2000, although many travelers still prefer to take the longer scenic route over gorgeous Tagaytay Ridge. Because of its proximity to Manila, Anilao is popular with locals as a weekend dive destination. It's possible to negotiate a midweek deal here, but many resorts are more or less shut down during the week. Make sure you are guaranteed access to boats, equipment and guides before making your reservation.

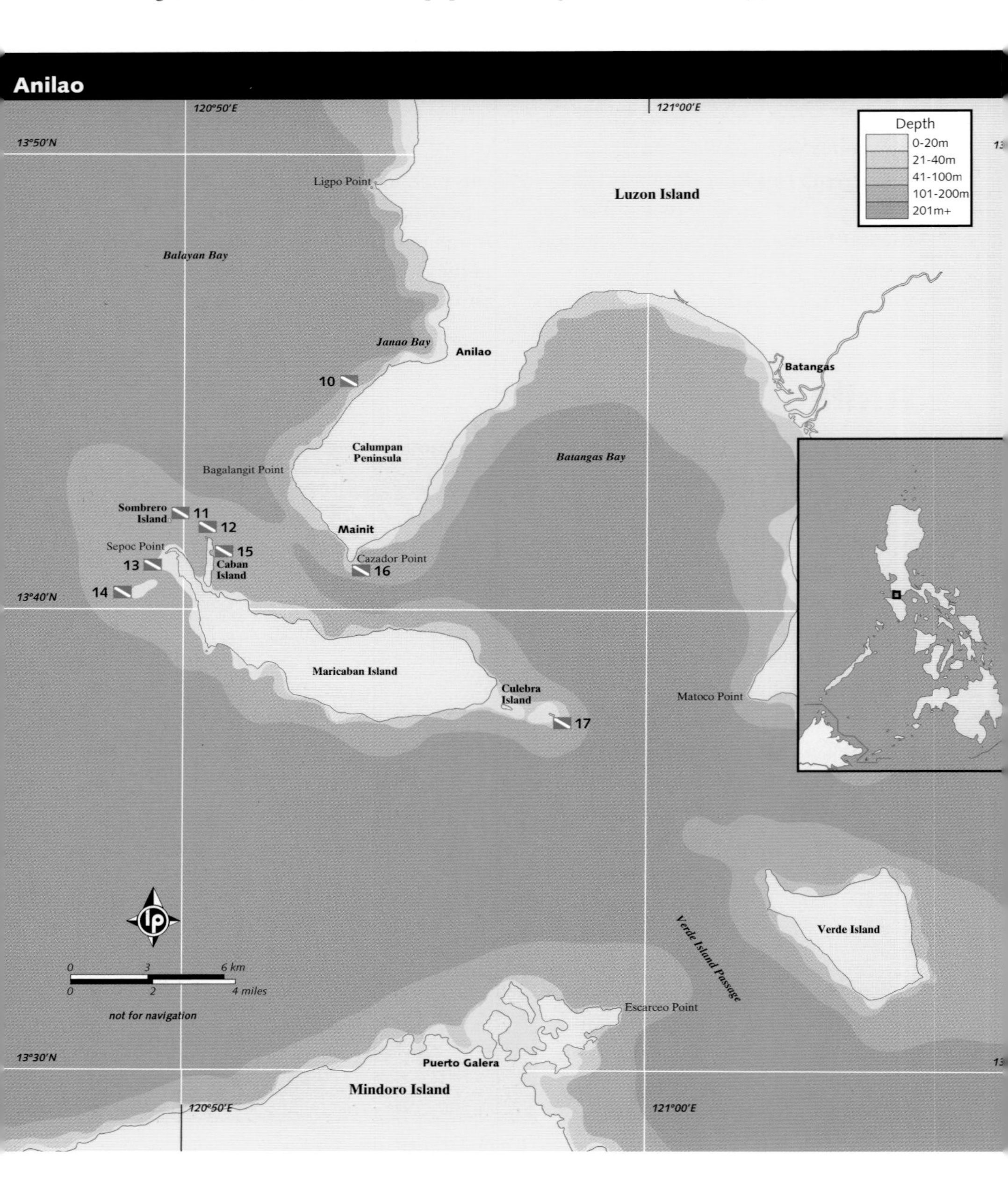

Anilao Dive Sites

	Good Snorkeling	Novice	Intermediate	Advanced
10 Cathedral Rock	●	●		
11 Sombrero Island	●			●
12 Bajura	●			●
13 Sepok Wall			●	
14 Mapating				●
15 Caban Cove	●	●		
16 Mainit	●		●	
17 Hot Springs			●	

10 Cathedral Rock

Location: NE of Bagalangit Point

Depth Range: 16-30m (53-100ft)

Access: Shore or boat

Expertise Rating: Novice

Most Manila-based divers do their open-water training dives at Cathedral Rock, a marine sanctuary and probably the most famous dive site in the Philippines. Cathedral is actually a flourishing artificial reef developed in 1967 by scuba enthusiast Dr. Tim Sevilla. This pioneer transplanted the now-prodigious live

TIM ROCK

Cathedral Rock, a prolific transplanted reef, is a popular open-water training site.

corals—at the time an act thought to be impossible—onto the previously barren twin rocks. These rocks are now teeming with fish awaiting a handout from divers, who for years have been feeding them.

On weekends in season, a huge number of divers are in the water at the same time. A great place to snap a few photos, Cathedral's main drawbacks are the sometimes aggressive feeding frenzies the fish can fall into when divers approach. This can upset those with a nervous disposition, as well as those who condemn fish feeding for creating unnatural behavioral patterns.

You come upon the reef at around 16m and will undoubtedly notice the small cross from which the site gets its name. The cross was blessed by Pope John Paul II and placed here in 1983 by then-Gen. Fidel V. Ramos, who went on to become president of the Philippines.

It is possible to go deeper than 30m, but there isn't much to see below the Cathedral's localized action, which typically includes nudibranchs, Moorish idols, butterflyfish, clownfish hanging around some copious anemones, angelfish, triggerfish, wrasses, parrotfish, damsels, puffers, surgeons and a host of other species. Most of the fish here are quite small, which is a blessing considering they can be very persistent, butting at your mask and even swimming inside your BC looking for scraps of food.

TIM ROCK

Sombrero's shallow corals are ideal for snorkeling.

11 Sombrero Island

Sombrero looks exactly like its namesake (a high-crowned hat with a wide brim) from almost any angle. Its shallow fringing reef, which stretches a long way north to south but is narrower from east to west, has some impressive drop-offs falling away from its edge that further enhance the illusion. It's home to some great diving as well, most notably at adjacent **Beatrice Rock**.

Location: North of Maricaban Island's western point

Depth Range: 6-27m (20-90ft)

Access: Boat

Expertise Rating: Advanced

Crevices, tunnels and piles of large boulders are scattered off Sombrero Island's northern cliffs, and the drop-off delves to 27m on the island's western side. Currents are usually strong here, though less so to the west and south, so you can expect some pelagic action, most notably rainbow runners and yellowtails. Divers sometimes see a few species of larger rays, including the odd eagle ray. The reef itself is festooned with gorgonians, black coral, shells and lots of soft corals. Grunts, jacks, snappers and, if you're lucky, hawksbill turtles are common visitors here. As at Cathedral Rock, a small shrine was placed here at around 13m.

12 Bajura

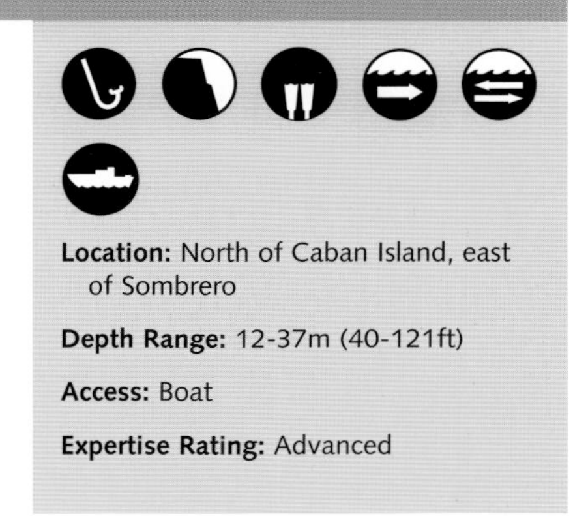

Location: North of Caban Island, east of Sombrero

Depth Range: 12-37m (40-121ft)

Access: Boat

Expertise Rating: Advanced

Bajura reef, just off the northern point of Caban Island, is more than a kilometer long. It's a challenging snorkeling site because of the strong currents and often-rough sea conditions.

Bajura's fish life is similar to Sombrero's but perhaps a little more prolific. Lots of caves and overhangs provide resting places for whitetip sharks, and the reef is also home to parrotfish, butterflyfish, wrasses, lionfish, sweetlips, scorpionfish, surgeonfish, snappers, angelfish, batfish and an occasional eagle ray, among others. The current is usually strong here, which has helped support the prolific coral population. These include table, staghorn and mushroom corals, as well as a lot of soft corals and crinoids.

TIM ROCK

Curious batfish often approach divers, providing up close photo opportunities.

13 Sepok Wall

Sepok Wall, covered in a variety of soft and hard corals, drops off impressively from west of Sepok Point to the southwest. Many nudibranchs reside at this site, so bring a camera with a macro lens. Of course, then you won't be able to take too many pictures of the copious small reef fish or the occasional pelagics that cruise by.

Location: Westernmost point of Caban Island

Depth Range: 4.5-30m (14-100ft)

Access: Boat

Expertise Rating: Intermediate

14 Mapating

This open-ocean reef is, surprisingly, not teeming with marine life from the shallow reeftop to the wall's abyssal depths. The layout of the reef can be very confusing, and the currents are sometimes strong, so this is a site for experienced divers only and should not be done without a guide.

Divers often see an impressive parade of pelagics, including large rays, whitetips and other shark species. The shallower portions of the reef are festooned with nudibranchs going about their business surrounded by prolific soft coral and some hard corals. The wall, which starts at around 18m, runs quite a distance. A ledge at 20m is sometimes used by resting nurse and cat sharks. Expect to see schools of surgeonfish and snappers along the wall. For qualified deep divers, the entrance to a massive cave lies between 43 and 48m.

Location: SSW of Sepok Wall

Depth Range: 3-40m+ (10-130ft+)

Access: Boat

Expertise Rating: Advanced

TIM ROCK

Nudibranchs festoon the shallower portions of Mapating.

15 Caban Cove

Location: Caban Island

Depth Range: 3-25m (10-82ft)

Access: Shore or boat

Expertise Rating: Novice

Caban Cove is a sheltered dive site, but watch out for the currents at the end of the cove. A great snorkeling and training area, Caban has some interesting coral formations (mostly bommies scattered across a sandy sea floor) and a progression of drop-offs that descends in steps. You can't overlook the many and colorful small tropical fish species that call this site home.

Caban Cove also has a good beach for picnicking, making this an ideal place to dive if you are traveling with folks who prefer to snorkel or sunbathe while you explore underwater.

16 Mainit

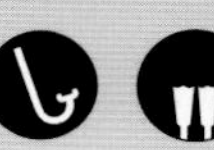    

Location: Off Cazador Point

Depth Range: 5-35m (16-115ft)

Access: Boat

Expertise Rating: Intermediate

Currents sweep this rocky, boulder-strewn, ridged, sloped reef, supporting lots of soft and hard corals. Although the wall goes quite deep, the shallower areas hold much more to see. Fish life includes Moorish idols, barracuda, sharks, pufferfish, snappers, surgeonfish, wrasses and jacks. Lots of angelfish live here as well, though not too many big ones.

A small cave at 6m is occasionally graced by resting whitetip sharks, and a submerged pinnacle at 21m offers a good vantage point from which to see the passing parade of pelagics when the current is running.

Mainit means "hot" in Tagalog—you might want to take a dip in the hot springs on the beach while you're there.

TIM ROCK

Moorish idols flit above Mainit's coral-covered slope.

17 Hot Springs

Location: Off Maricaban's eastern tip

Depth Range: 10-21m (33-70ft)

Access: Boat

Expertise Rating: Intermediate

A fascinating and unusual dive site, Hot Springs' main feature is—you guessed it—hot springs. Volcanically heated fresh water gushes from cracks in the seafloor (which is covered in unusual bright green, yellow and pastel-hued soft corals) into the cooler seawater, creating a naturally heated underwater pool.

The endearing frogfish and several species of sharks and rays, among others, find this area most appealing. Because of the unique underwater environment, the visibility is almost always good here.

A further bonus is that you can cook lunch while diving. At the start of your dive simply place an egg over one of the vents—it will be hard-boiled and ready to eat by the time you finish your dive.

STEVE ROSENBERG

The unusual frogfish is easily mistaken for a piece of sponge.

Donsol—Home of Gentle Giants

Luzon's southeasternmost province has not really been developed for diving. Despite the fact that few dive sites in this area are worth the 12-hour road trip or 45-minute flight from Manila, the waters off the small town of Donsol—with a resident whale shark population—most certainly are.

ROBERT YIN

Filter-feeding whale sharks cruise Donsol's nutrient-rich bay.

Backdropped by the famous, impressive Mt. Mayon (2,420m/7,940ft), an active volcano that boasts an almost perfect cone shape, Donsol leapt to international fame in 1998 when visiting divers filmed fishermen from outside of the local community dissecting the carcass of a huge whale shark. After the ensuing outcry from environmentalists scared the poachers away, it was discovered that Donsol Bay has been home to a group of adult whale sharks thought to number more than 90 individuals. These *buntandings*, as they are known locally, have been cruising the murky, often-rough waters of Donsol for generations.

Environmental groups, nongovernmental organizations and other interested parties swiftly set up research programs to study these gentle giants of the sea. Meanwhile, as word of the phenomenon spread, hundreds of divers and snorkelers arrived in sleepy Donsol with the hope of swimming with the whale sharks. Realizing the need to both protect the animals and cater to the swelling crowds of visitors, the local government, together with groups such as the WWF, has established visitor guidelines and strictly enforces them.

The official season for whale watching runs from February 1 to May 31. Though snorkeling with the whale sharks is permitted, diving is strictly forbidden. Bring your own snorkeling gear, as rental equipment is limited and quality varies. Flash photography is not allowed, nor is physical contact with the whale sharks.

Only authorized boats may carry guests out to the whale watching area, and a registered guide must accompany visitors at all times. Visitors should expect to pay a minimum of US$100 for each boat, sometimes more depending on the number of guests in the boat.

Donsol Bay's waters, as mentioned, are quite turbid, and the weather turns soon after May 1, making boat trips unsafe and snorkeling impossible. Consequently, as yet no one knows if the sharks stay here year-round or make an annual or semiannual pilgrimage to Donsol. We do know that this is the single most unique and unusual whale shark gathering so far discovered on the planet.

One further word of advice: Mt. Mayon is an active volcano. Since 1998 the volcano has had several minor eruptions. When it is showing signs of activity, you should not visit Donsol—getting to the town may be impossible under such circumstances. For more information you can contact any of the dive centers in Metro Manila, the Sorsogon Provincial Tourism Council or call Fernando's Hotel in Sorsogon: ☎ (63-56) 211 1357.

Mindoro Dive Sites

This rugged, mountainous island is one of the most popular, if not *the* most popular, destinations for divers visiting the Philippines. Most of the diving is near Puerto Galera (Spanish for "Port of the Galleons"), a perfect, natural harbor endowed with a stunningly beautiful tropical topside as well as some of the best underwater scenery in the islands.

In the gorgeous coves and bays east of Puerto Galera you'll find more than 30 excellent dive sites within 20 minutes of most diving services, and more dive sites farther out. Accessible snorkeling is just offshore, where marine life abounds even in shallow water. Dive safaris (live-aboard trips) are also arranged from Puerto Galera and usually visit Maestre de Campo and the Sibuyan Sea (see Sibuyan Sea Dive Sites, page 72) to the southeast and Apo Reef, Hunter's Rock and Coron Bay (see Palawan Dive Sites, Coron, page 137) to the southwest.

The coastal waters of Puerto Galera were declared a marine sanctuary several decades ago. As a result, the reefs have become amazingly diverse and prolific

Mindoro Dive Sites

	Site	Good Snorkeling	Novice	Intermediate	Advanced
18	Talipanan Reef				●
19	Manila Channel (Northwest Channel)	●	●		
20	Coral Gardens (The Hill)	●	●		
21	Big La Laguna Beach	●	●		
22	Monkey Beach	●	●		●
23	Ernie's Cave	●		●	
24	West Escarceo	●	●		
25	Hole in the Wall		●		
26	Shark Cave				●
27	Pink Wall & Canyons	●	●		●
28	Sinandigan Wall		●		
29	Washing Machine	●			●
30	Verde Island Wall	●		●	

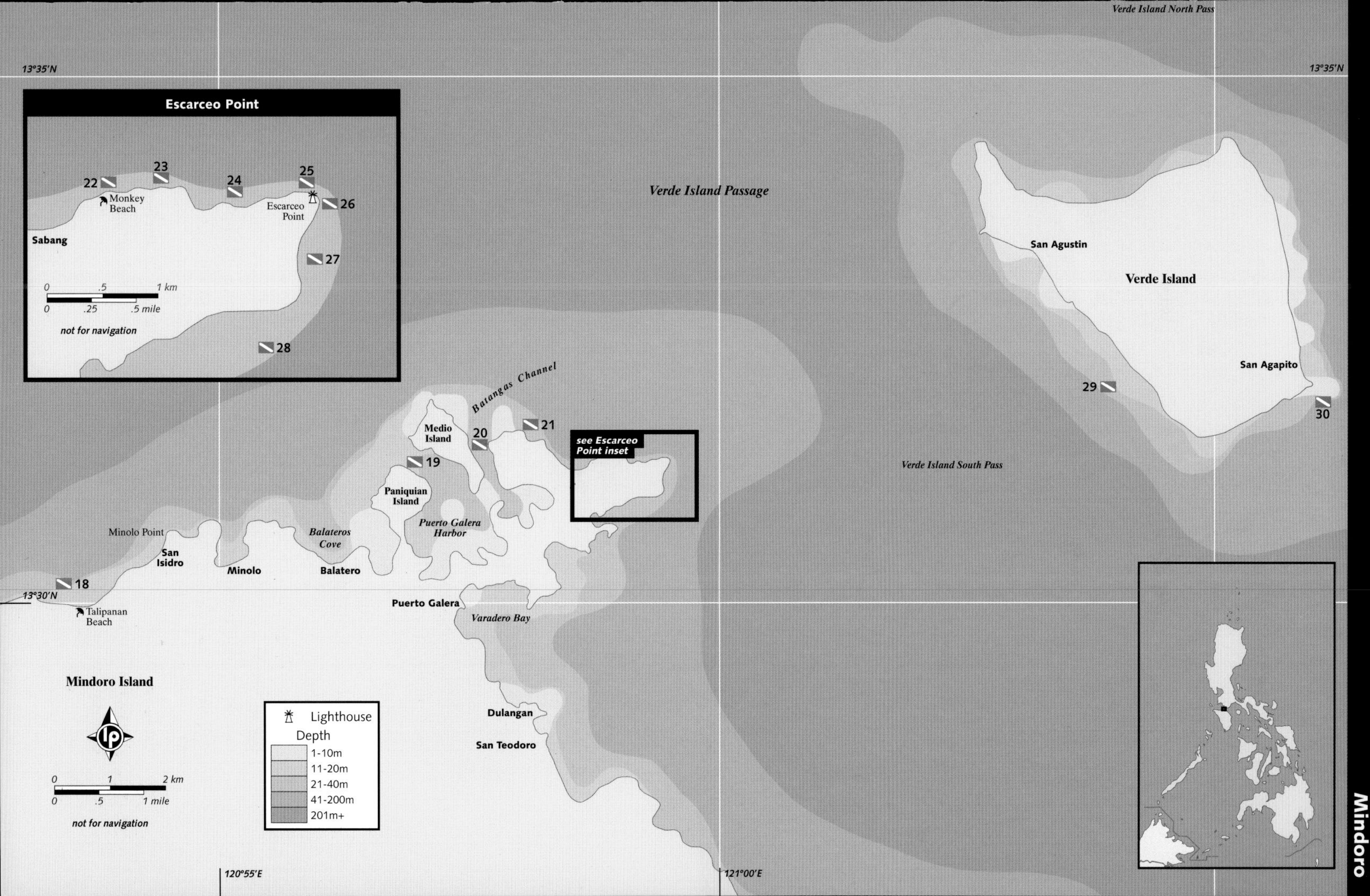

Escarceo Point
Sabang
Monkey Beach
Escarceo Point
22
23
24
25
26
27
28
0 .5 1 km
0 .25 .5 mile
not for navigation
Verde Island North Pass
Verde Island Passage
13°35'N
Verde Island
San Agustin
San Agapito
29
30
Verde Island South Pass
Batangas Channel
see Escarceo Point inset
Medio Island
Paniquian Island
Puerto Galera Harbor
Balateros Cove
Minolo Point
San Isidro
Minolo
Balatero
Puerto Galera
Varadero Bay
Dulangan
San Teodoro
Talipanan Beach
13°30'N
18
19
20
21
Mindoro Island
Lighthouse
Depth
1-10m
11-20m
21-40m
41-200m
201m+
0 1 2 km
0 .5 1 mile
not for navigation
120°55'E
121°00'E

TIM ROCK

Hotels, restaurants and dive shops line Big La Laguna Beach, west of Sabang.

over the years. The general consensus is that locals benefit more by maintaining and preserving the reefs and marine life—and by catering to divers' needs—than by fishing.

Diving is possible year-round, most of it done from boats, although there are a few possible shore entries. Visibility can exceed 24m (80ft), but is usually less. Currents can be quite strong at some of the sites, and unwary divers have been swept out to sea on occasion, so always dive with a knowledgeable local guide, of which there is no shortage. Puerto Galera is a major dive-training location with many professional instructors and courses ranging from basic Open Water certification to technical diving. A wide selection of rental equipment is available. PADI is the predominant agency here, as it is throughout the country.

A two-hour bus ride from Manila to Batangas followed by a one-hour crossing of the Verde Island Passage, Puerto Galera is easily accessible. Most resorts and dive centers can arrange transfers from anywhere in Manila. Accommodation is plentiful, ranging from simple beach cottages to air-conditioned resorts. Many expatriates from around the world call Puerto Galera home these days, drawn as much by the business opportunities it offers as by the wealth of natural assets it enjoys. Consequently, visitors will have no shortage of dining and entertainment options.

18 Talipanan Reef

Location: Off Talipanan Beach

Depth Range: 15-40m+ (50-130ft+)

Access: Boat

Expertise Rating: Advanced

Talipanan Beach is about 8km west of Puerto Galera's town proper. It's the last beach you'll come to before the coast becomes a cliff face. Although not visited as often as many of the other sites in the region (presumably because it's farther from the dive centers clustered east of Puerto), Talipanan is a great dive site with everything an experienced diver could hope for. Visibility ranges from a few meters to 25m, depending on the currents, tides and season.

Talipanan's reef, which lies about a kilometer or so offshore, is teeming with life. Divers usually see large pelagics, including Spanish mackerel, rainbow runners, tuna, yellowtail, wahoos and whitetip and blacktip sharks. Divers should watch for several species of rays, including eagle and leopard rays. The reef itself, subjected to strong currents most of the time, consists of jumbled hard corals that compete for every square inch of space. Gorgonians poke out from its sides, and you'll find a fair representation of most of the hard corals and many of the soft corals you would expect to find in these waters. Surgeonfish, sweetlips, triggerfish and squirrelfish hide in the many cracks and fissures, while angelfish, emperors and a host of other tropical fish vie for survival on this vibrant rock.

TIM ROCK

Sweetlips and sea whips are a small part of what make Talipanan worth visiting.

19 Manila Channel (Northwest Channel)

Location: Puerto Galera Harbor

Depth Range: 1-22m (3-72ft)

Access: Boat

Expertise Rating: Novice

The remains of an ancient interisland trading vessel are in many ways responsible for putting Puerto Galera on the diving map. This ship apparently caught fire and sunk hundreds of years ago. After identifying the wreck, discoverer Brian Homan and the National Museum salvaged Chinese pottery from the surrounding mud. Proceeds from the salvage project helped fund the area's fledgling dive centers, enabling them to expand and eventually capture a large share of the Philippines' diving market.

TIM ROCK
Sea fans thrive in the channel's moderate current.

Not much is left of the wreck now, but the site is a fun dive and has some healthy corals. Two small walls drop off progressively to 18m, beyond which the seafloor slopes away more gradually. Some medium-sized groupers live here, but they're difficult to spot, as they are well camouflaged and disappear into various holes and cracks at a diver's approach. With this site's moderate current, dives are best attempted on a flood tide.

Sunken Treasure

For centuries, Chinese traders and Spanish galleons roamed the often-perilous waters of the Philippines. Many ended up on the bottom of the ocean, their precious cargoes lost forever. Well, perhaps not forever...

Every year, spectacular discoveries of sunken treasures are announced—and more are probably kept tight-lipped secrets. Ancient Chinese pottery worth millions of dollars, as well as historical wrecks full of valuable artifacts, are frequently found off the reefs and islands of the Philippines, even in such well-dived locations as Coron Bay and Puerto Galera.

While the odds are remote that you'll stumble onto an ancient Spanish galleon loaded with gold and jewels or a Chinese junk loaded to the gunwales with priceless Ming pottery, it could happen. And there's nothing like the thought of discovering a king's ransom in ancient treasure to add a little spice to a remote dive trip!

20 Coral Gardens (The Hill)

Location: Batangas Channel

Depth Range: 3-15m (10-50ft)

Access: Boat

Expertise Rating: Novice

If you are heading by boat to any of the beaches northeast of Puerto Galera, you'll pass this attractive site on your way out of the channel—you can't miss the prolific corals and sponges that grow in the shallow water here.

Provided there's no current running, this is an easy dive that is frequently used for training and is also a great snorkeling spot. Staghorn and basket corals are prolific, and shell fanciers will appreciate the variety of cowry species that are common at this site. Clams, morays, lionfish and the occasional frogfish also inhabit the area.

TIM ROCK

This snowflake moray shelters within the coral's crevices.

21 Big La Laguna Beach

Location: Off Big La Laguna Beach

Depth Range: 2-15m (7-50ft)

Access: Shore

Expertise Rating: Novice

This is a shallow but interesting dive, making it ideal for training and snorkeling. Currents are typically negligible, though if you swim too far out, you can get caught in them, so watch out!

You'll find lots of hard and soft corals and plenty of small tropical reef fish, including an occasional frogfish. Look for morays, clams and lots of nudibranchs in the reef's nooks and crannies. These critters and others make this an ideal macrophotography site and a popular night dive.

22 Monkey Beach

Keep an eye on your depth gauge here, because it's easy to go deeper than you planned. Monkey Beach is, in fact, an easy dive down a gentle slope festooned with small coral bommies. You'll find fairly good snorkeling here for experienced snorkelers who are accomplished free-divers. Current can be a factor, so time your dive according to your preferences—an outgoing tide will carry you along, while slack tide is a bit more calm.

Location: East of Sabang Point

Depth Range: 3-40m+ (10-130ft+)

Access: Boat or shore

Expertise Rating: Novice (off beach)
Advanced (wall and wreck)

TIM ROCK

Monkey Beach Wreck is a popular technical dive.

Expect to find stingrays, leatherjackets, surgeonfish and an occasional turtle or two. The bommies, ideal breeding grounds, are home to lots of smaller blennies, wrasses, juvenile groupers and other small tropical reef fish. This is also a very popular night dive, where divers often see cuttlefish.

Follow the wall down from Monkey Beach and, if your guide knows where he is going, you'll run into **Monkey Beach Wreck**, the remains of a 25m-long wooden vessel, one of several boats scuttled over the years by local dive operators in an effort to create additional dive sites—as if there were not already enough in Puerto Galera! This particular effort was only partially successful in that the boat corkscrewed down deeper than was intended, apparently disintegrating as it did so, and settled upside down to boot.

Nonetheless, with the advent of technical diving in the

area, this has become a popular dive in its own right.

Not much remains of the actual vessel, but what's left is home to a colony of cod and snappers, and it's visited by cuttlefish on occasion. Soft corals have attached themselves to much of the remaining timber.

23 Ernie's Cave

Ernie was a large, solitary grouper that used to hang out in this cave named after him. Alas, poor old Ernie is no longer with us, having departed for the great fishbowl in the sky, but his memory lives on at this site.

Location: East of Monkey Beach

Depth Range: 10-28m (33-92ft)

Access: Boat

Expertise Rating: Intermediate

TIM ROCK

Strong currents make for great visibility here.

Here you'll find not one, but two small caves—one at 22m, the other at 28m. Ernie's surviving compatriots include shoals of snappers, fusiliers, surgeonfish and unicornfish. At the deeper part of the dive you can marvel at some very attractive gorgonian corals. Be aware that the current can be quite stiff.

24 West Escarceo

Location: West of Escarceo Point

Depth Range: 3-30m (10-100ft)

Access: Boat

Expertise Rating: Novice

West Escarceo can be a relatively relaxing dive for a novice or a challenging one for an intermediate diver, depending on the current. Again, having a dive guide who knows your specific skill level will enhance both your safety and enjoyment of this site.

Depending on the direction of the current, you'll either get pushed along the steep slope, which drops away to 30m, toward Canyons and Hole in the Wall, or you'll find yourself drifting among shoals of fusiliers and tuna. You'll see some impressive boulder and table corals here, and it's a popular site for photographers.

25 Hole in the Wall

Location: Off Escarceo Point

Depth Range: 9-18m (30-60ft)

Access: Boat

Expertise Rating: Novice

This site off Escarceo Point is renowned for its sometimes ferocious currents and riptides, whirlpools and eddies. As with any dive in this vicinity, always take a qualified and experienced dive guide along to make sure you don't end up in the middle of the South China Sea.

One of the more popular sites around Puerto Galera, Hole in the Wall is reached by dropping in over a field of stunning table corals at about 9m. Several 3m-high drop-offs festooned with hard and soft corals lead down to the namesake hole at around 13m. The hole itself is about 1.5m wide, which allows a fully equipped diver to easily pass through. It's covered with brightly colored sponges, crinoids and soft corals.

The wall falls away beyond this, and you'll have a good chance of running into large pelagics and even a turtle or two beyond the hole. Local divers have from time to time reported seeing mantas, whale sharks and other big fish here and at the adjacent Canyons. You will certainly see sweetlips and lionfish, probably jacks and tuna, a moray eel and maybe even a whitetip or two. Technical divers or advanced deep divers with quick finning techniques and good air consumption may well decide to go deeper from here to visit the Canyons.

TIM ROCK

The ornate lionfish's delicate fins belie their potent venom. Keep your hands out of harm's way.

26 Shark Cave

Location: Off Escarceo Point

Depth Range: 18-28m (60-92ft)

Access: Boat

Expertise Rating: Advanced

One of the most popular dives in Puerto Galera, this cave is really more of an overhang. Shark Cave is usually done as part of a dive at Canyons—when the current is right, you'll pass over Shark Cave on your way there. You can drop down into the small dip at the mouth of the cave to shelter from the current. It's also dived as the deeper section of a multilevel dive ending at Pink Wall.

During the daytime, one or two whitetip sharks often rest in this cave. Photographers love this dive because you can get really close to the sharks. The cave is not big, and neither are the sharks. A little deeper, a narrower cave occasionally hosts whitetips.

TIM ROCK

Shark Cave offers abundant fish and corals, as well as occasional whitetips.

27 Pink Wall & Canyons

Location: Off Escarceo Point

Depth Range: 12-40m (40-130ft)

Access: Boat

Expertise Rating: Novice (Pink Wall) Advanced (Canyons)

When the tide is right, Pink Wall, just off of Escarceo Point, is an ideal spot for novice divers. Actually an overhang festooned with pink cauliflower corals, the Pink Wall is a favorite night dive as well. It's popular with photographers for its colorful corals.

Nearby is an advanced site, Canyons, worthy of more than one dive. Local knowledge of the currents is imperative here, as you must rely on the prevailing current to sweep you into position on this dive. After racing with the current over several small drop-offs festooned with soft corals and sponges, you'll find yourself in an area with several crevasses (the canyons) cleaved into the wall. These afford some respite from the usually raging current.

Expect to see large schools of trevallies, snappers, emperors, sweetlips, jacks, barracuda and sometimes whitetip sharks. Lionfish, surgeonfish and angelfish are also often present. The usual end point of this dive is a large anchor (about 1.5m across) embedded in the reef. It's covered with soft corals and is home to a couple of lionfish. You may get lucky here and spot the legendary Barnacle Bill, a large hawksbill turtle that frequents the area.

28 Sinandigan Wall

Location: SW of Escarceo Point

Depth Range: 3-40m (10-130ft)

Access: Boat

Expertise Rating: Novice

This impressive wall has some outstanding coral formations. The usual array of tropical reef fish call this home, and occasionally pelagics pass by, especially when the current is running. Of special interest at this site are the nudibranchs: At least seven different species are present. Divers may also see surgeonfish, lionfish, groupers, snappers, a few morays and the odd pufferfish.

TIM ROCK

Nudibranchs are colorful, willing photo subjects.

29 Washing Machine

Location: Off Verde Island's west coast

Depth Range: 3-15m (10-50ft)

Access: Boat

Expertise Rating: Advanced

As the name implies, the current here can be ferocious. While this site may not be everybody's cup of tea, when the current is running at full tilt, the Washing Machine beats the heck out of any amusement park ride! The fun occurs over a series of seven gullies on the gently sloping seafloor that runs out from the rocky shore of Verde's west coast. There is nothing particularly impressive about the dive site itself other than the current. When the current is not running, it's a relatively easy and not particularly interesting dive compared with many of the other local sites. When it's running, you fairly fly over the bottom, swooping down into a gully to get out of the raging torrent whenever you feel like taking a break.

30 Verde Island Wall

Location: SE point of Verde Island

Depth Range: 5-25m+ (16-82ft+)

Access: Boat

Expertise Rating: Intermediate

Recognized as one of the best wall dives in the country, Verde Island Wall is this area's diving highlight. Although it's closer to Puerto Galera and popular with divers based there, Verde is also regularly visited by divers staying in Anilao and can be dived from the island's own luxury resort and dive center.

The wall itself is easy to find: Look for the two rocks jutting out of the sea 100m or so off the island's southeast point. Drop in a few meters south of them, then head north. The wall is hard to miss, but be careful of the current, which can whisk you away in the wrong direction if you plan your dive wrong.

The visibility is usually excellent here, and the wall itself has lots of cracks and crevices that you can use to duck out of the current, but remember that it falls away to great depths—take care not to exceed your limits. Most divers remain above 25m, and frankly there is no good reason to descend any deeper than that.

Whitetips and other sharks, occasional mantas, eagle rays, tuna and jacks, rainbow runners, wahoos and Spanish mackerel are among the pelagics you could see along this mighty wall. Napoleon wrasses, parrotfish, unicornfish, legions of soldierfish, surgeons, batfish, tangs, gobies and sweetlips and emperors are found throughout the area.

The wall itself is festooned in an impossible array of colorful corals. Some especially impressive gorgonians decorate the wall, jutting out between vast slabs of star corals. Huge, colorful riots of soft corals drape and dangle from the drop-off, and sea fans and anemones sway endlessly in the current. When making your recommended safety stop on the reeftop, look for the bubbles of volcanic gases escaping from the reef's cracks.

TIM ROCK

Sea fans festoon the Verde Island Wall.

Sibuyan Sea Dive Sites

The Sibuyan Sea lies between the east coast of Mindoro, the west coast of Bicol, the south coast of Marinduque Island and the northern Visayas. Though it's too remote to be dived by dayboats, live-aboard trips to the area are organized by dive centers from Puerto Galera and Boracay and usually last from three to five days. Yet, due to unpredictable weather patterns and sea conditions, schedules sometimes change. The diving season runs from January to June, with March to May

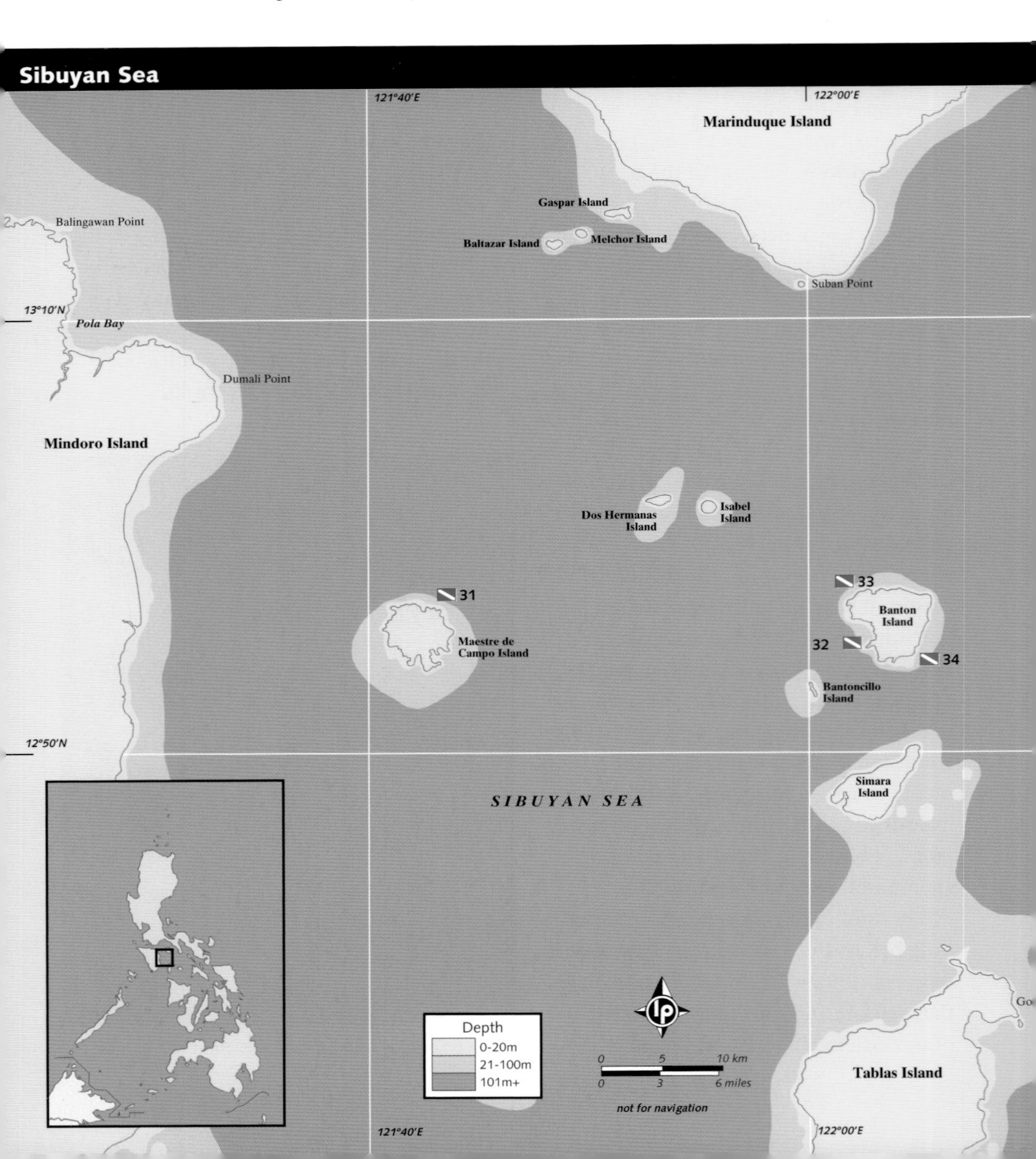

being the best months to visit, but it's possible to dive year-round at some of the more sheltered sites.

Dive sites here are varied, ranging from the popular wreck of the MV *Mactan* (an interisland ferryboat that went down off the coast of Maestre de Campo a few decades ago) to tiny colorful Banton Island and the sheltered Romblon and Tablas Islands. The waters surrounding Marinduque are home to a number of more sheltered sites, such as Tres Reyes, Dos Hermanos and Nantanco, which are usually only visited when the seas are too rough to get to preferred destinations.

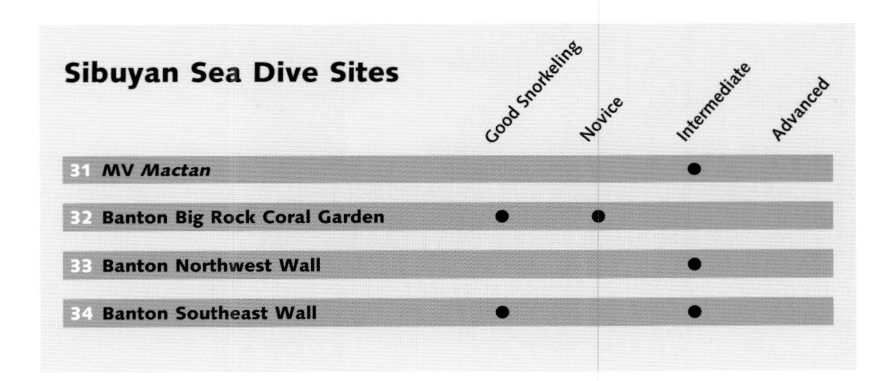

Sibuyan Sea Dive Sites

	Good Snorkeling	Novice	Intermediate	Advanced
31 MV *Mactan*			●	
32 Banton Big Rock Coral Garden	●	●		
33 Banton Northwest Wall			●	
34 Banton Southeast Wall	●		●	

31 MV *Mactan*

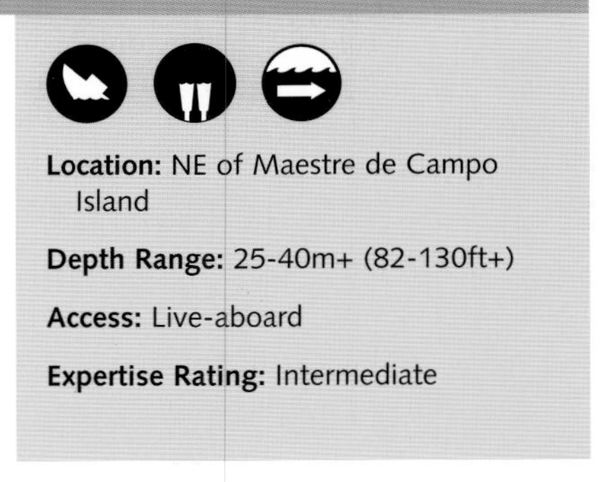

Location: NE of Maestre de Campo Island

Depth Range: 25-40m+ (82-130ft+)

Access: Live-aboard

Expertise Rating: Intermediate

This old ferryboat capsized in the late '70s in a freak wave just off the coast of Maestre de Campo Island. The passengers and crew were saved by hauling themselves along a rope that a couple of brave swimmers managed to attach to the sinking vessel from the mainland. No lives were lost, and the diving community gained one of the country's better wreck dives.

The hull sits more or less upright and north to south on the 25 to 55m-deep sandy bottom. It's now home to groupers, snappers, sweetlips, shoals of barracuda, plenty of lionfish and lots of small tropical reef fish. The wreck is penetrable, but because of its depth, only experienced and trained wreck divers should attempt to do so. It's an excellent technical dive. Current can be a factor here, and though the visibility is not always perfect, it can reach more than 20m.

Maestre de Campo's harbor, Port Concepcion, is the final resting place of the remains of two small Japanese warships and a couple of small WWII planes. Visibility is not normally that good here, but the muddy seabed can often reward a diligent searcher with a relic or bottle to keep as a souvenir. (While the National Museum regards anything older than 100 years old as an antiquity and therefore sacrosanct, any object newer than this, apart from gold, precious metals, etc., is technically salvageable. To perform an actual salvage operation, a permit is required.)

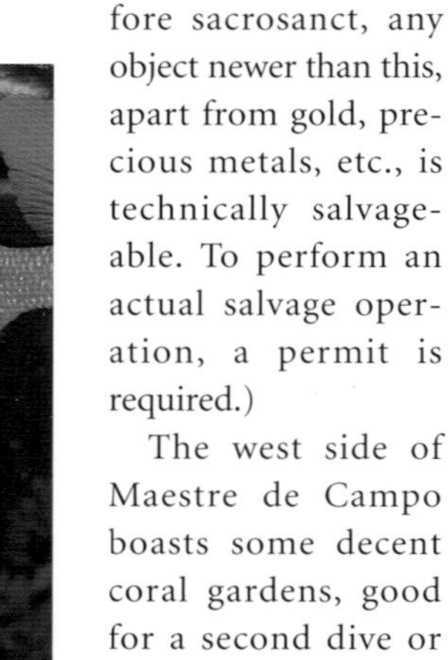

STEVE ROSENBERG

The *Mactan's* hull is now home to sweetlips and other groupers.

The west side of Maestre de Campo boasts some decent coral gardens, good for a second dive or snorkeling when the sea is calm.

32 Banton Big Rock Coral Garden

Location: Banton Island's west coast

Depth Range: Surface-12m (40ft)

Access: Live-aboard

Expertise Rating: Novice

After diving Banton's Northwest Wall, head southwest around the corner to a small bay with a large rock sticking out of it. This is a colorful shallow dive (you needn't exceed 12m) and is also an excellent snorkeling site.

Swim over the pristine coral reef, where sea whips and a host of other corals—table, boulder, brain and more—carpet the sandy seafloor. Groupers, snappers, sweetlips, cuttlefish and lots of small reef fish are everywhere, and they don't seem overly shy of divers or snorkelers. The large rock's seaward face has a huge cleft that is penetrable for several meters.

33 Banton Northwest Wall

Location: Banton Island's NW point

Depth Range: Surface-40m+ (130ft+)

Access: Live-aboard

Expertise Rating: Intermediate

About 30km from Marinduque Island's southern tip, Banton is a nearly circular island with a diameter of just 3km. The islanders rely on copra farming for subsistence (the entire island is covered in coconut trees), and they don't maintain a fishing fleet: In fact, they discourage off-islanders from fishing in their waters.

Serious currents can rip around the island and it's not always possible to reach it in a small boat. Once you get there, you can usually dive on one side of the island or the other.

Though the island has two main sites and a number of lesser ones, Banton's Northwest Wall is one of the most impressive in the country. And it's easy to find—just get in the water a few meters offshore from the graffiti written on the cliff by an overzealous scholastic fraternity member.

Huge gorgonians, sheer slopes, overhangs, cracks, caves, crevices, some outstanding hard- and soft-coral formations and a host of reef and pelagic fish make this relatively short section of the rugged Banton Island coast a place that divers want to visit again and again. You'll always find something new, whether it be a manta ray, sharks, Napoleon wrasses, tuna, barracuda, sweetlips, large groupers or snappers. Look for soldierfish and surgeons swimming in shoals, pennant butterflyfish flitting about, morays poking out of holes and pufferfish puffing around. Gobies, blennies, anthias and chromis weave their way in and out of the soft corals, table gorgonians and other stony corals that adorn the wall.

SCOTT TUASON

Banton's reefs and walls offer healthy corals and colorful fish.

34 Banton Southeast Wall

When the current or waves are too much to dive the Northwest Wall, it's usually OK to dive along the southeast side of the island. A gently sloping healthy coral garden runs from the seashore to around 10m, where the wall drops off steeply. Some good overhangs, crevices and some really big soft corals cascade in places over the lip of the wall, forming bulbous pastel curtains. You'll find plenty of fish, but the visibility is not usually as good here as at Northwest Wall.

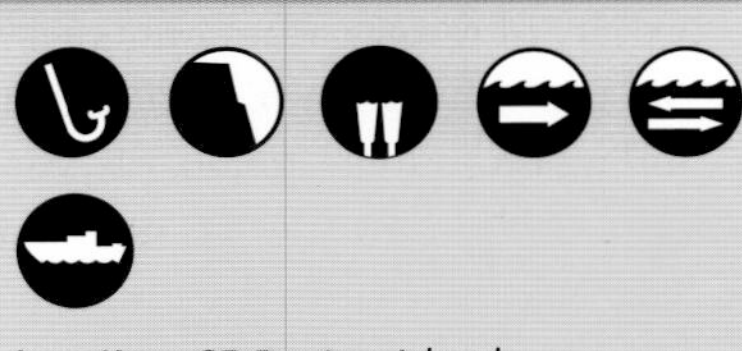

Location: SE Banton Island

Depth Range: Surface-40m+ (130ft+)

Access: Live-aboard

Expertise Rating: Intermediate

The Visayas Dive Sites

Encompassing a broad swath of central Philippine territory that includes dozens of islands large and small, the Visayas is a treasure trove of underwater delights for both divers and snorkelers. Some of the prime spots are near Boracay Island, Cebu City and Mactan Island, the Visayan Triangle (which includes Moalboal, Dumaguete and Bohol) and Southern Leyte. Though dive trips can be booked year-round here, check the weather report first. Between July and October this region is sometimes hit by typhoons.

Cebu City is the region's transportation hub. Ferryboats are the most common way to get around the Visayas. An assortment of vessels, from fast Super Cat ferries to aged wooden hulks, ply the Visayan Sea's waters. Many of the islands are served by regular airline flights from both Manila and Cebu.

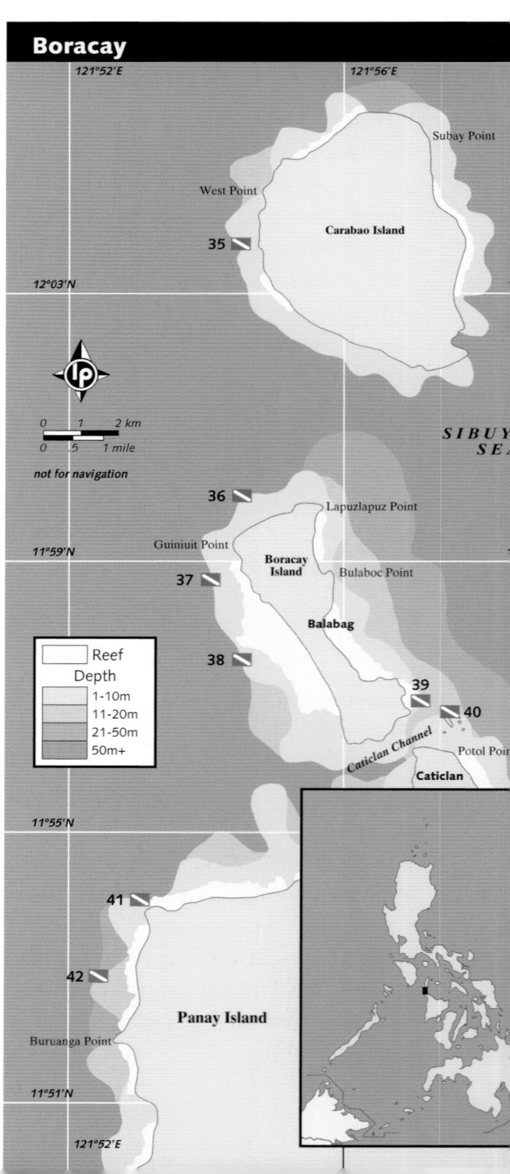

Boracay

Sand like talcum powder, a booming cosmopolitan beach scene and outstanding natural beauty have all contributed to making Boracay one of the most famous beach destinations in the Philippines. On the main west-facing beach you'll find more than 20 dive centers, a large variety of resorts, restaurants serving everything from Thai cuisine to English muffins, sailboards, banana boats and sailing bancas for rent, a golf course, a couple of discos and countless souvenir shops. Although the diving isn't the country's best, the island has several sites worth checking out, as well as some great dive areas not far away.

Though the weather is best between January and June, it's possible to dive year-round in Boracay, as there are several sheltered sites that can be reliably dived most of the time. This is a good place to learn diving or to upgrade your certification. A couple of PADI IDC and IE courses are held here most every year, and technical diving is quite popular—some local sites, such as Yapak, lend themselves well to mixed-gas exploration.

A number of vessels ply the local dive-safari route, visiting places that other Visayan dive centers don't, including the Sibuyan Sea (see Sibuyan Sea Dive Sites, page 72), Romblon and Tablas to the north, the impressive east coast of Panay (the large island south of Boracay) and Semirara to the west.

Several small aircraft fly daily to the small strip at Caticlan (across the channel on Panay Island), and regular flights from Manila and Cebu land at Kalbo Airport (about two hours away by air-conditioned buses, which ferry travelers to Caticlan for the 2km, or 1¼-mile, crossing).

MARK DAFFEY

Boracay offers clear water and sandy shores.

Boracay Dive Sites

	Good Snorkeling	Novice	Intermediate	Advanced
35 Cathedral Cave			●	
36 Yapak				●
37 Punta Bonga 1 & 2	●		●	
38 Friday's Rock	●	●		
39 Crocodile Island	●		●	
40 Laurel Island	●		●	
41 Nasog Point	●		●	
42 Dog Drift	●		●	

35 Cathedral Cave

The sometimes-thrilling boat ride (which means it can get rough quite quickly) across the channel separating Carabao Island from Boracay isn't everyone's idea of a good day out. But when the sea conditions warrant it, the trip to Cathedral Cave rewards you with its unusual diving.

Location: West Carabao Island

Depth Range: 25-40m (82-130ft)

Access: Boat

Expertise Rating: Intermediate

STEVE ROSENBERG

Colorful corals adorn Cathedral's nearby walls.

The wide-mouthed cave entrance is at 28m, and the cave goes well back into the reef. No cave diving experience is necessary to enter this cave—it's more of a large hollow with plenty of cracks and crevices in its walls than it is a system of passageways. In addition to the many reef fish that proliferate inside and around the cave, you may see some large groupers. Whitetip sharks and other large fish often rest in the cave's cracks and crannies.

Adjacent to Cathedral are some good wall dives, with caves and caverns and lots of fish and corals. This area is usually visited as a second dive during a trip to Carabao Island.

36 Yapak

Yapak is the most exciting, vibrant and prolific dive site around Boracay. Visibility is often good, usually more than 20m. Unfortunately, the conditions can be hairy—it's deep, and the currents are often strong. Definitely not for inexperienced or nervous divers, Yapak epitomizes the best of deep diving, with big, BIG fish.

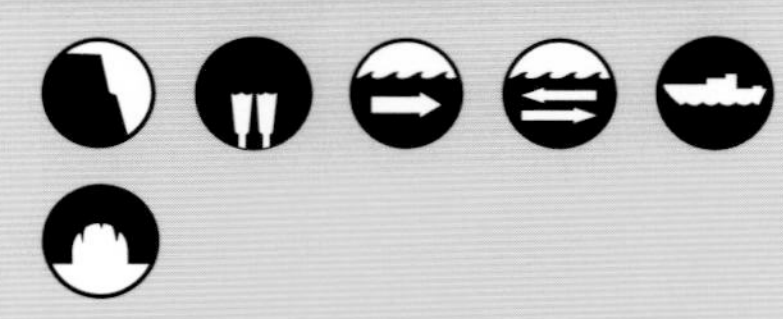

Location: North of Boracay

Depth Range: 30-40m+ (100-130ft+)

Access: Boat

Expertise Rating: Advanced

The reef wall is decorated in colorful sea fans, barrel sponges and a variety of soft corals. Despite the stunning reefscape with its endless profusion of life, it's to the deep blue waters that most divers direct their attention. Pelagics are the name of the game here, and you will seldom be disappointed. Chances are you will see a couple of shark species—perhaps whitetip and blacktip, maybe hammerheads and on rare occasions a whale shark. Tuna, jacks, wahoos, Spanish mackerel, barracuda, rainbow runners and (if you're lucky) mantas and other rays pass by in the often-swift currents, accompanied by sweetlips, surgeonfish, Napoleon wrasses, groupers and pennant butterflyfish. At the south end, also known as Yapak 1, the tunnel leading to 40m is fun to pass through if you can find it.

This is a deep dive. Remember that the nearest recompression chamber is far away in Cebu and very hard to reach. Bottom time, depth and buoyancy are critical at Yapak: If you are not confident in your ability to successfully keep up with an experienced group, consider diving Punta Bonga instead. If this is your kind of diving though, don't miss it.

Deep Diving

Opportunities to dive deep abound in the Philippines. Many attractions are beyond 40m (130ft), the recognized maximum depth limit of sport diving. Before venturing beyond these limits, it is imperative that divers be specially trained in deep diving and/or technical diving.

Classes will teach you to recognize symptoms of nitrogen narcosis and perform proper decompression procedures. Remember, emergency facilities in the Philippines are limited. Know your limits and don't push your luck when it comes to depth.

37 Punta Bonga 1 & 2

Location: North of Friday's Rock, west Boracay

Depth Range: 8-40m+ (26-130ft+)

Access: Boat

Expertise Rating: Intermediate

These sites mark the point at which the sea topography starts to change—the drop-off comes closer to shore here than at the more southern sites and also becomes deeper and steeper. The shallower section (Punta Bonga 1) has lots of soft corals, though you'll see fewer stony corals than at other sites in the region. Punta Bonga 2, to the north, is similarly covered, but the wall here gradually descends to small ledges, like steps cut into the reef.

Lots of fish and some larger pelagics, such as tuna, jacks, barracuda and occasionally whitetip sharks, find their way here. Triggerfish and stingrays are quite common, as well as groupers, angelfish, sweetlips and cornetfish.

STEVE ROSENBERG

Look for clown triggerfish at Punta Bonga.

The bottom of the wall runs into a sandy seafloor with scattered coral bommies, but at 45m you don't have a lot of time to explore, unless you are a technical diver, in which case this is a good training area with lots to see.

38 Friday's Rock

Location: Just off Balabag, west Boracay

Depth Range: 7-18m (23-60ft)

Access: Shore or boat

Expertise Rating: Novice

A popular training and snorkeling site, Friday's Rock is a large, 11m-high boulder that sticks up from the sandy seafloor, with a reasonable coral garden just a few meters inshore. Local divers have established fish-feeding stations here, so the fish are "friendly." Because of the feeding, you're likely to see more fish here than is typical at such a site.

Butterflyfish, tangs, wrasses, damselfish, groupers, sweetlips, sergeant majors and snappers abound, while morays, ribbon eels and a variety of sea stars litter the sandy bottom. Large lionfish and scorpionfish hide amid the rocks and corals, so be careful. It's possible to swim out to Friday's, but it's far enough from shore to tire most divers and snorkelers. Boat diving is more common and is usually the best way to go.

39 Crocodile Island

Location: Off Boracay's SE tip

Depth Range: 5-25m (16-82ft)

Access: Boat

Expertise Rating: Intermediate

Don't worry, no crocodiles ply these waters, but the island does resemble a croc, hence the name. What you will find are some pretty corals and a decent cave full of wrasses. Because the island is at the eastern mouth of the Caticlan Channel, which divides Boracay from the mainland, a fair current usually passes through here, its direction depending on the tide.

Crocodile is one of the most popular dive sites around Boracay—it has something for everyone. Snorkelers will enjoy the large shallow reeftop, which is well covered in corals and has a number of tropical reef fish to look at. The wall is festooned in places with some really pretty blue gorgonians, as well as other sea fans, sea whips and many types of hard and soft corals and sponges.

Large sea snakes are often seen here—they are used to divers and leave them alone. Lots of fish call Crocodile home, including sweetlips, butterflyfish, snappers, squirrelfish, triggerfish, groupers, parrotfish, pipefish, cornetfish, Moorish idols, surgeonfish and fusiliers among others. Quite a lot of nudibranchs live here as well. It's no surprise that this is a good macrophotography site.

Visibility is not always the best here, but it can reach more than 25m from late February to June. You won't see too many pelagics cruise through the water, but the abundant reef life more than makes up for that.

STEVE ROSENBERG

Nudibranchs make for colorful macrophotography subjects.

40 Laurel Island

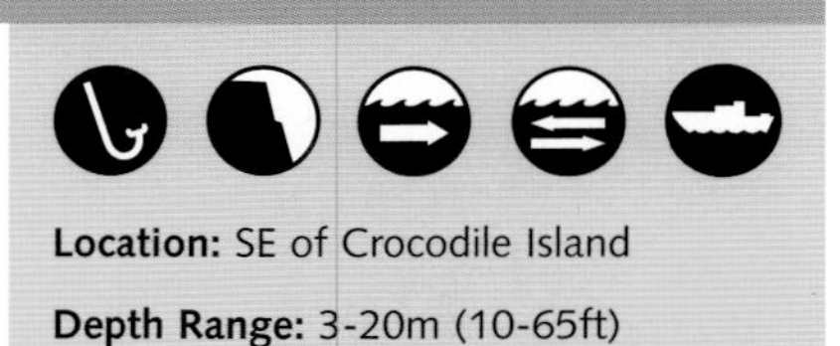

Location: SE of Crocodile Island

Depth Range: 3-20m (10-65ft)

Access: Boat

Expertise Rating: Intermediate

The shallow reef around Laurel Island is another good snorkeling area and is great for divers, too. Actually, the island has two dive sites, called **Laurel 1** and **Laurel 2.** Because both sites are in the Caticlan Channel, the current can be quite strong, but it feeds the corals and sustains a great diversity of fish life. Laurel 2, to the east, is favored in the rainy season because it's more sheltered than Laurel 1.

The reeftop at Laurel 1, on the northeast side of the island, is well covered with both soft and hard corals—some impressive boulder corals dominate the seascape.

The most interesting diving feature of Laurel 1 is an 8m-long cave (more of a tunnel really). When the current is running, yellow and orange coral polyps open up inside the tunnel, creating a gorgeous display. After swimming through the tunnel, you'll emerge into a bowl that drops to the bottom of the reef. The bowl is itself a remarkable area, with plenty of hard corals (including some black corals), barrel sponges and assorted stony coral heads.

You'll see lots of fish at both Laurel 1 and 2, similar to those at Crocodile, but again, not a lot of pelagics. This is also a great night dive. Photographers should make sure they have a full roll of film in their camera.

SAMMY ANG

Bright orange cup corals open in the current.

41 Nasog Point

Location: NW Panay

Depth Range: Surface-35m (115ft)

Access: Boat

Expertise Rating: Intermediate

A good snorkeling site when the current is not too strong, Nasog Point has an interesting bottom composition of massive boulders and canyons with some good coral cover, including gorgonians and soft corals.

Though you won't find a lot of interesting fish life here, some large snappers, triggerfish, sweetlips and (depending on the current) tuna, barracuda and other pelagics may pass by. Turtles are quite common. Nasog is visited by dive centers from Boracay and is usually dived in conjunction with Dog Drift or Black Rock.

42 Dog Drift

Location: South of Nasog Point

Depth Range: 5-30m (16-100ft)

Access: Boat

Expertise Rating: Intermediate

No need to wonder how the reef got its name—this is usually a drift dive with plenty to see when the current is running. This relatively small wall has lots of caves and crevices to explore, some of them with painted crays (spiny lobsters) waving their antennae around. Turtles are not uncommon and are often seen nosing around in the cracks and crannies looking for a bite to eat. Pelagics pass by frequently.

The reef is a healthy, vibrant dive with gorgonians and soft corals, similar to Nasog Point but with lots more fish life. Fusiliers, groupers, snappers, batfish and sweetlips are just some of the many species that thrive here. Watch out for lionfish and stonefish, and keep your hands out of holes and cracks because there are all sorts of potentially hazardous critters lurking in them, such as morays, that could easily mistake your fingers for lunch.

STEVE ROSENBERG

Turtles ply the waters at Dog Drift.

Malapascua Island

With some of the region's best dive sites, this newcomer on the Visayas' dive circuit has created quite a stir. Malapascua's fabulous sugar-white soft-sand beaches are oft described as "better than Boracay." This once-remote, tiny island is now trying to cope with the influx of divers and beach lovers wanting to experience its undeniable charms.

You can reach Malapascua by taking the bus from Cebu City's Northern Bus Terminal (4 hours) or by taxi (2½ hours) to the town of Maya on the northwest coast of Cebu Island. From there, you can rent a private banca or take the passenger-ferry banca for the 30-minute crossing to Malapascua. Four dive centers and several modest resorts now service the island.

SCOTT TUASON

Beachcombers are silhouetted against the sky.

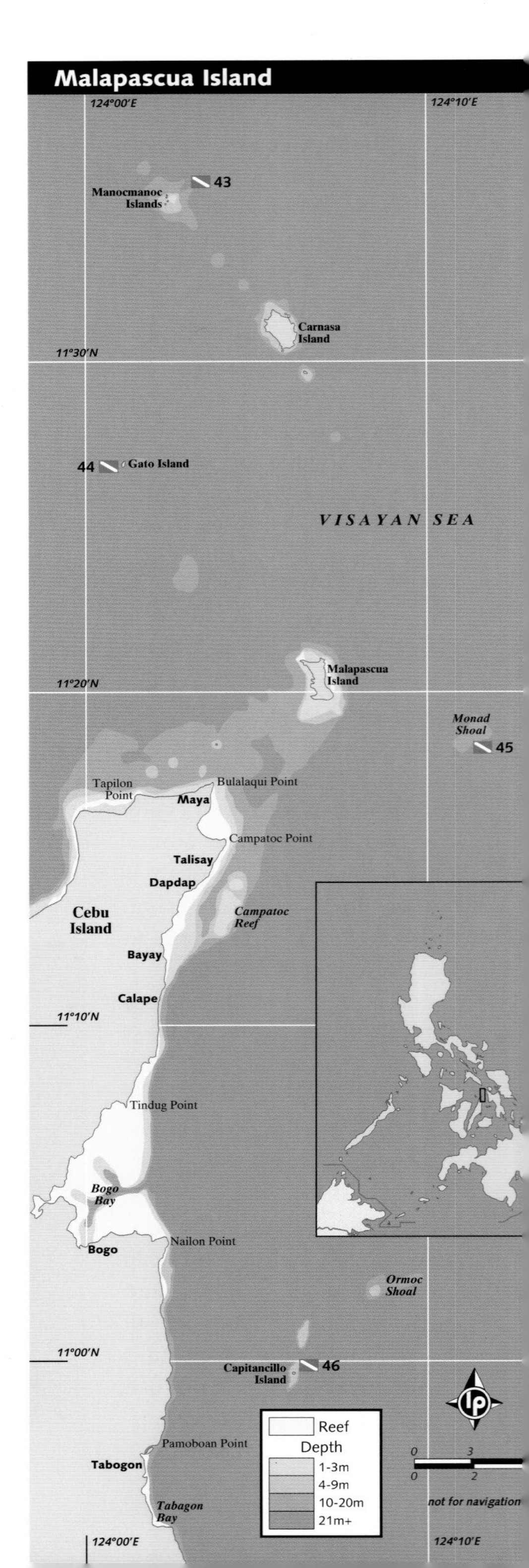

Malapascua Island Dive Sites

	Good Snorkeling	Novice	Intermediate	Advanced
43 Wreck of the *Doña Marilyn*				●
44 Gato Island	●		●	
45 Monad Shoal			●	
46 Capitancillo Island	●			●

43 Wreck of the *Doña Marilyn*

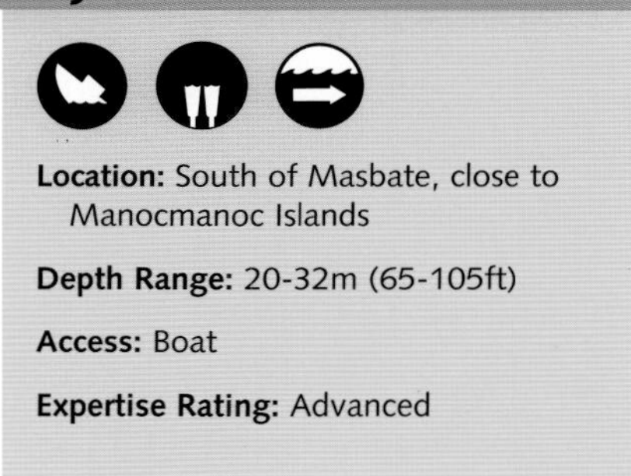

Location: South of Masbate, close to Manocmanoc Islands

Depth Range: 20-32m (65-105ft)

Access: Boat

Expertise Rating: Advanced

A passenger ferry that went down more than 20 years ago, this wreck, accessed from Malapascua Island, is now carpeted in gorgeous soft corals. Lying on its starboard side at 32m, the wreck is penetrable by qualified divers. Much of its cargo now lies scattered over the seafloor, home to nurse sharks and black-blotched rays.

The port side of the wreck is festooned with blue and red soft corals, and a wide variety of marine life now resides within and on this hulk. This very pretty site is good for several dives, but only experienced divers need apply—the stiff current and remote location allow no room for error.

SCOTT TUASON

The port side of the *Doña Marilyn* is festooned with corals.

44 Gato Island

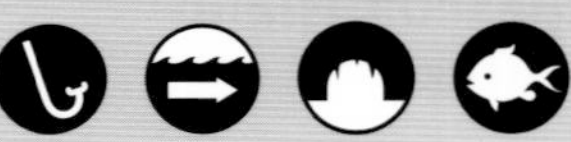

Location: North of Cebu Island

Depth Range: 5-25m (16-82ft)

Access: Boat

Expertise Rating: Intermediate

Gato means "cat" in the local dialect, but after circumnavigating the island, you'll still wonder why it's called that.

Gato has a fisheries protection plan in place, manned by University of Cebu researchers and some armed guards. Once they know you're not fishing (and that you have no spearguns with you), they're happy to let divers explore. It's a good idea to bring some fresh vegetables, ice and liquid refreshment along for the staff, as they are stuck on what is basically a bare rock in a hut perched over the sea with no access to the mainland for long periods of time. They'll appreciate your concern for their well-being. Divers may need to pay a fee to dive here, no doubt a reflection on the increased numbers of scuba enthusiasts turning up now that Malapascua dive centers have "discovered" Gato.

STEVE ROSENBERG

Gato Island's sandy seafloor is home to bluespotted stingrays.

Gato is the perfect environment for underwater photographers. The bottom is relatively flat, sandy and liberally festooned with colorful clumps of hard and soft corals, sea fans, sea whips and black coral. The sand is home to lots of shell life and bluespotted stingrays. Several shark species like to rest under the scattered large boulders. You'll likely run into groupers and snappers here, as well as the usual assortment of reef fish. Several large cuttlefish and an emperor angelfish may even get in the way of your camera. Macro enthusiasts will appreciate the diversity of subjects hereabouts as well, especially the many nudibranchs.

The island is quite small, although it would be a chore to swim all the way around it in one dive. Usually it's best to select whichever side has the lightest current and plan to do the first dive there.

Of course, if you simply must see what's on the other side, there is an option: A cave runs through the middle of the island, and you can swim all the way through it—a fascinating experience, but not for those who suffer from claustrophobia or who might panic upon encountering sleeping sharks and banded sea snakes along the rocky passageway. The cave entrance is at 5m on the west side of the island and runs for around 80m before exiting at 14m on the east side. Be sure to bring your dive light. The inside is lined with pretty flower-like soft corals and sponges. Lobsters, crabs and cleaner shrimp scurry around in the nocturnal environment. Near the exit at around 14m are a couple of smaller caves where whitetip sharks often rest.

45 Monad Shoal

Location: East of Malapascua

Depth Range: 15-40m+ (50-130ft+)

Access: Boat

Expertise Rating: Intermediate

Monad Shoal isn't just any old seamount. It's where a large group of thresher sharks (*Alopias vulpinus*) gathers. Uncommon in Philippine waters, this rare congregation is the reason so many divers are flocking to Malapascua.

Thresher sharks grow to a maximum of 3.3m. With their long, sweeping tails and bulbous bodies, threshers are easy to differentiate from other species. Like hammerheads, they prefer to swim and hunt together as a school. Though the sharks are not generally regarded as a threat, divers should nonetheless keep away from a thresher's powerful tail,

STEVE ROSENBERG

Monad shoal displays impressive sea fans.

which it uses to hit and stun prey. In fact, divers should not approach a school of threshers at all, as to do so could disrupt the cohesiveness of the school and affect the sharks' behavior patterns.

Threshers, as with other members of the mackerel shark family, give birth to live pups, usually between two and four at a time. Interestingly, researchers have recorded a form of intrauterine cannibalism among threshers, where pups in the womb attack and eat their siblings before birth.

Other shark species are commonly seen here, including whitetips, hammerheads and silvertip sharks. Mantas visit frequently, making this a pelagic fish lover's heaven. As if that weren't enough, reports that a whale shark occasionally visits is certain to get many big-fish lovers packing their dive bags and booking the next flight to Cebu for the road and banca trip to Malapascua.

Most divers will want to do several dives here, as there's a lot of territory to cover. The reef has two major dive sites, **Shark Point** and **The Hole**. Both lend themselves to repeated dives, as they offer plenty to see at different depths. Diving depths here average between 25 and 30m.

The reeftop runs from about 15 to 23m deep, at which point it drops to a ledge at around 45m and then plunges into the briny deep. Obviously, this is a good site for technical divers who know what they're doing, but strong currents can cause problems, so do be careful.

The shoal has some impressive gorgonians and sea fans and features some interesting black corals and white sea anemones, as well as some very pretty curtains of soft corals hanging along the wall. Look carefully and you may be rewarded with a glimpse at a peculiar yellow frogfish hiding amid the soft fronds.

Thresher Sharks

At Monad Shoal, divers are almost guaranteed to see the powerful and graceful thresher sharks, but some experts are concerned that increased contact with divers is beginning to affect the sharks' habits—and may soon drive them away.

ROBERT YIN

Divers mustn't disrupt a thresher shark's swimming pattern.

Threshers, a shoaling shark species, follow precise swimming patterns based on a triangular grid with repeated circular patterns at each corner. When divers get in the sharks' way, the sharks may become confused. It's possible that Malapascua's threshers may simply leave for less confusing waters if proper protocol, which includes staying well above the shoaling creatures, is not enforced by local dive operators.

46 Capitancillo Island

Location: Northern Cebu, SE of Bogo

Depth Range: 9-40m+ (30-130ft+)

Access: Boat

Expertise Rating: Advanced

Capitancillo Island has several sites, such as **Nuñez** and **Ormoc Shoals**, all of which share similar features. Unfortunately, the reeftop has suffered some significant damage, in part from typhoons but also from unscrupulous dynamiteros (dynamite fishers) who have devastated some sections of the reef. However, plenty of areas on the expansive reef are still worth diving, and the walls are pretty good.

Currents can get vicious: Though good for attracting pelagics, currents can cause major problems for inexperienced divers. Better to dive as close to high tide as possible for the best chance of reduced current, and make sure your divemaster knows the area well.

The reeftop is colorful in places, but it's the walls that interest most divers. You'll see gorgonians and plenty of corals, as well as some black corals deeper down. Overhangs, caves and clouds of reef fish, such as damsels, wrasses and snappers and the occasional turtle, whitetip and grey reef shark, make this an interesting dive. Divers sometimes spot barracuda, tuna and rainbow runners in the swift-running current, and mantas visit at times.

Mactan Island & Cebu City

Hardly a tropical paradise when viewed from the air, Mactan—a large, flat, rocky island with little abundant greenery—has a huge number of dive centers (more than 100 at the last count) catering to divers from around the world.

Both international and domestic flights land at the Mactan-Cebu International Airport. Mactan's abundant resorts range from small and inexpensive to impressive luxury properties. Most are on the island's eastern side, which has a fringing reef with an impressive wall along its length. Unfortunately, in many areas the reef has been badly affected by typhoons and dynamite fishing.

Mactan has a few areas worth diving and is also the jumping-off point for many sites in the Visayas, several of which are less than an hour away by banca boat. Most resorts and dive centers throughout Mactan offer dive training, much of it PADI oriented, but the prices tend to be higher here than in other parts of the country.

Cebu City, a short taxi ride across the channel that divides it from Mactan, has no dive sites, but several retail dive centers supply equipment and services to the region's many dive operators and their customers. Cebu's harbor is a convenient boarding point for live-aboard boats and fast ferries to outlying islands, and its north and south bus stations see a steady stream of divers making pilgrimages to Sogod (home to Alegre Beach Resort and some fair diving) and points north, as well as to Moalboal, on the southwest coast of Cebu Island.

Mactan Island & Cebu City Dive Sites

	Good Snorkeling	Novice	Intermediate	Advanced
47 Tambuli Fish-Feeding Station	●	●		
48 Kon Tiki House Reef	●	●		
49 Marigondon Cave	●		●	

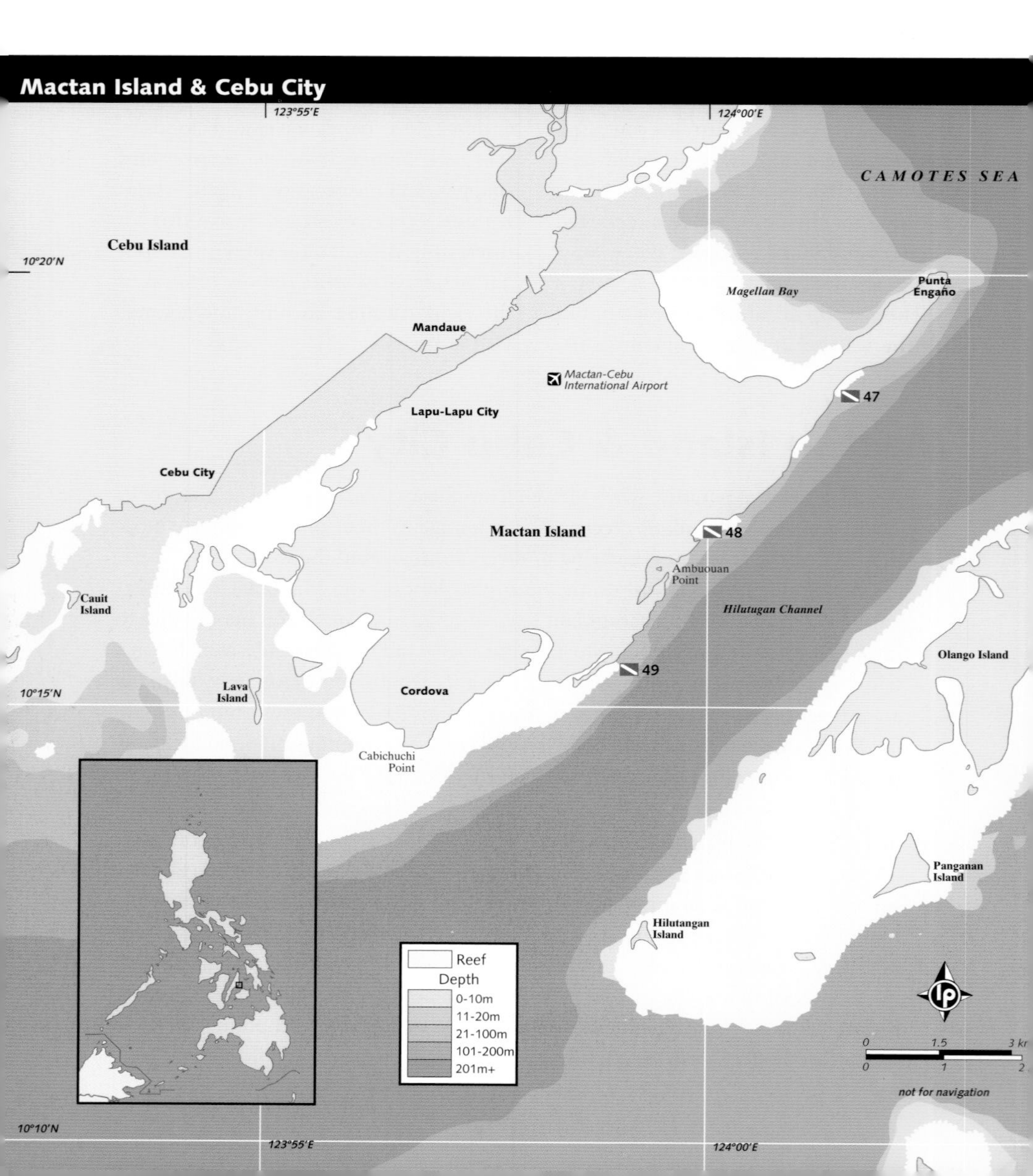

47 Tambuli Fish-Feeding Station

Location: Off Tambuli Beach Club

Depth Range: Surface-30m+ (100ft+)

Access: Shore

Expertise Rating: Novice

A popular training site and a good orientation to local dive conditions, Tambuli is a comfortable and long-established dive resort at the northeastern end of Mactan. The reef itself, like much of the diving along this coast, is nothing spectacular and shows evidence of damage and poor garbage management—on some dives the largest object you'll find in the shallows is an old tractor tire. But the fish, looking for a handout, swarm over divers, so this is a good place for underwater photographers to shoot the local inhabitants up close.

The reef, more of a sandy bottom with straggly lumps of stressed coral outgrowths, slopes down gently to the lip of the wall, which then plummets to abyssal depths. No need to go down the wall here, as it isn't particularly impressive. This is a shallow dive in usually clear water with minimal current.

For more experienced divers, an unusual artificial reef lies between 17 and 22m. Tambuli Beach Club anchored an old twin-engine Bonanza aircraft to the sea bottom. It is now home to a variety of marine animals and is quickly being covered by small hard and soft corals and barnacles. To permit easy penetration, the doors were removed, as were the propellers, most of the wings and the avionics. Pufferfish, porcupinefish, brown tangs, groupers and surgeonfish have taken up residence in the plane, and an occasional eagle ray sometimes passes by. Lobsters and crabs reside between the fuselage and the sandy sea bottom. Surrounding the site are sea whips, anemones and clownfish, bubble corals, sea pens, urchins and triggerfish. Seamoths, dragonfish and trumpetfish, ghost pipefish, sea snakes, lionfish and stonefish are also well represented. Watch out for the stinging hydroids that are liberally festooned around the area.

Another annoying factor to consider is the large amount of water traffic, including many banca boats and the obnoxious Jet Skiers who love nothing more than to use a diver's safety buoy as a marker to race around. Listen carefully for the sound of motors before ascending to the surface.

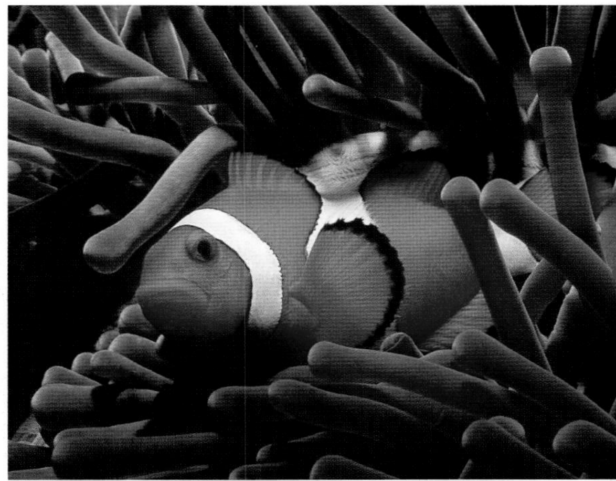

STEVE ROSENBERG

Anemones and clownfish abound on Tambuli's reef.

48 Kon Tiki House Reef

Although it's possible to dive beyond 30m here, this is a fairly easy dive and is used as a training ground by many instructors teaching on Mactan. Unlike most of the reef dives along this extensive reef system, the Kon Tiki House Reef is actually alive and flourishing.

Kon Tiki is a dedicated budget dive resort that was one of the first properties developed along the coast. The owners have zealously guarded the reef, which starts right off the seawall (there is no beach here, only a few rocks). Their efforts have paid off—Kon Tiki House Reef is a showpiece that attracts divers from all over the island. It's unlike the rest of the Mactan coast, where the once-impressive fringing reef has seen significant destruction through illegal fishing, coral collection and environmental neglect.

Location: In front of Kon Tiki Resort

Depth Range: 3-30m+ (10-100ft+)

Access: Shore

Expertise Rating: Novice

The top of the reef is covered in boulders and coral bommies and small sandy patches, sloping gently to the lip of the wall a few meters offshore, which then plummets irregularly down into the depths of the Hilutugan Channel, the seemingly bottomless body of water that separates Mactan from nearby Olango Island. As a result, despite the usual lack of strong currents, these waters are often visited by large pelagics, including occasional whale sharks. Mactan's

STEVE ROSENBERG

Look for small critters, such as ghost pipefish, hiding amid a crinoid's arms.

wall, despite its often scarred and barren face, is a convenient draw for big-fish lovers to visit.

The **Kon Tiki Wall** is one of the better areas to spot pelagics—even if they don't show up, the reef itself is worth the visit. It's covered in big gorgonians, sea whips and fans, sea stars, feather stars and crinoids. Lots of colorful corals cover every part of it. The ledges, cracks and crevices are home to a variety of crustaceans and plenty of reef fish, such as snappers, groupers, angelfish, parrotfish, gobies and wrasses. Tuna, barracuda and jacks are often spotted finning by, and larger pelagics are likely visitors. Worth more than one dive, the Kon Tiki House Reef stands as proof that dive resorts can and should make a difference in protecting the underwater environment.

49 Marigondon Cave

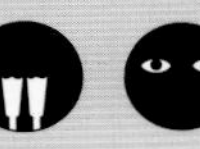

Location: East of Marigondon

Depth Range: 5-35m (16-115ft)

Access: Boat

Expertise Rating: Intermediate

Marigondon Cave is a particularly impressive dive at the southern part of Marigondon Reef. You can reach the wide cave entrance by descending the wall to around 28m. The bottom of the cave is at around 35m (the cave itself slopes slightly downward from the large entrance before rising up again), so watch your depth. The cave is massive, stretching back for almost 45m, the floor and ceiling rising as you move farther in.

At the far end of the cave is a tiny aperture (just large enough to get your head into) that opens to a small subterranean grotto. At first glance it's pitch black, but as you become accustomed to the dark, you'll notice dozens of pairs of "eyes" winking at you in the darkness. These are the bioluminescent patches on the faces of dozens of flashlight fish, a species that made this amazing adaptation to survive in dark interiors.

Watch your bottom time in this cave, because you will have to descend several meters again to get out of the entrance, and you don't want to incur a decompression penalty by overstaying in the shallower interior. The reeftop is a good place to do a safety stop, as it is relatively shallow and has a few coral heads and some skittish fish around.

Moalboal

Moalboal, whose name means "bubbling water," a reference to some nearby freshwater springs, is a quiet, peaceful little village that has become a mecca for divers. To get here from Cebu City you must cross the mountainous spine of skinny Cebu Island, a potentially noisy, dusty, 90-minute bus ride from Cebu's south bus terminal. It's useful to bring earplugs, as well as a scarf to cover your mouth and nose. Alternatively, you can arrange for a clean and quiet private car and driver or negotiate a taxi ride.

Ahead of its time, Moalboal started to attract divers in the late 1970s. Then, it was a raggedy collection of cheap cottages and restaurants—a backpackers' paradise—where a dive cost less than US$5 and a training course (of sorts) not much more. Times have changed: Moalboal is now an internationally recognized center of diving excellence, with more than a dozen high-quality dive centers teaching reasonably priced courses to all levels of divers. Several local operators offer nitrox and technical training and diving. Another indication of the local dive operators' professionalism is that every local dive site now has a mooring buoy.

Aside from visiting local sites, Moalboal dive centers organize dive safaris to many other parts of the Visayas, including the not-so-distant Apo Island.

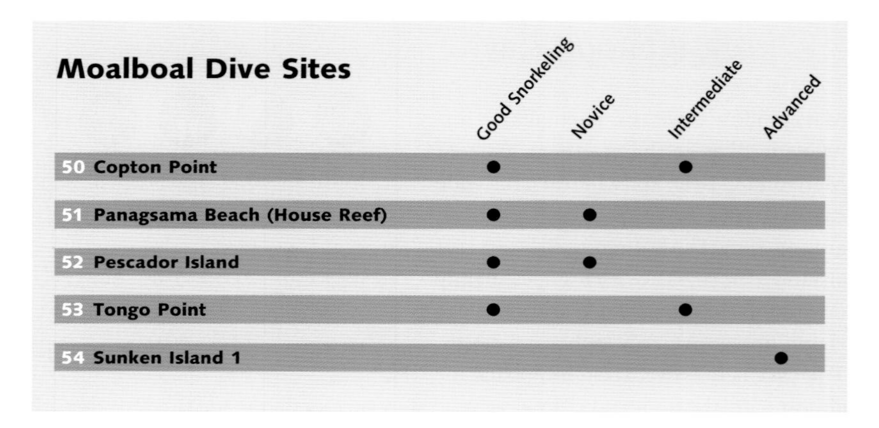

Moalboal Dive Sites

	Good Snorkeling	Novice	Intermediate	Advanced
50 Copton Point	●		●	
51 Panagsama Beach (House Reef)	●	●		
52 Pescador Island	●	●		
53 Tongo Point	●		●	
54 Sunken Island 1				●

Moalboal

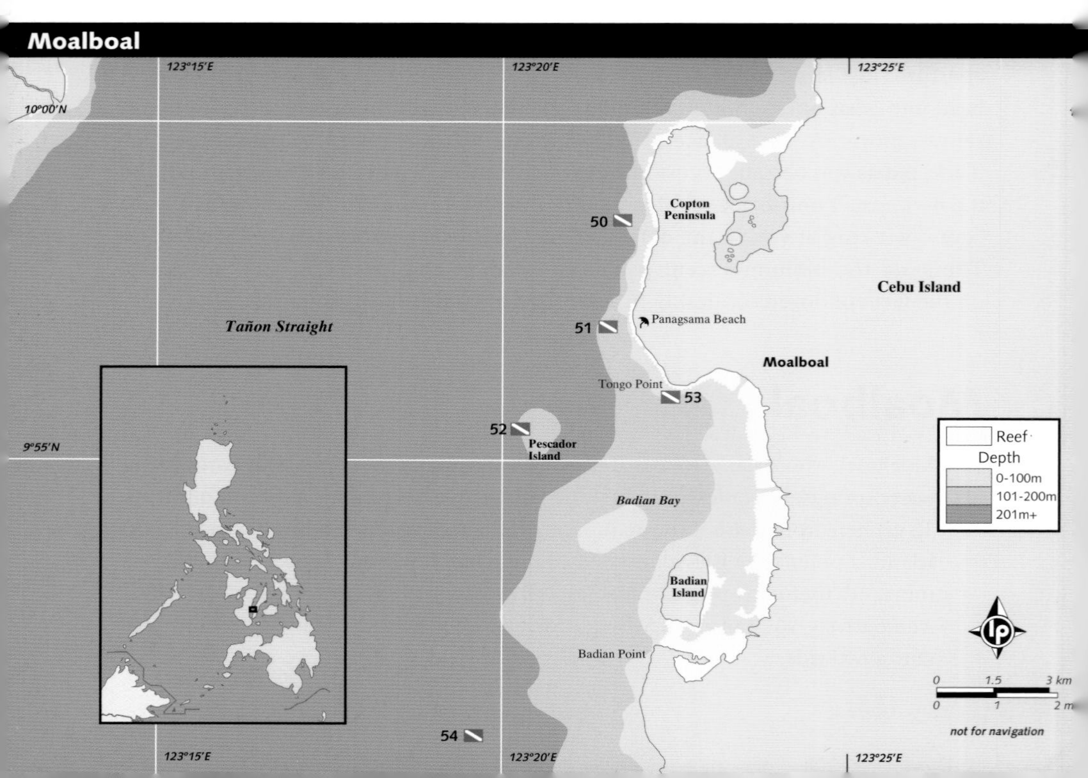

50 Copton Point

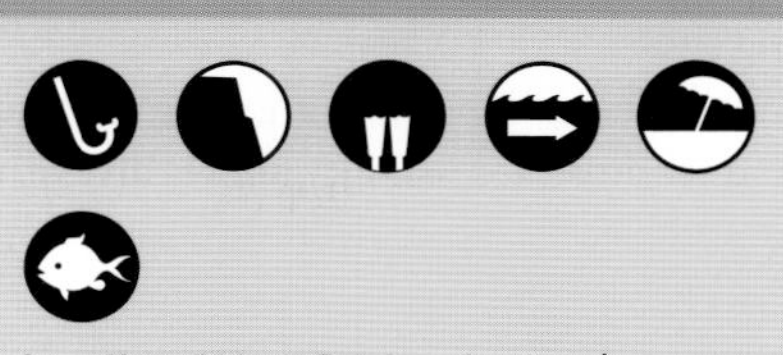

Location: West Copton Peninsula

Depth Range: Surface-40m (130ft)

Access: Shore or boat

Expertise Rating: Intermediate

The diving at Copton (part of the Ronda Bay Marine Park) is reliably good, but access is limited. You can make a beach entry, and snorkelers often do, but divers tend to get here by boat. Strong, unpredictable currents often pass through.

The top of the reef is sandy and home to plenty of hard and soft corals (including some lovely staghorn and sea whips), as well as sponges. Watch out for the sea urchins! You might spot some rays in the sand, and you'll see plenty of anemones billowing in the current.

At the northern end of the reef the wall starts at around 5m, making it ideal for snorkelers. The bottom slopes steeply away to the south, and the lip of the wall deepens to around 23m at the southern end. As the current is usually south to north, this makes for an intelligent deeper first section and a perfect safety stop on the shallower, prolific northern end of the reef. The wall itself has some fair-sized sea fans and gorgonians on it.

Fish you might expect to find include almost anything you can think of. Several species of triggerfish and angelfish abound, some stunning chromis and anthias lurk in the table corals, and sea snakes hunt here, morays too. Garfish, pipefish, puffers, snappers, groupers (some large individuals are deeper down the wall), fusiliers and Napoleon wrasses all call this area home.

TIM ROCK

It is easy to mistake a still pipefish for seagrass.

51 Panagsama Beach (House Reef)

Location: Off Panagsama Beach

Depth Range: Surface-40m+ (130ft+)

Access: Shore

Expertise Rating: Novice

This used to be a really impressive reef, the drop-off a short swim over stunning corals off any point along the beach. Unfortunately, a typhoon in 1984 ravaged the reeftop, ending decades of fantastic snorkeling. Thankfully, although not yet fully recovered, the reeftop is almost back to its former glory and is once again as good as or better than many of the region's other shallow snorkeling and diving sites.

The reef is a popular training ground, and its shore accessibility allows dive centers to pass the transportation savings to their customers. The wall stretches quite a way along the coast. Divers and snorkelers may enter from several areas between Panagsama and Bas Diot (just out from Moalboal Reef Club).

Take a flashlight to explore the various small caves along the wall. The wall, which drops down in stages to more than 40m, is still impressive in many places, with gorgonians and plenty of hard and soft corals. Morays and sometimes sea snakes prowl this area, and you'll see lots of species of crinoids.

SAMMY ANG

Sunlight shines through this nearly transparent jellyfish.

In early 2001 a pair of whale sharks made an appearance just off the town pier. A few lucky snorkelers were able to swim with them and photograph them.

A shoal of bigeye trevallies is often stationed near Moalboal pier's barnacle-encrusted legs, and you can study plenty of small fish and fry on the reeftop. Deeper down the wall, you may encounter catfish, some snappers, gobies, angelfish, chromis and anthias, morays, anemones and clownfish.

52 Pescador Island

It was Pescador that put Moalboal on the diver's map and Pescador that remains its biggest draw today. The island is the most obvious landmark off the coast of Moalboal: You can see it from just about anywhere along Panagsama Beach. An almost constant stream of dive bancas makes its way back and forth from Moalboal to Pescador, carrying load after load of happy divers.

For many years its gorgonians and fan corals set the standard by which other Philippines dive sites were judged. Another of its claims to fame are the Spanish dancers, a species of large nudibranchs that wiggle and shimmy their way across the reef.

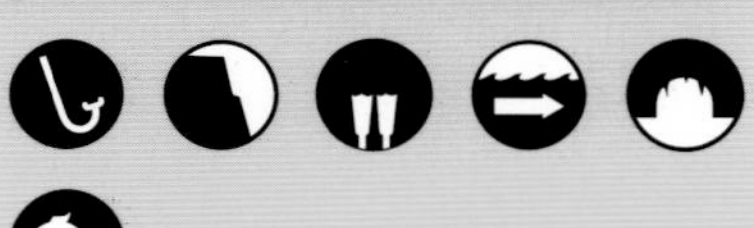

Location: West of Panagsama Beach

Depth Range: Surface-40m+ (130ft+)

Access: Boat

Expertise Rating: Novice

Local dive operators have placed mooring buoys at several locations to protect the reef from anchor damage—a sensible precaution given the volume of traffic that moors here daily. If several boats are at your dive site, make sure you get on the right one at the end of the dive! Currents are usually strong, but the visibility is great, often more than 25m.

It's possible to swim around the entire island in one dive, but Pescador deserves several dives to be fully appreciated. Snorkelers can swim over the shallower sections of the reef, which range from around 3 to 10m, to the wall. There is plenty to see, but watch out for banca traffic and the current.

The top of the reef is festooned with many kinds of corals, including staghorns and sea whips, table and boulder corals. Deeper down the wall you'll see lots of tube and basket sponges and plenty of colorful, well-developed soft corals all over the place, as well as some fair-sized clumps of black coral. The vertical wall boasts some impressive overhangs and crevices. The wall's north face reaches below 50m, so watch your depth.

Fish life encompasses virtually every tropical reef species you can imagine. Prevalent species include scorpionfish, sea snakes and moray eels. Mantas and sharks are occasionally seen, and some very lucky divers have spotted whale sharks. Reef species include lizardfish, anthias, gobies, groupers, snappers, tuna, rabbitfish, barracuda, turtles, parrotfish, Napoleon wrasses and more.

One of the most popular areas of Pescador is **The Cathedral**, a stunning crevice that descends to 34m. At midday, shafts of light dapple the corals and illuminate the interior in an ethereal light show. You can also look for another smaller cave, known as **Lionfish Cave**.

TIM ROCK

Spanish dancer nudibranchs lay lacy red egg masses.

53 Tongo Point

Tongo Point is a good site year-round, though currents are sometimes strong and unpredictable. Snorkelers who don't mind a long swim can access this area from the beach, but divers will most likely arrive and depart by boat.

Though you won't see a lot of fish here, the corals are exceptionally healthy,

Location: South Copton Peninsula

Depth Range: 3-40m+ (10-130ft+)

Access: Shore or boat

Expertise Rating: Intermediate

especially the sea fans along the wall. Some luxuriant soft corals grow here too. Reasonably sized groupers often hang out along the wall between 30 and 45m.

At the north end of the point, snorkelers can explore impressive coral archways. Off the reef's south end, the very healthy corals are also worth checking out.

54 Sunken Island 1

Location: SW of Badian Point

Depth Range: 25-40m+ (82-130ft+)

Access: Boat

Expertise Rating: Advanced

Strong currents and an open-ocean free descent to 25m are the hallmarks of this remarkable seamount. Obviously, only advanced divers escorted by a knowledgeable dive guide need apply.

The mount is covered by healthy corals and some impressive sponges, especially barrels, as well as the ubiquitous gorgonians, which are quite grand here. Mantas occasionally pass by this site, and it's common to see plenty of pelagics, such as tuna, mackerel and barracuda. Grey reef sharks are sometimes spotted, and you'll certainly see large lionfish. The funny looking frogfish, or anglerfish, are quite common here, as are triggerfish, Napoleon wrasses, surgeons, pufferfish, groupers, snappers, sea snakes, angelfish and many of the others you'd expect to find on a current-swept seamount.

TIM ROCK

A pufferfish takes shelter from the current.

Dumaguete

Dumaguete, a university town on the east coast of Negros Island, faces the southern tip of Cebu Island, which lies to the east. It can be reached by fast ferryboats from Cebu and is served daily by domestic airline flights from Manila. With some cozy beach resorts nearby, Dumaguete is becoming popular with divers from around the world. Several dive centers now operate resorts with dive services, and several worthwhile dive sites are in the area.

The most popular dive area is Apo Island, a couple of hours by banca from Dumaguete and one of the better sites in the Visayas. Several dive sites on the southern tip of Cebu, as well as Sumilon Island just around the corner on the east coast of Cebu, are also easily accessed from Dumaguete and are well worth the trip. Local dive centers can take you to many other sites, including one or two around Siquijor Island, home of Filipino witches and warlocks. Unfortunately, the local wizards have pointedly failed to protect much of the reef around Siquijor: Blast fishing has caused some major devastation, and the reef is generally overfished.

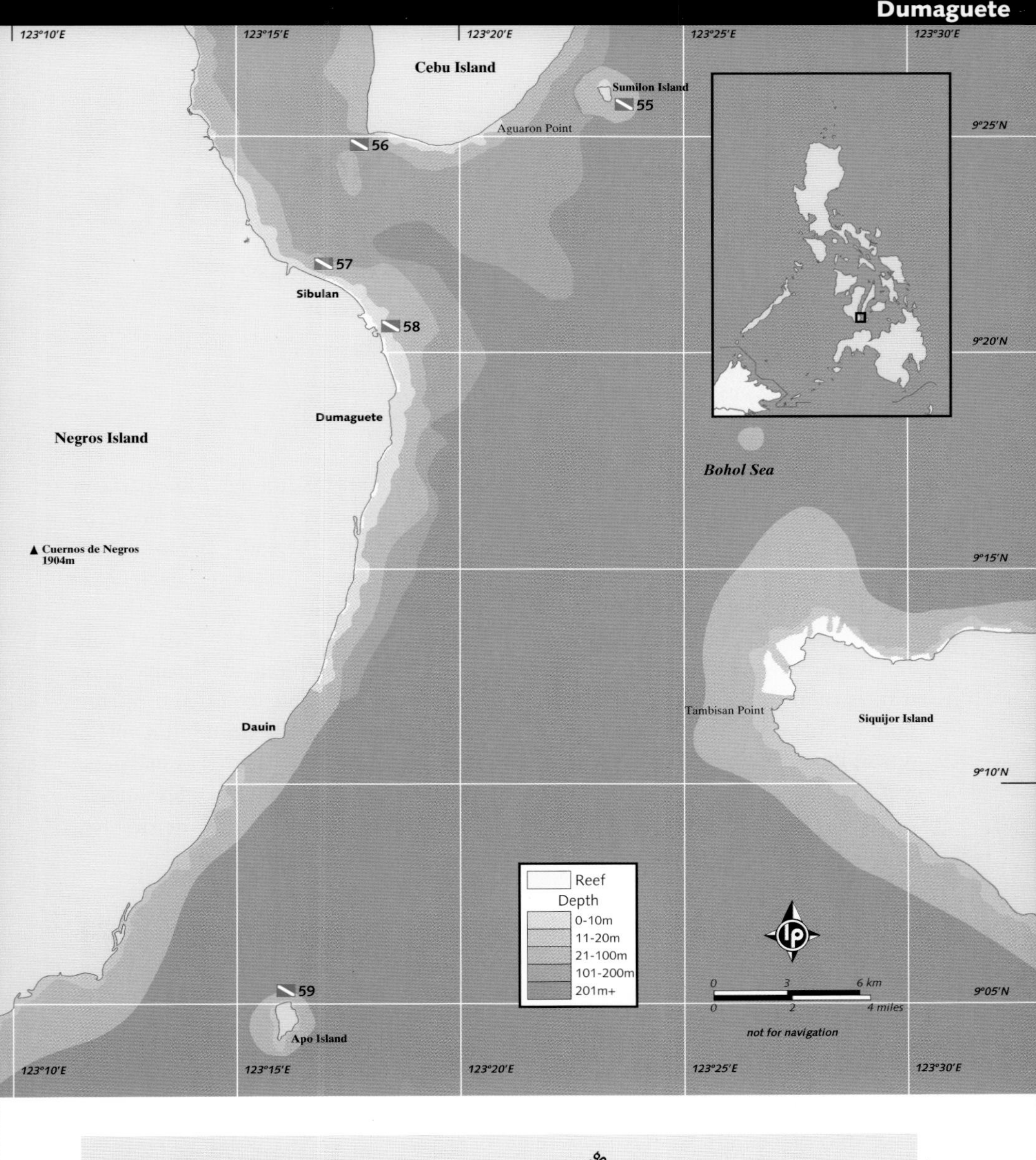

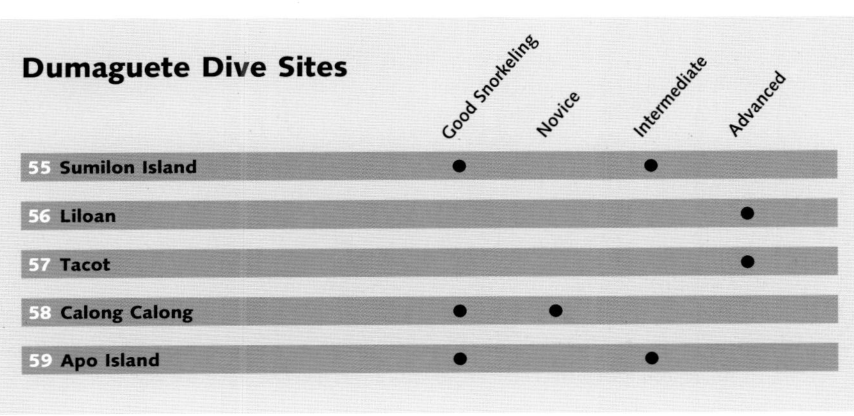

Dumaguete Dive Sites

	Good Snorkeling	Novice	Intermediate	Advanced
55 Sumilon Island	●		●	
56 Liloan				●
57 Tacot				●
58 Calong Calong	●	●		
59 Apo Island	●		●	

55 Sumilon Island

Location: East of Cebu's south tip

Depth Range: 3-24m (10-80ft)

Access: Boat

Expertise Rating: Intermediate

Sumilon Island, the first marine reserve in the Philippines, was once a fantastic dive site. Somehow its protected status became defunct, and it took no time at all for the dynamiteros, the gillnetters and the spearfishers to move in and wipe out years of patient conservation efforts.

As a result, the abundant marine life of yore is a distant memory, but the reef is showing signs of recovery, especially along the walls. You still have a fair chance of seeing some large pelagics in the usually great visibility that surrounds the island. Hammerheads are sometimes seen during the dry season, though manta and leopard rays are much rarer in these waters than they used to be, and the numbers of yellowfins and jacks are also down, though they are still seen off the reef's walls.

The current that usually runs here can sometimes be quite strong. Snorkeling conditions are OK, though some parts of the reef are better than others. As divers descend along the wall, the corals get better, and some crevices and small caves beg for exploration.

The reef southeast of the island is in much better condition—reasonable coral bommies, and table, brain and mushroom corals are quite common. Quite a few eels live here too, as well as snappers, tangs, wrasses, parrotfish, a few angelfish and, a little deeper, some skittish groupers, among other species.

TIM ROCK

At Sumilon Island, the corals improve as divers descend along the wall.

56 Liloan

Location: SW tip of Cebu

Depth Range: 10-40m+ (33-130ft+)

Access: Boat

Expertise Rating: Advanced

At this drift dive over a nominally sandy bottom, experienced divers will want to drop down to the sloping reef and investigate the large rocks and bommies that litter the seafloor. Lurking around inside the structures are a good selection of reef fish, such as snappers, groupers, parrotfish, pufferfish and so on.

Large pelagics cruise by here frequently—jacks, barracuda, tuna and mackerel are all likely candidates for an encounter. Divers sometimes spot whitetip sharks. Mantas are not uncommon late in the dry season.

Check out the seafloor for shrimp gobies and their roommates (the blind cleaning shrimp), as well as a variety of shells, quite a few bluespotted stingrays and garden eels. Also look for the assorted crustaceans that dwell in the nooks and crannies.

At the far west end of Liloan the reef becomes what local divers call the "wall of death." It plummets beyond sport-diving limits and has hellacious currents that threaten to rip your mask and regulator away. Don't attempt this dive unless you're a very experienced diver. If you are an experienced diver who loves drifting rapidly along (and sometimes down) a great wall, then this is for you. But watch your depth and bottom time and make sure you have adequate buoyancy to compensate for potential down-currents.

STEVE ROSENBERG

Shrimp gobies and blind cleaning shrimp live symbiotically along the seafloor.

57 Tacot

Location: Offshore of Sibulan

Depth Range: 12-23m (40-75ft)

Access: Boat

Expertise Rating: Advanced

This underwater seamount often attracts large pelagics, usually has great visibility (more than 20m) and always has strong currents. It is not a dive for amateurs. You'll drop off the boat into blue water and follow the anchor line down to the top of the underwater mountain. When a current is running, you'll know how it feels to be a flag on a pole.

The reef itself is surrounded by a fair selection of fish life (groupers, snappers, puffers, parrotfish and angelfish, among others), and the corals are healthy and large as a consequence of the nutrient-filled currents. Gorgonians, pretty soft corals and some reasonable outcroppings of table, brain and boulder corals decorate the seamount.

As the dive is relatively shallow, most divers will have enough air to explore the reef quite thoroughly, especially if you do two dives here. Unfortunately, a second dive isn't always possible—if the sea conditions are rough, even the saltiest sea dog may get seasick riding over the reef in lumpy weather. Do watch your bottom time to avoid a decompression penalty, as this is not a good spot to hang out at 3m. A keen pair of eyes on the dive boat is a must to spot divers who may get swept off the reef in the current.

SAMMY ANG

Schooling fish surround Tacot.

58 Calong Calong

Location: North of Dumaguete

Depth Range: 3-25m (10-82ft)

Access: Boat

Expertise Rating: Novice

A popular training site and a reasonable snorkeling area, this large reef has some fair-sized corals sprouting from it, including table and basket corals and, of course, sea fans. Among others, spotted rays, groupers, snappers, puffers, gobies, parrotfish, some angelfish, a variety of tangs and a few frogfish reside on the reef.

There's plenty to see on this large reef, which deserves more than one visit. Snorkelers beware that currents can be strong here. The dive boats usually follow divers, but carrying a safety sausage isn't a bad idea—divers in a group can get dispersed over the reef, making it difficult for the banceros to keep track of every buddy team.

59 Apo Island

Location: Off SE tip of Negros Island

Depth Range: 3-35m (10-115ft)

Access: Boat

Expertise Rating: Intermediate

Since the early '70s, Apo Island has enjoyed marine sanctuary status. Unlike Sumilon Island, the rules have been consistently applied here, and the results speak for themselves. The island now has a couple of dive resorts, and dive trips are mounted to Apo from all over the Visayas. Apo is best visited between December and May. The rest of the year, sea conditions can make diving here uncomfortable if not impossible.

Snorkeling is great over most of the fringing reef, which runs around the conically shaped island from 3m to around 25m before dropping off to the seafloor. Currents are usually moderate to strong here though, so sea conditions are often not ideal for snorkeling. Only experienced snorkelers should consider Apo as a destination.

The reef is festooned with a multitude of large, prolific corals and sponges, including table, star and brain corals, barrel sponges and sea whips, and some good-sized clumps of black coral a little deeper. Anemones and clownfish, as well as some giant clams (some of which have been seeded) abound at Apo. Some impressive gorgonians sprout from the walls.

The fish life is similarly prolific, with plenty of groupers, glasseye snappers, gobies, tangs, wrasses, chromis, damsels, surgeons, squirrelfish, butterflyfish, drums, fusiliers and parrotfish. Blacktip and whitetip sharks are quite common, and an impressive array of pelagics, including tuna, jacks, barracuda, wahoos and mackerel, regularly visits the usually clear water. Stinging hydroids seem to grow everywhere, so (as always) look but don't touch.

SAMMY ANG

Descend along the anchor line when currents sweep Apo.

Bohol

The lovely island of Bohol is another well-kept secret. A proud and independent people, Boholanos have taken care of their island's many natural wonders. The result has been an increase in nature-loving visitors who are eager to experience what Bohol has to offer, as well as an improved infrastructure to accommodate and entertain them. Alona Beach on Panglao Island, which is connected by a causeway to the mainland and is a few kilometers away from Bohol's sleepy capital of Tagbilaran, is the place most divers will call home.

Alona Beach is all about diving: Resorts, ranging from simple cottages and guesthouses for a few dollars a night to delightful medium-sized developments with adequate luxuries for a few dollars more, cater to divers. More than a dozen well-equipped, professionally run dive centers operate along the beach. Even the nightlife (what little there is of it) is geared toward the diving community—tall tales of deep encounters are heard at most restaurants and bars along the beach.

Alona Beach is a jumping-off point for dive safaris throughout the Visayas. Safaris are usually undertaken on larger banca boats and often involve camping and barbecuing on remote islands during a two- to five-day trip.

The airport at Tagbilaran receives several flights daily from Manila and nearby Cebu, and every day several Super Cat ferries ply the route from Cebu's port for the one-way, 40-minute transfer. You can arrange in advance for transfers from Tagbilaran to Alona Beach through dive centers and resorts, or you can easily arrange your own trip by tricycle, taxi, jeepney or private coaster (minivan).

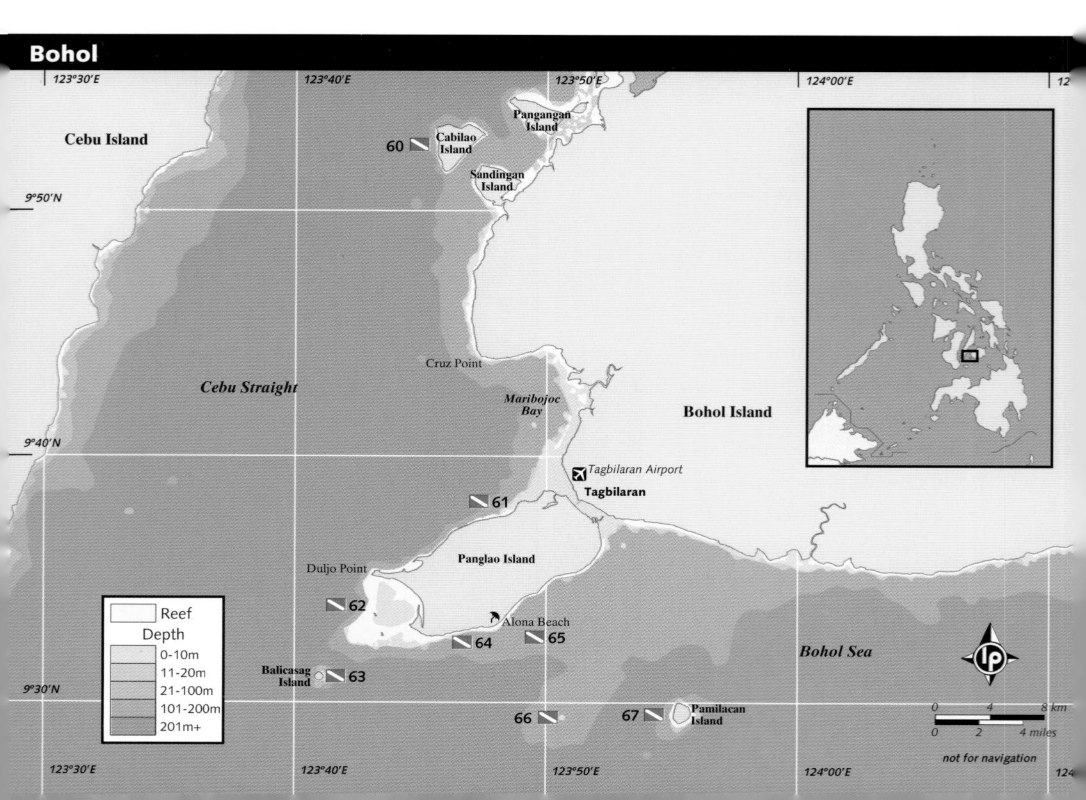

Bohol Dive Sites

	Good Snorkeling	Novice	Intermediate	Advanced
60 Cabilao Island	●		●	
61 Napaling	●		●	
62 Tangnan Wall			●	
63 Balicasag	●		●	
64 Kalipayan (Happy Wall)	●	●		
65 Arco Point (Hole in the Wall)	●		●	
66 Cervera Shoal			●	
67 Pamilacan Island	●		●	

60 Cabilao Island

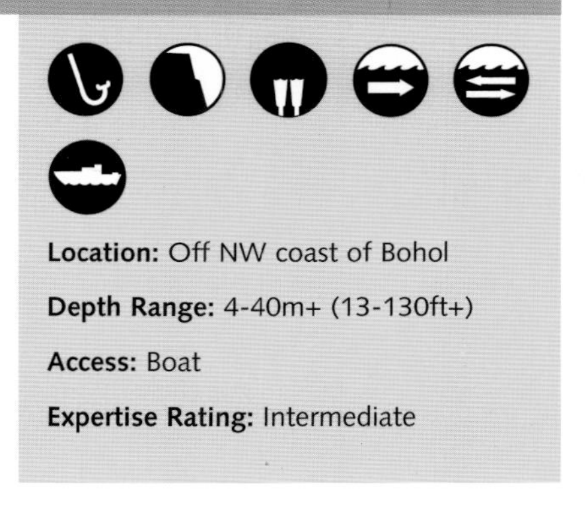

Location: Off NW coast of Bohol

Depth Range: 4-40m+ (13-130ft+)

Access: Boat

Expertise Rating: Intermediate

Cabilao, off the northwestern coast of Bohol, is an immensely popular dive area. When sea conditions are bad, it's impossible to reach Cabilao by conventional means. Even if you travel on a large boat, diving is often out of the question if the waves are too high.

Divers come to watch the shoals of hammerhead sharks at **Hammerhead Point**, which is easy to find due to its proximity to the island's lighthouse. The sharks are here every year between December and June, though you are more likely to see them in the earlier part of the season. This site can get quite crowded and, like all sites around Cabilao, is often afflicted with hellacious currents, though visibility is often well over 30m. If lots of dive boats are around, it's obviously important to stick with your dive guide.

The reef off the point has many cracks, overhangs and coral gardens on it. It drops off to a ledge at 30m, and then drops again to much deeper water. This is a popular meeting point for the ubiquitous hammerheads, which shoal off the point in deeper water. Despite the fantastic visibility, divers here tend to exceed reasonable depths to get a closer view of the deep-swimming hammerheads, large groupers and Napoleon wrasses.

Hammerheads, despite their ferocious appearance, are actually extremely wary of divers and tend to disperse to even deeper water if they feel provoked or threatened, such as by divers who approach too closely. Pay attention to the dive briefing and stick to the planned depths and times.

The reef is home to some reasonable gorgonians, and large barrel sponges, whips, sponges and crinoids festoon the walls. Whitetip and grey sharks are frequently seen, and barracuda, jacks, mackerel and tuna round out the pelagic menu. Butterflyfish, Napoleon wrasses and triggerfish are common reef inhabitants, and you'll probably encounter fusiliers, snappers, Moorish idols and sweetlips.

Along **Southwest Cabilao**, the strong currents make this a perennial drift dive that often has better than 30m of visibility. Though the drop-in point is a mundane section of shallow reef, the scenery improves as you drift either north or southeast.

The shallow southern portion of the reef is torn up from years of passing typhoons—not much to see here but rubble and dead coral. Drifting north, you'll soon arrive at a wall that drops down to a ledge and then descends beyond the sport-diving limit. The wall is liberally covered with small gorgonians and sea fans, some impressive barrel sponges, baskets, lots of soft corals and sea whips and a clump or two of elephant ear corals. Watch out for the abundant fire coral. If you accidentally brush against it, you'll regret it—the local treatments for fire coral and jellyfish stings include urinating on the wound and pouring gasoline over it, both of which are effective, but neither of which is particularly enjoyable.

You'll see lots of sea stars around, as well as crinoids and many nudibranchs. Check out the colonies of ribbon eels and garden eels, as well as the small rays, on the sandy sections of the reef.

At the deeper end of the reef you'll find large groupers and Napoleon wrasses. The higher you go the more likely you will encounter squirrelfish hiding in dark recesses, lots of fusiliers and soldierfish, snappers, sweetlips,

ROBERT YIN

Shoaling hammerheads draw divers from around the world to tiny Cabilao Island.

some lionfish and damselfish, among others.

A southeasterly current will sweep you over the dead section of the reef to a wall that drops to more than 40m, again with similar features and marine life as that to the north, although the gorgonians are larger here, and you'll probably see some tube anemones. The major attractions on this dive are the impressive clumps of black coral along some of the deeper sections of the wall.

61 Napaling

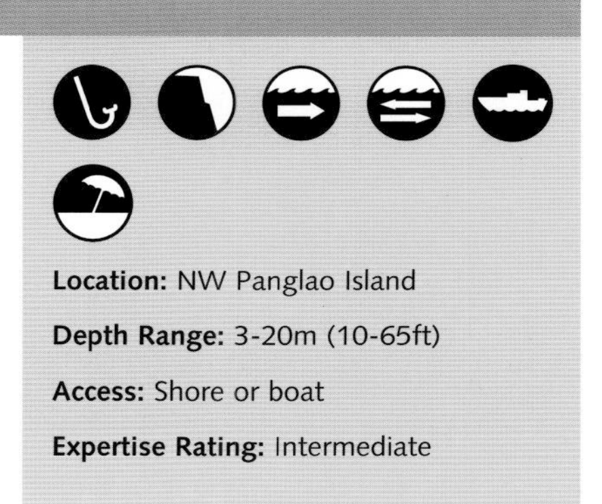

Location: NW Panglao Island

Depth Range: 3-20m (10-65ft)

Access: Shore or boat

Expertise Rating: Intermediate

Though not the easiest site to get to when the weather is rough, this is nonetheless a great dive. Because of the frequent current, Napaling is often dived as a drift dive. The dive boats usually follow your bubbles and pick you up when you surface. Though it can also be dived from the adjacent beach, the current can make it difficult to get back to shore again.

The reeftop runs a fair distance and is quite shallow (about 8m deep)—excellent for snorkeling. Dynamite fishing has caused some damage, but aside from these areas the reef is relatively healthy, with impressive table and pillar corals. Anemones, replete with the standard-issue clownfish, are quite prevalent here, and you'll probably find razorfish, damselfish, butterflyfish, parrotfish and a large shoal of anthias lurking about as well.

The wall and overhangs are quite impressive, covered with a good selection of hydroids, gorgonians, sponges and crinoids and lots of soft and tubastrea corals. Whitetip sharks often make an appearance, and a good variety of nudibranchs and various worms pose for macrophotographers. Use a flashlight to see inside the wall's many holes—you'll likely be rewarded with glimpses of angelfish, morays and various crustaceans. Jacks, tuna, rainbow runners and barracuda represent the pelagic visitors, while several species of groupers, coral trout and Napoleon wrasses are usually hanging out around the reef.

STEVE ROSENBERG

Impressive table corals grace Napaling's reef.

62 Tangnan Wall

Location: Off Panglao Island

Depth Range: 6-35m+ (20-115ft+)

Access: Boat

Expertise Rating: Intermediate

This steep wall is pocked with lots of small caves and crevices that are home to some large groupers. The wall itself supports a number of fans and gorgonians that sprout from its steep sides, as well as a fair assortment of sponges, tunicates and soft and hard corals. You may also spot wrasses, soldierfish and surgeons flitting about the coral growth, and an occasional barracuda swimming through the blue.

SAMMY ANG

Leathery soft coral sprouts from Tangnan Wall.

63 Balicasag

Location: SW of Panglao Island

Depth Range: Surface-40m+ (130ft+)

Access: Boat

Expertise Rating: Intermediate

About 6km from the southwest point of Panglao Island (45 minutes by banca boat), Balicasag is one of the Visayas' best dive areas. Stunning corals, a great variety of fish life and visibility that often exceeds 35m attract dive operators from around the Visayas. Unfortunately, as with other popular regions, this may mean that sites are crowded with divers who come for the world-class diving. Balicasag's marine sanctuary status has helped it to flourish. Despite the volume of divers, neither marine life species nor coral growth has diminished.

As with most reefs off Balicasag, **Southeast Wall** is festooned with a huge variety of corals, including table and star corals, sea whips, leather and soft corals. Anemones flourish, as do hydroids, sea stars, crinoids and sea cucumbers. In fact, this is one of the richest dive sites around, with nudibranchs competing for space with sea worms and shrimp.

Fish life is prolific, with favorites such as the stunning tiny blue chromis, which live here in the fingers of huge table corals. You'll find fusiliers, Moorish idols, anthias, bannerfish, pennantfish, lionfish, jacks, snappers and wrasses, batfish and parrotfish. And that's just in the shallow sections of the reef.

The wall is garlanded with impressive gorgonians and sea fans, elephant ear sponges, barrel sponges and basket sponges everywhere, with crinoids and various worms wiggling around all over the place. Several holes and crevices along the wall are home to soldierfish, squirrelfish and morays. Whitetip and grey reef sharks and barracuda cruise the wall frequently, and you may spot schools of rainbow runners and tuna on patrol as well.

Currents along the wall range from sluggish to "oh my God." Try to find out which to expect before you get in the water, but be prepared for either. If you can head east, you'll eventually run into **Rudy's Rock**. It's similar to Southeast Wall, but with the added chance of spotting green turtles and a shoal of bigeye trevallies that are accustomed to divers.

Black Forest, along Balicasag's northeast shore, is another popular dive area. The reef itself is really more a sandy slope dropping away to well beyond safe sport-diving limits, so watch your depth. This can be another great site for techies, of course. Again, currents can be quite vicious here and can head in almost any direction, so prepare for a drift dive accordingly. Obviously, an experienced local dive guide is a prerequisite for safe diving anywhere off Balicasag.

Massive clumps of black coral are the most significant feature of this site. You won't start to see the forest until you reach 30m. On the way down you'll pass many coral bommies, sea whips and small gorgonians sprouting out of the sand. Garden eels and moray eels are frequent neighbors here, sharing the waters with emperor and royal angelfish, Moorish idols, bannerfish, puffers, surgeons and a couple different types of triggerfish, among others. At the deeper sections of the reef, you may encounter some large skittish groupers, tuna, batfish and Napoleon wrasses.

Due to the depth of the black corals and the probable current, you should start your ascent with plenty of air left in your tank and plan a safety stop at around 5m at the top of the reef. Prepare to be washed off the reef into blue water during your safety stop if the current isn't cooperating.

STEVE ROSENBERG

A silver curtain of bigeye jacks schools before a diver.

64 Kalipayan (Happy Wall)

Location: Off Alona Beach

Depth Range: 2-20m (7-65ft)

Access: Boat

Expertise Rating: Novice

Minimal current and good visibility (often more than 20m) make this a popular training site. Kalipayan is a small drop-off with moderate coral coverage, including some small gorgonians, leathery corals, sponges and tunicates. You are likely to spot wrasses, juvenile groupers and snappers, and occasionally a barracuda or two will cruise by for a look.

This site is also good for night diving, and snorkelers will enjoy the shallow parts of the reef, which offer assorted colorful reef fish.

65 Arco Point (Hole in the Wall)

Location: Off Arco Point

Depth Range: 6-25m (20-82ft)

Access: Boat

Expertise Rating: Intermediate

Arco Point is a fish-feeding station, so the local reef residents are unusually friendly. Some sea snakes roam the reef, and you can find wrasses, triggerfish, morays and butterflyfish flitting around the corals, which are reasonably varied.

This site's most interesting feature is a small cave (the hole in the wall that the site gets its secondary name from) that you can enter at 8m and exit at 18m. Covered with colorful soft corals, the cave's interior is home to lots of small fish, including copper sweepers, wrasses, tangs and butterflyfish. Current is not usually a factor here, and visibility can be quite good, so bring a camera for a chance to take some good shots.

STEVE ROSENBERG

A cloud of copper sweepers parts as a diver swims by.

66 Cervera Shoal

Location: West of Pamilacan Island

Depth Range: 5-40m+ (16-130ft+)

Access: Boat

Expertise Rating: Intermediate

Currents can be quite strong on this seamount, which rises from more than 60m to just below the surface. You'll need to watch your depth, but, frankly, the deeper you go the less there is to see.

Though the corals are not particularly impressive, the large resident colony of banded sea snakes is. Aside from the sea snakes, which aren't everybody's favorite underwater resident, pelagics are what most divers come here to see—you may spy tuna, jacks, whitetip sharks, rainbow runners and barracuda. Schools of damsels, scorpionfish, surgeons and butterflyfish flit above the reef.

67 Pamilacan Island

Location: 23km (14 miles) SE of Panglao Island

Depth Range: 5-30m (16-100ft)

Access: Boat

Expertise Rating: Intermediate

In the local dialect *pamilacan* means "resting place of the mantas." You'll have a good chance at spotting some of these impressive animals cruising the unusually clear, current-swept waters here. Visibility often exceeds 30m.

The northwest side of the island is a marine sanctuary. The wall that drops from the reeftop within the sanctuary is festooned with good-sized gorgonians, tunicates, sponges, anemones, sea fans and a wide variety of hard and soft corals.

On other parts of the island the bottom is quite sandy, sloping gently away from shore, with scattered coral bommies. You'll find anemones (with clownfish, of course), fusiliers, small groupers and snappers among others at this site. Pelagic visitors include Napoleon wrasses, jacks, barracuda and some large dogtooth tuna.

ROBERT YIN

Mantas glide gracefully by Pamilacan Island.

Southern Leyte

The newest diving destination in the Philippines is Southern Leyte (to the northeast of Cebu City), where local divers have researched and documented more than 20 excellent sites. Three dive centers operate in the area now, so adventurous divers looking for the epitome of pristine diving may well want to plan a trip here. The friendly locals, mostly into subsistence agriculture, lead simple lives in a very laid-back rural setting.

Southern Leyte is served by a fast Super Cat catamaran ferry that departs daily from Cebu Port 4 at 8:30am for the 2½ hour trip to Maasin, the capital of Southern Leyte.

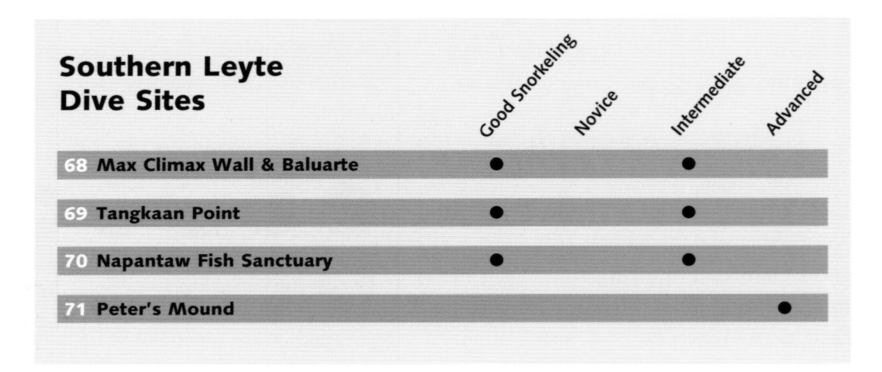

Southern Leyte Dive Sites

	Good Snorkeling	Novice	Intermediate	Advanced
68 Max Climax Wall & Baluarte	●		●	
69 Tangkaan Point	●		●	
70 Napantaw Fish Sanctuary	●		●	
71 Peter's Mound				●

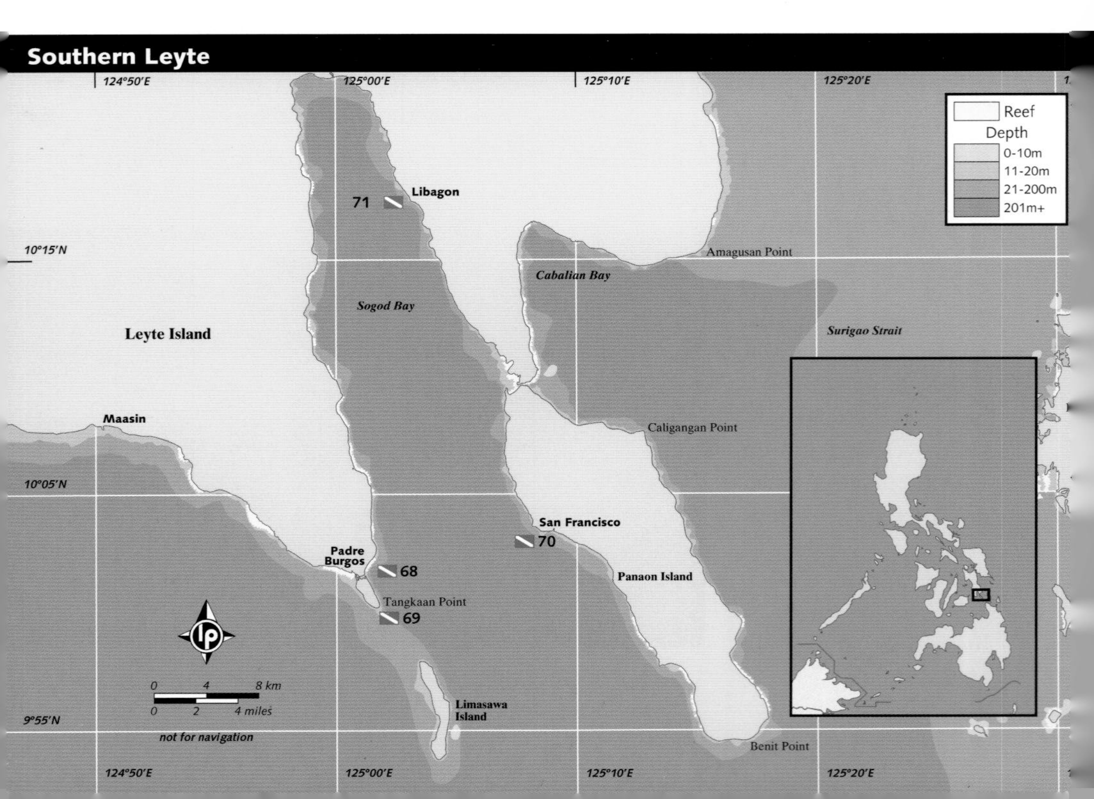

68 Max Climax Wall & Baluarte

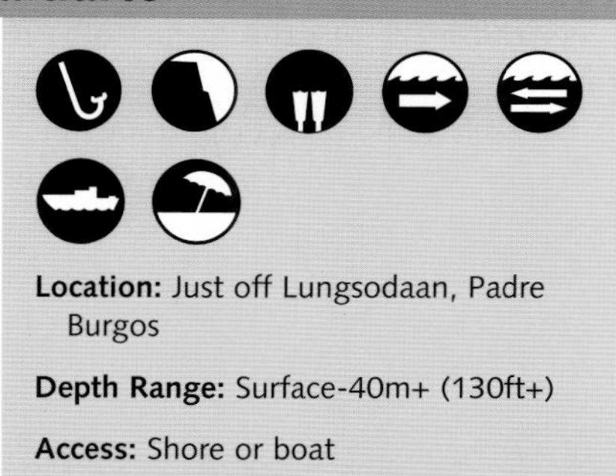

Location: Just off Lungsodaan, Padre Burgos

Depth Range: Surface-40m+ (130ft+)

Access: Shore or boat

Expertise Rating: Intermediate

Max Climax Wall starts a few meters from shore, so it's possible to do a beach dive here. Divers usually arrive and depart by tricycle or pickup—a new experience for most. The wall is riddled with crevices that shelter angelfish, snappers, sweetlips, Napoleon wrasses and groupers.

A little farther along the coast is Baluarte, which is very similar to Max Climax. Pelagics seen at both sites include jacks, tuna and barracuda. Sharks, turtles and eagle rays are also frequent visitors. Gorgonian fan corals are well represented at these sites, as are some black corals and soft corals. The reef is in very good condition, and as yet very few divers have visited these sites, or indeed any of Southern Leyte's sites.

69 Tangkaan Point

Location: Padre Burgos

Depth Range: Surface-40m+ (130ft+)

Access: Shore or boat

Expertise Rating: Intermediate

Divers have discovered several sites in and around Sogod Bay, and more are being found as the large reef systems are explored. The topography is diverse; reef flats and walls interspersed with interesting limestone and rock formations. Much of the reef has been declared a fish sanctuary, and fishing is regulated by the local communities, so the corals and marine life thrive. Sogod Bay is a good place to see whale sharks, whales, dolphins, manta rays and several species of shark. Whaleshark watching cruises are a good option between dives.

Tangkaan Point, a half hour by road from Maasin, is a long land mass with

STEVE ROSENBERG

Barrel sponges grow only 2cm per year.

some outstanding and varied pristine reefs and walls to explore just off the shore.

Snorkelers and divers will enjoy much of the area, like **Barrel Sponge Garden**, a small drop-off with massive barrel sponges, table corals and a huge variety of colorful hard corals. Sites are more easily accessed by boat, but locals can point snorkelers in the right direction to find the shallow coral gardens that characterize most of the area.

Turtle Rock is great for big-fish lovers. Green turtles are common here, as well as batfish, eagle rays and groupers. The corals are prolific and diverse, including gorgonians, tables, brain and sea whips, as well as sponges galore.

70 Napantaw Fish Sanctuary

Location: Napantaw, San Francisco

Depth Range: 10-40m+ (33-130ft+)

Access: Boat

Expertise Rating: Intermediate

This wall dive goes by many names, including **Rio's Wall** and **Toshi's Wall.** Of the many walls in Southern Leyte, this one stands out not only for its huge gorgonians, black corals and soft corals, but also for its generally prolific and colorful marine life. The corals, fed by the often-strong currents that sweep by, are especially healthy here. Reef inhabitants include batfish, groupers, sweetlips and many other reef fish. Turtles and barracuda also frequent the area.

Take a flashlight to peer inside the cave at 40m. If you don't locate it within the first few minutes of the dive, it's better to forget about it and avoid risking the bends—concentrate on the amazing reef life a little higher up the wall.

Local divers are setting up a mooring buoy to protect the reef from anchor damage at this increasingly popular dive site. A dive fee is being charged to help finance monitoring and protection measures undertaken by the Barangay Council of Napantaw.

71 Peter's Mound

Location: Offshore Otikon, Libagon

Depth Range: 10-40m+ (33-130ft+)

Access: Boat

Expertise Rating: Advanced

A seamount just 200m offshore, this fascinating site serves as a cleaning station for large pelagics.

To fully appreciate the experience, you should dive here when a strong current is flowing. For this reason, a boat is the preferred way to access the site. Be sure to descend and ascend using a shot line.

The reef is abuzz with fish racing about and feeding, including Napoleon wrasses, groupers, sweetlips, surgeons, fusiliers, tuna and jacks.

Mindanao Dive Sites

One of the largest but poorest of the Philippines' 7,107 islands, Mindanao has some great diving but a lackluster infrastructure. The island has one or two luxury resorts, but in general the accommodations and transportation options remain in the medium- to low-budget range.

Some parts of the province, especially the southwestern islands of Tawi Tawi, Basilan Island and the Sulu Archipelago, have been hotbeds of piracy, kidnappings and assorted violence for centuries and still remain a virtual no-go for visitors. However, despite all the bad press and negative associations that the Abu Sayaf, MILF and other extreme insurgent groups have created over the years, some parts of Mindanao—particularly Cagayan de Oro, Davao and General Santos—have become popular with visitors. Mindanaoans of all religious and tribal persuasions are, in general, a welcoming and gracious people who make every effort to entertain and impress a foreign guest.

Divers will be happy to learn that some outstanding dive sites are within reach of the above-mentioned cities, and amenities are in place to facilitate hassle-free diving once you get there. Here you'll find good hotels and resorts at reasonable prices, a choice of dining and entertainment options and a law and order situation on a par with the rest of the country—attractive enticements for adventurers and tourists alike.

ERIC L. WHEATER

Detail of a bolo and belt worn by the T'boli, one of Mindanao's many tribes.

Camiguin

Camiguin is a charming island off the coast of the Misamis Oriental province in northern Mindanao, just 88km (55 miles) from Cagayan de Oro. You can easily access Camiguin by combining public bus and fast ferry services from there. Although it's technically a part of Mindanao, divers often visit Camiguin on dive safaris organized from the divers' mecca of the Visayas, particularly from Alona Beach, Bohol, which isn't far away. Domestic flights are scheduled to resume to Camiguin's quaint airport, but at the time of writing these had not yet materialized.

Many small- to medium-sized resorts dot the island. All are reasonably priced, and most are attractive. A few dive services operate on the island, and Mantangale Alibuag Dive Resort on the mainland (close to Cagayan de Oro) also visits the island regularly.

Shallow, prolific coral gardens attract divers and snorkelers to Camiguin.

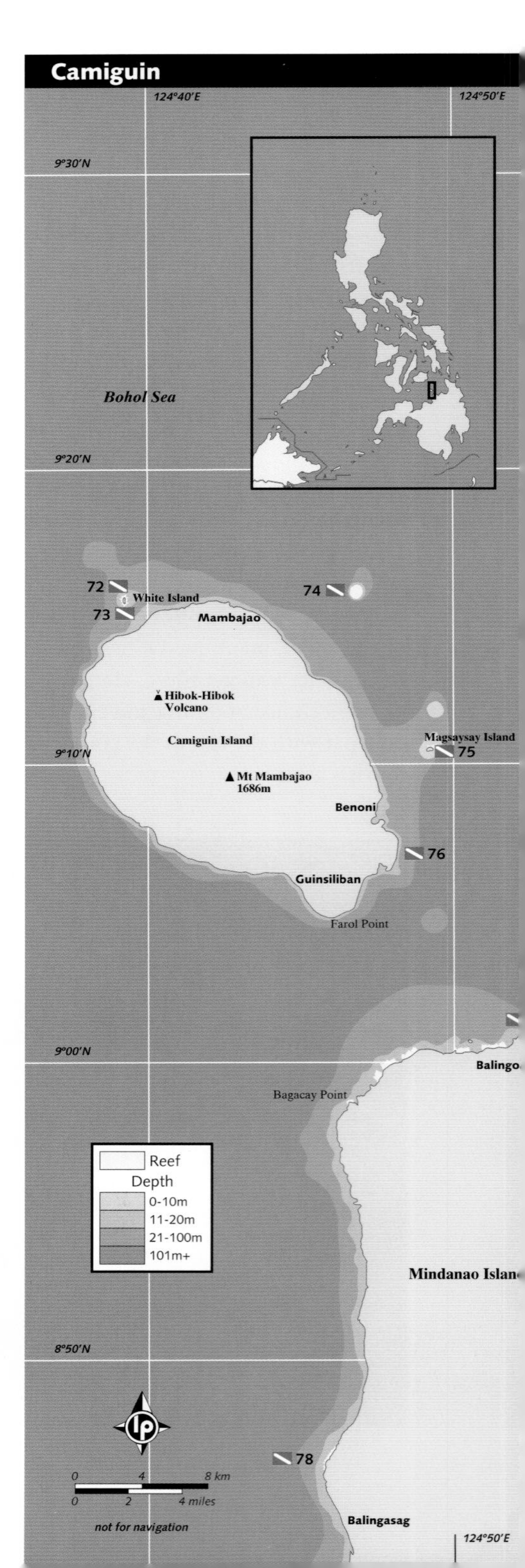

Camiguin Dive Sites

	Good Snorkeling	Novice	Intermediate	Advanced
72 Agutaya Reef	●		●	
73 Medina Underwater Springs	●	●	●	
74 Jigdup Shoal	●		●	
75 Punta Diwata	●		●	
76 Cabuan Point	●	●		
77 Sipaka Point	●			●
78 Constancia Reef	●		●	

72 Agutaya Reef

Location: Off White Island

Depth Range: 5-40m+ (16-130ft+)

Access: Boat

Expertise Rating: Intermediate

With the towering bulk of Hibok-Hibok Volcano watching over you from Camiguin Island, this idyllic sandy cay is a great place for snorkelers and divers alike.

Reef fish dart about the coral.

The large, shallow Agutaya Reef has some healthy corals and lots of small reef fish darting around, and some larger specimens are holed up in the nooks and crannies of the corals and rocks.

The eastern portion of the reef drops away from around 15m. Here you can explore a multitude of cracks, caverns and crevices that are home to a variety of larger fish such as barracuda, surgeons, tuna, eagle rays and sometimes sharks.

73 Medina Underwater Springs

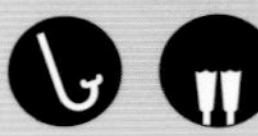

Location: Off White Island

Depth Range: 6-33m (20-108ft)

Access: Boat

Expertise Rating:
Novice (The Aquarium)
Intermediate (Paradise Canyon)

You will find two dives here, both interesting and unusual, that feature cold freshwater springs (known locally as *alibuag*) bubbling out of the seafloor. These sites are both about 300m west of White Island's beach and are at the edge of the coral reef.

Descending to around 28m, **Paradise Canyon**'s walls are punctured with plenty of cracks and holes, home to a wide variety of marine life. Take a dive light with you and look for the cavern that you can enter and explore.

A second dive in the area, known as **The Aquarium**, is (as the name implies) well endowed with corals and assorted marine life. This is an excellent training site and snorkeling spot, as it's relatively shallow (from 6 to 20m deep).

74 Jigdup Shoal

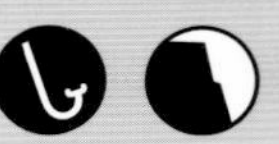

Location: 2km from Mambajao

Depth Range: Surface-40m+ (130ft+)

Access: Boat

Expertise Rating: Intermediate

One of the best sites hereabouts, this shoal rises from the seafloor to form a sprawling reef more than 10 hectares across. Teeming with all sorts of marine life, this reef is a wide-angle photographer's dream. Lush corals, excellent visibility year-round and a never-ending diorama of tropical reef fish, pelagics and macrophotography subjects make this a favorite repeat site for many divers. Barracuda, tuna, several species of sharks and rays, wrasses, angelfish, surgeons, snappers and groupers are all likely candidates for observation.

The current can be fierce at times, so be prepared to deal with it accordingly. If you have any doubts, turn around and head for the boat while your tank is still two-thirds full.

TIM ROCK

Jigdup is a wide-angle photographer's dream.

75 Punta Diwata

The reef here has stepped ledges of coral that descend to the depths. The walls and overhangs are covered in sea fans, sponges and a variety of multicolored gorgonians, sea whips and hard and soft corals. Commonly seen fish species include groupers, sweetlips and snappers, while mantas are occasionally spotted. This is yet another excellent wide-angle site with usually good visibility unless it's been raining recently.

Location: Eastern tip of Gingoong Bay, Magsaysay Island

Depth Range: Surface-40m+ (130ft+)

Access: Boat

Expertise Rating: Intermediate

76 Cabuan Point

A delightful dive that's sure to attract the interest of wide-angle photographers, this site features stunning sea fans, branching corals and a huge variety of hard and soft corals and sponges. You are sure to see angelfish, tangs, colorful cuttlefish and parrotfish, and the usually light currents make diving here a breeze.

Location: Between Benoni and Guinsiliban Ports

Depth Range: Surface-30m+ (100ft+)

Access: Shore or boat

Expertise Rating: Novice

Visibility ranges from 12 to 35m, depending on the recent weather conditions. This is a good training ground and ideal for snorkelers.

TIM ROCK

Kaleidoscopic cuttlefish are often seen by divers, especially at night.

77 Sipaka Point

Location: Close to Mantangale Alibuag Dive Resort, Balingoan

Depth Range: Surface-25m (82ft)

Access: Boat

Expertise Rating: Advanced

A strong current can make this a wild ride, so the site is best suited for more experienced divers. The currents bring nutrients, which in turn nourish the fantastic assortment of huge corals that abound here. Massive basket sponges, sea fans and table corals are common, together with a wide array of hard and soft corals, sponges and feather stars.

Look for stingrays hiding in the sandy spots, and groupers, snappers, wrasses, surgeons, parrotfish, angelfish and many other species darting in and out of the corals and rocks.

Photographers will have a hard time deciding whether to use a macro or wide-angle lens—you'll probably have to do several dives to see Sipaka's full potential.

78 Constancia Reef

Location: Offshore north of Balingasag

Depth Range: 6-40m+ (20-130ft+)

Access: Boat

Expertise Rating: Intermediate

Although some distance from shore, this tiny shoal with healthy corals on the south side is worth visiting because of the pelagic life you're likely to encounter. Eagle rays are quite common, and you may run into a turtle or two. Keep an eye out for the occasional manta. Tuna, jacks, barracuda, several species of sharks, rainbow runners and Spanish mackerel also frequent Constancia's tumbling walls.

TIM ROCK

Cleaner shrimp go to work on a grouper.

On the reeftop, parrotfish spend much of their time resting and gathering above the lettuce corals, which cover much of the area. Sea fans and sponges proliferate, and a variety of reef fish, such as angelfish, wrasses, blennies, groupers, snappers and surgeonfish dart about between the coral cover.

This is a good site for photographers, but the current can be a factor. Visibility is usually more than 25m.

Davao

Davao is geographically the largest city in the Philippines. However, as with Puerto Princesa in Palawan, the published boundaries of the city don't reflect the demographics of the inhabitants. Much of the "city" is sparsely inhabited farmland and forest. Despite apparent attempts to impose some form of grandeur on what is in actuality a pleasant provincial town, Davao retains a charm and appeal all its own.

Only a few degrees north of the equator, the Davao region enjoys a Hawaii-like weather pattern. It rains briefly most days, the hot sun shines almost every day and typhoons are unknown here (indeed, all of Mindanao is well south of the typhoon belt). Davao is a genuine year-round diving destination, something that is not lost on the local dive entrepreneurs, who visit sites around nearby Samal Island.

SCOTT TUASON

The Pearl Farm Resort's stilt houses are styled after those of the Sulu archipelago's seafaring tribes.

As luck would have it, two Japanese ships lie in 40m (130ft) in the Malipano anchorage of the Pearl Farm Resort—a bit deep for normal recreational diving, but a good drawing card nonetheless. However, much of the reef life that once flourished close to Davao has been seriously compromised for a number of reasons, including illegal fishing techniques, overfishing and anchor damage to the reefs. This notwithstanding, some pretty good sites are within reasonable striking distance of Davao, providing the chance to interact with plenty of tropical marine life.

Feast or Foul?

Davao is the Philippines' capital of durian, an oversized, rank-smelling, spiky-sheathed fruit. In his *Malayan Trilogy*, Anthony Burgess described the experience of devouring durian as similar to "eating a custard pie while sitting on the toilet." Be warned: If planning to take a sample back to the folks at home, airlines, buses and ferries refuse to carry durian onboard, as its smell upsets passengers and crew alike. However, you can buy durian-flavored ice cream in Davao, as well as a smorgasbord of other processed durian delights that act as a fine substitute and are far more socially acceptable.

VERONICA GARBUTT

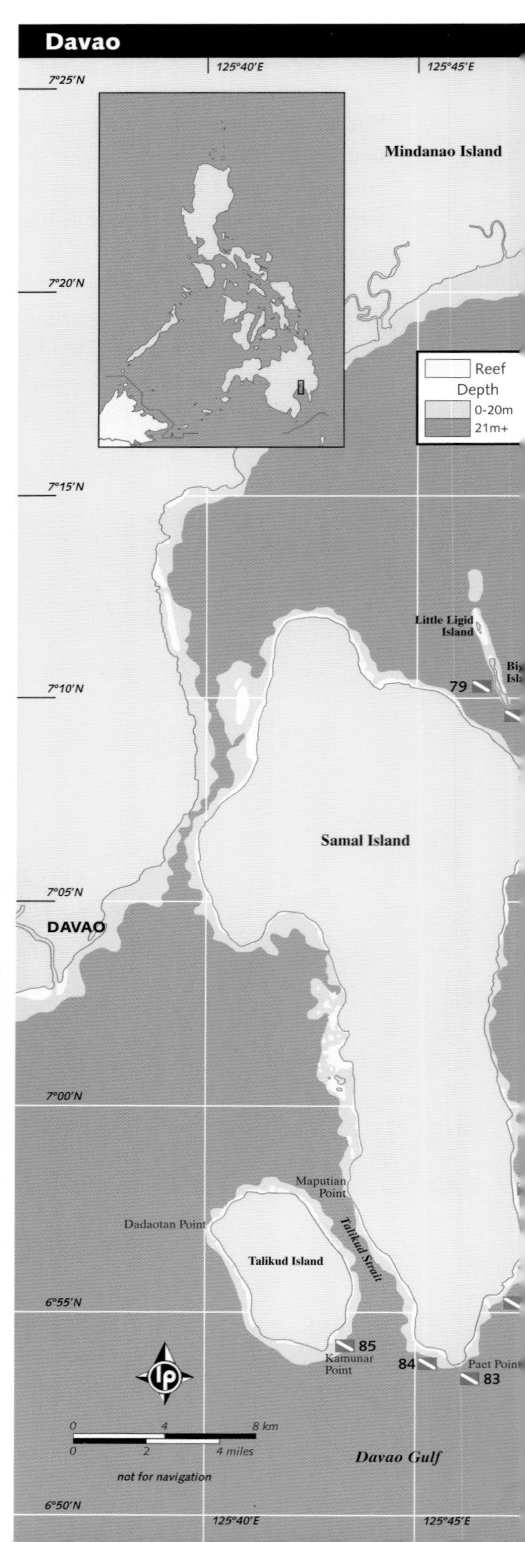

Davao Dive Sites

	Good Snorkeling	Novice	Intermediate	Advanced
79 Ligid Caves	●		●	
80 Pinnacle Point	●		●	
81 Pindawon Wall	●		●	
82 Mushroom Rock	●		●	
83 Marissa 1, 2 & 3	●	●		
84 Malipano Japanese Wrecks	●			●
85 Linosutan Coral Gardens	●	●		

79 Ligid Caves

Location: Big Ligid Island, NE of Samal Island

Depth Range: Surface-30m (100ft)

Access: Boat

Expertise Rating: Intermediate

You can find the Ligid Caves by swimming over the leather-coral encrusted reef, past where the wall drops sharply from 16m, then descending a few meters farther until you reach the two cave systems.

One of the caves has three entrances that all lead to a central chamber filled with black corals, a variety of sponges and tunicates, soft corals and crustaceans such as sponge crabs.

Lionfish, scorpionfish, parrotfish and rabbitfish hang out near the caves' entrances. Look for a large harp-shaped gorgonian and check out the resident razorfish, ideal subjects for a well-strobed photo shoot.

Atop the reef, especially on night dives, look for the many golden sea cucumbers, hydroids and basket stars. This is also a fair snorkeling site for experienced snorkelers.

TIM ROCK

Golden sea cucumbers emerge at night.

80 Pinnacle Point

Location: SE tip of Big Ligid Island

Depth Range: 8-35m (26-115ft)

Access: Boat

Expertise Rating: Intermediate

Expect strong currents here—try to get in the water at high tide for the least current and best visibility. Head southeast along the wall, current permitting, taking in views of the gorgonians and fans. Check out the cracks and holes in the wall, where you can find bigeyes and cardinalfish. Some octopuses and morays also dwell in the smaller holes.

Southeast of the point are three reef formations where schools of surgeonfish, pennant butterflyfish, jacks and several types of angelfish frequently visit. The center structure is covered in delightful pink soft corals, while the leeward side is festooned with large gorgonians, black coral and a host of anthias and tubastrea.

Macrophotographers will appreciate the many nudibranchs and similar subjects. Watch your depth on this dive, and make sure you have enough air left to get back to the boat's anchor line with enough time for a safety stop, which could be affected by strong currents.

81 Pindawon Wall

Location: East side of Samal Island

Depth Range: 10-40m+ (33-130ft+)

Access: Boat

Expertise Rating: Intermediate

Pindawon is one of the better walls in the area, with some impressive overhangs and good hard-coral cover. Some spectacular table corals and black corals are features at this site, as well as major cabbage coral colonies. You may well run into some sea snakes, as the pickings are quite good for them.

Some interesting nudibranchs live around the numerous crevices and cracks, and there is an average amount of fish life, including colorful harlequin shrimps and razorfish. You may also spot snappers and a few skittish groupers.

STEVE ROSENBERG

Shrimps hide amid an anemone's tentacles.

82 Mushroom Rock

Location: SE side of Samal Island

Depth Range: 5-35m (16-115ft)

Access: Boat

Expertise Rating: Intermediate

Sticking out of the water, this dive site's namesake rock has been eroded by millennia of unceasing aquatic friction. Watch out for the currents here, as they can be ferocious. For the best conditions, dive this site during the amihan (northeast monsoon) season, and at high tide.

The strong currents bring out the pelagics, of course, so you might run into tuna, rainbow runners and jacks, among others. Divers commonly see dolphins in the surrounding area, but seldom encounter them underwater.

The reeftop is well covered with leather corals, table corals and a variety of hard and soft corals. The reef itself has some interesting formations, crevices and bulges that are home to a variety of tropical reef fish. A wall plummets to a sandy bottom at 35m. Watch your depth on this dive, and remember that currents can pick up fast, so return to your anchor line or shot line with enough air to do a safety stop, and be prepared to hang on to the line if the current picks up. In such a case you risk getting washed out to sea or even onto the rocks.

83 Marissa 1, 2 & 3

Location: South of Samal Island

Depth Range: 8-18m (26-60ft)

Access: Boat

Expertise Rating: Novice

Marissa is a good training area and not a bad night dive either. Snorkelers may also enjoy this site. Named after the daughter (a keen diver) of the Pearl Farm Resort's owner, the three reefs here share similar features.

The Pearl Farm maintains the reefs as a marine sanctuary, so there is plenty of life bubbling around. The rills, undercuts, small walls and drop-offs interspersed with gentle slopes are home to a variety of corals, including staghorn, elkhorn and table. Moray eels and tube worms vie for space on some parts of the reef, and there is a profusion of sea stars. At some times of the year, especially around Easter, you'll see hydroids by the thousands. (Though they aren't particularly vicious ones, be sure you are properly covered before entering the water.)

TIM ROCK

Sea stars are profuse at the Marissas.

84 Malipano Japanese Wrecks

Location: Off Pearl Farm Resort

Depth Range: 18-40m (60-130ft)

Access: Boat

Expertise Rating: Advanced

The lack of currents here has prevented much coral from growing on the hulls of these two Japanese ships, which both went down in WWII. Though just a few sponges and tunicates, a couple of whip corals and the odd shell or two decorate the wreck site, its proximity to the Pearl Farm Resort has ensured the site is visited frequently.

The wrecks are only about 40m apart, so you can visit both on the same dive.

This site is recommended only for those with suitable deep-dive training.

85 Linosutan Coral Gardens

Location: SE Talicud Island

Depth Range: 5-40m+ (16-130ft+)

Access: Boat

Expertise Rating: Novice

A good snorkeling and photography site, this 4km-long stretch of reef offers the best diving near Davao City. Its most attractive features are above 20m, but the reef slopes (gently in some places and more steeply in others) down to the sandy bottom at 43m, with less cover and more sand the deeper you go. Visibility is often good here, usually between 18 and 27m. The many species of hard and soft corals make this a colorful and entertaining dive, appreciated by novice and advanced divers alike.

ROBERT YIN

Shallow coral gardens are ideal for snorkeling.

Anthias, shrimp, gobies, damsels, fusiliers, flounder, butterflyfish, sea stars, sponges and tube worms are everywhere. Several species of mollusks navigate the sandy bottom, and you'll find a sizeable colony of ribbon eels, their heads poking out of the sand. It's not uncommon to encounter hawksbill turtles here, and tuna and eagle rays are also frequent visitors.

General Santos City

Usually referred to simply as Gen San, this relatively recent addition to the Philippine dive circuit offers some of the most outstanding wall dives in the country. Much of the diving is in Sarangani Bay, where the massive drop-off and its colorful fringing reef run for kilometers just off the beach. Well over 20 world-class sites have been discovered and are dived regularly, and others are sure to follow as more divers venture into the many unexplored pristine areas. For the time being, Tuna City Scuba Center is the only dive center in town.

Gen San is also called Tuna City, a reference to its large tuna fishing fleet. Dining options are predictably slanted toward fresh seafood (try the local delicacy, *sinugba*, charcoal-broiled tuna served with a special sauce), but cattle are raised locally, so beef is usually on the menu. You'll find a range of hotels and

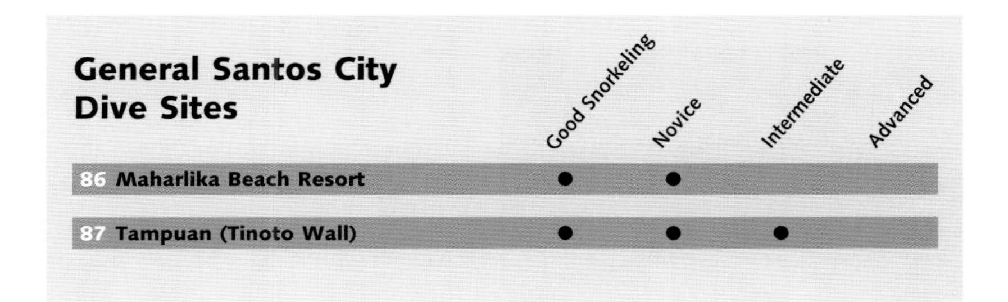

General Santos City Dive Sites	Good Snorkeling	Novice	Intermediate	Advanced
86 Maharlika Beach Resort	●	●		
87 Tampuan (Tinoto Wall)	●	●	●	

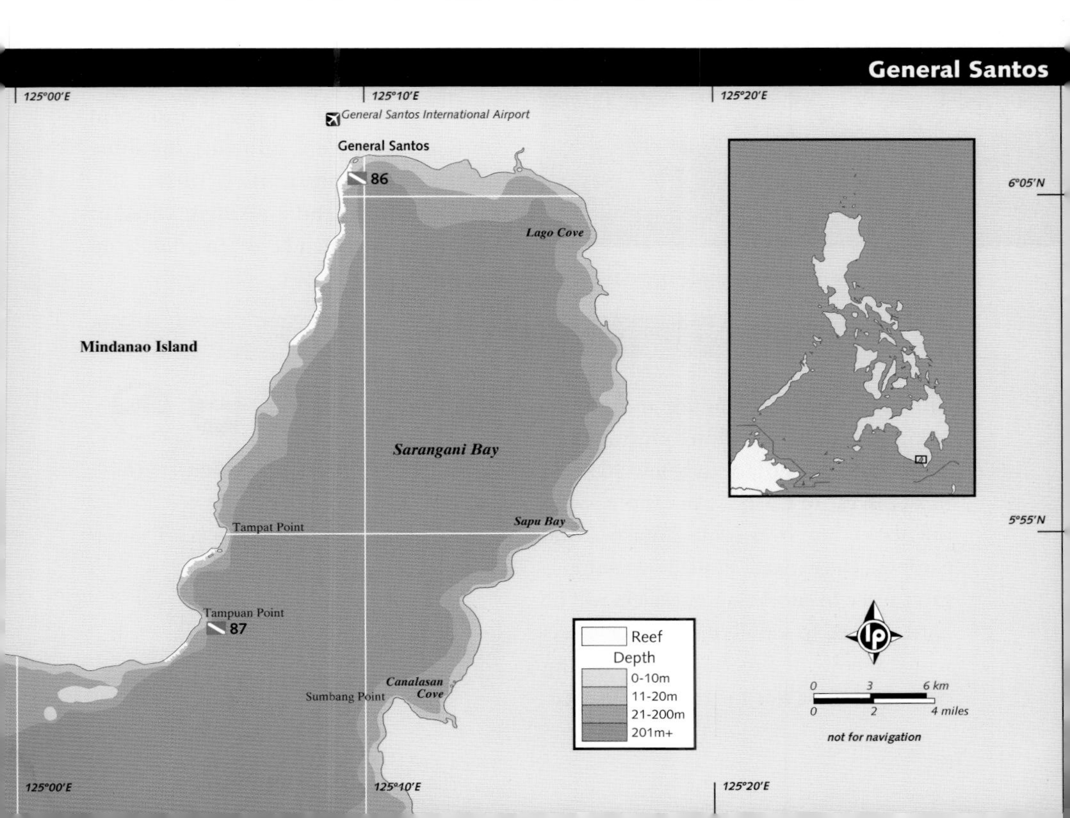

pension houses in town, as well as several budget to medium-priced resorts on adjacent beaches. Air Philippines and Philippine Airlines fly daily from Manila to Gen San. Negros Navigation offers ferry service from Manila on Mondays; WG&A offers the same on Wednesdays and Saturdays.

86 Maharlika Beach Resort

This is an ideal training site, with plenty to see, healthy corals and lots of fish. Snorkelers will also really enjoy this spot. It's the nearest site to the center of town and the largest beach resort in the area.

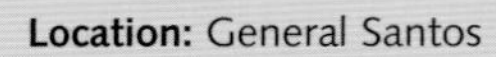

Location: General Santos

Depth Range: Surface-21m (70ft)

Access: Shore

Expertise Rating: Novice

TIM ROCK
An arceye hawkfish seeks shelter amid the coral.

Huge staghorn corals are the main attraction here, providing homes to a variety of reef fish including parrotfish, wrasses, emperors, Moorish idols, sweetlips and groupers. Cowfish, turretfish and filefish are also commonly seen here, and you may see lots of shrimp gobies here in June and July. Big squid lay their eggs on the staghorn corals and seem oblivious to divers, allowing for some great photo opportunities. Turtles also visit regularly, and a resident shoal of yellowtail barracuda often makes an appearance.

87 Tampuan (Tinoto Wall)

This massive wall runs for more than 10km along the coastline, plummeting down from the surface to below 200m in most places. To reach it from shore, swim out about 50m over some fantastic coral gardens. The expansive, shallow reeftop is great place to snorkel—snorkelers will be hard-pressed to see all of it. Novice divers will also enjoy the reeftop, but plunging over the wall is not for the fainthearted.

Location: 50km (31 miles) from General Santos

Depth Range: Surface-40m+ (130ft+)

Access: Shore or boat

Expertise Rating: Novice (reeftop) Intermediate (wall)

Currents can be strong sometimes, but usually not for long.

The wall itself is truly impressive, with massive gorgonians, hydroids, sponges, tunicates and sea cucumbers along its length. Crustaceans and nudibranchs hide in the thick hard- and soft-coral growth, crevices and cracks.

Plenty of tropical reef fish, such as groupers, snappers, puffers, surgeons, soldierfish, gobies, anthias, angels, parrotfish and butterflyfish swarm everywhere, but it's the big fish and pelagics that will draw your attention. The deeper you go, the larger they are. Napoleon wrasses and bumphead parrotfish, manta and eagle rays, tuna and rainbow runners are frequently spotted, as well as several species of sharks, including hammerheads on occasion.

As the wall has not yet been explored thoroughly, there are still plenty of opportunities for new discoveries. Some areas that are visited regularly include **Amadora's** Diving Resort and **Lau-Tengco Point** (also called **Barracuda Point**). Though Amadora's has only one cottage, the diving off the beach and down the wall is probably the best yet discovered in the area and is much visited.

Lau-Tengco Point is a little farther along the reef from Amadora's, where the wall does an S-bend. Although the top of the reef is still recovering from being dynamited, the scenery along the wall is markedly different from that described above.

Barracuda are often seen shoaling in the depths, and the current can be quite ferocious at times. Usually the current gradually increases over a few minutes, allowing divers time to get out of the water and avoid experiencing its washing-machine effect.

STEVE ROSENBERG

Look for bumphead parrotfish along Tampuan's deeper reaches.

Sulu Sea Dive Sites

Tubbataha Reefs, a UNESCO World Heritage Site, and other nearby Sulu Sea sites offer some of the best diving you are ever likely to come across anywhere in the world. Awesome walls, a couple of wrecks, flourishing reefs, big fish and remote serenity make a trip to Tubbataha unforgettable. Many divers return year after year to rediscover the experience.

Live-aboard boats access the region from Puerto Princesa (central Palawan). Trips can also be arranged out of the western Visayas, although this is quite uncommon because the long transit time and unpredictable weather adds significantly to the operators' costs and risks. Because of the region's prolific marine life, specialty photography trips are often available. The season is relatively short—from February to mid-June—so book early to ensure you don't miss out on this unique destination. At other times of the year, the sea conditions are simply too rough to get to the sites, let alone dive them.

Tubbataha was discovered in the mid-'70s by pioneering diver Danny Sarmiento of Aquaventure, the largest and oldest established dive retailer in the Philippines. Word quickly spread, and before long Tubbataha became *the* place to dive for those lucky enough to get a berth on one of the few live-aboards then operating. The remains of one of these early pioneers, the *Tristar B*, now lie on Basterra Reef.

ROBERT YIN

The *Tristar B* now lies on the seafloor at Basterra's north reef.

Tubbataha is actually two separate reef structures housing three lagoons. The larger structure to the north has two lagoons. The southern system has a lighthouse on its southern tip. A tiny islet, Bird Island, is the most obvious topside feature of the northern system. The islet itself is off-limits to visitors to protect the thousands of terns and boobies that nest here and lay their eggs in the sand.

Tubbataha Reefs is a designated marine park, regulated by park rangers stationed at the remote Bird Island outpost. They inspect live-aboards, issue permits (US$50—permit may be included in your dive package but are also available in Puerto Princesa) and brief divers about local regulations. These include: no fishing in the marine park confines, no Jet Skiing or water skiing, no disposal of garbage or human waste, no spearfishing and no shell or coral collection. Nothing can be taken from these waters. Mooring buoys have been strategically placed around the reefs, but some can't hold a larger boat, and others have simply washed away in the current. Anchoring is forbidden within the park, so chase boats pick up divers while mother ships steam around off the reef, unless they can attach themselves to a buoy.

It's important to remember that the Sulu Sea sites are about 100 nautical miles offshore (about 180km, or 110 miles), so getting help to a distressed diver is not at all easy. Dive safely, watch your depth and bottom times, listen to your dive guide and follow the dive plan—if something goes wrong, you're on your own out here.

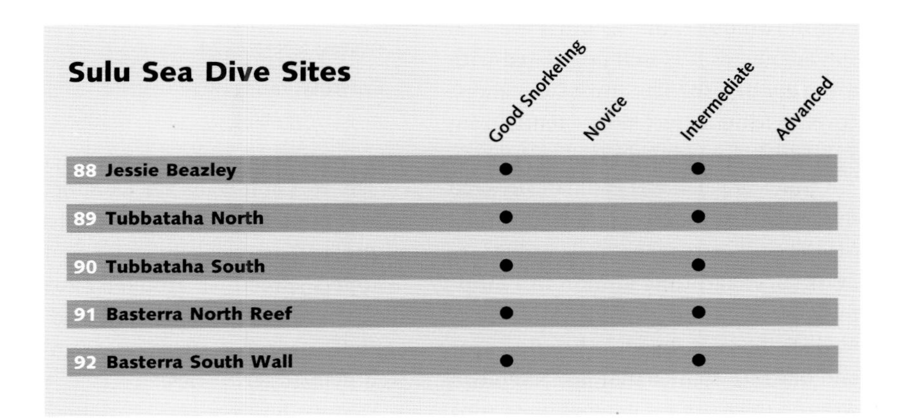

Sulu Sea Dive Sites	Good Snorkeling	Novice	Intermediate	Advanced
88 Jessie Beazley	●		●	
89 Tubbataha North	●		●	
90 Tubbataha South	●		●	
91 Basterra North Reef	●		●	
92 Basterra South Wall	●		●	

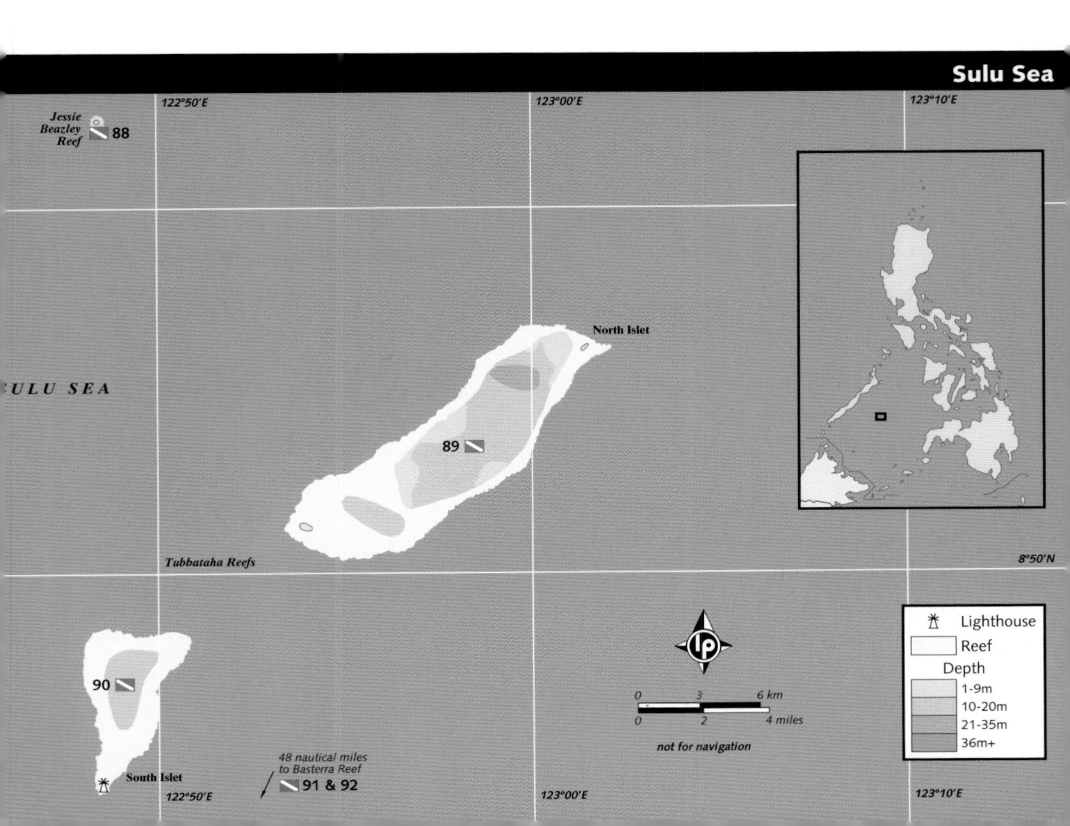

88 Jessie Beazley

Location: 18km (11 miles) NW of Tubbataha's North Islet

Depth Range: Surface-40m+ (130ft+)

Access: Live-aboard

Expertise Rating: Intermediate

A small seamount capped by a sandy cay with impressive walls plunging down to abyssal depths, Jessie Beazley is one of the Sulu Sea's treasures. It is named after the boat that discovered it and promptly sunk after hitting it.

Divers can explore most of this small reef in two dives, but you may want to stay longer, as it is well populated with a variety of fish. The top of the coral-covered fringing reef slopes gently from 7 to 12m before plunging below 1,000m.

Clouds of small reef fish dart between the corals, but the large pelagics cruising off the wall attract the most attention. Look for mako (uncommon in Philippine waters) and thresher sharks, as well as hammerhead, whitetip, grey and blacktip sharks, mantas, Napoleon wrasses, trevallies, rainbow runners, tuna and others. Turtles are frequent visitors here as well.

The wall and its impressive overhangs are decorated with sea fans and gorgonians, massive basket sponges (some of which are 3m across), tube sponges and black corals, all of which provide homes for a huge variety of reef life.

The reef and walls are teeming with fish—permanent residents in this remote outpost of tropical diversity. Batfish, snappers, sweetlips, groupers, lots and lots of triggerfish, angelfish and butterflyfish vie for space in seemingly well-defined territories.

Despite the often-swift currents, photographers will really like this site, but if they don't own two cameras and housings, they'll be hard-pressed to pick between their macro and wide-angle lenses. Mind you, handling two cameras in a strong current in not an easy task, so it's probably better to make two dives and take a different lens on each.

89 Tubbataha North

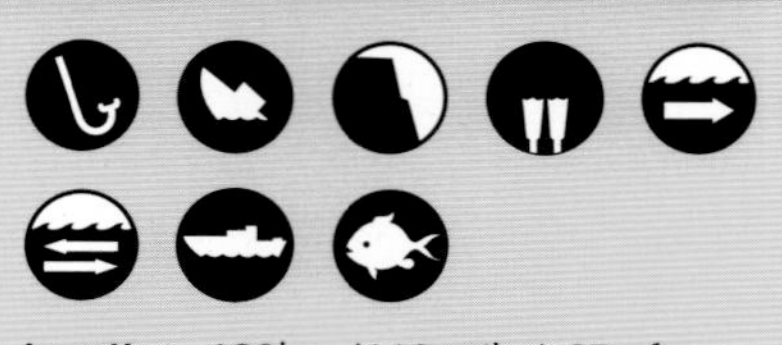

Location: 180km (110 miles) SE of Puerto Princesa

Depth Range: Surface-40m+ (130ft+)

Access: Live-aboard

Expertise Rating: Intermediate

You can dive at several spots around Tubbataha's North Islet, and odds are you'll encounter several species of large pelagics on every one.

The diving off the north shore of the islet is over a fissured, coral-covered sandy slope, home to shovelnosed rays (guitarfish), stingrays, lobsters hiding amid the large table corals, sea whips and coral bommies. The gently sloping wall itself starts at around 7m, and you can hope to find nurse, whitetip and sometimes leopard sharks resting in its cracks. Lots of black coral, tube sponges, gigantic gorgonians, colorful soft corals and barrel sponges grow along the plethora of overhangs and crevices that typify this area.

Pelagic life can be impressive. Mantas are often seen here—the top of the reef appears to be a nursery for young mantas, in fact. Several species of sharks roam these waters, as do tuna, snappers, Moorish idols, groupers, surgeons, soldierfish, trevallies and jacks.

To the east the wall continues to bear enormous gorgonians, and the pelagic action doesn't seem to diminish any. Turtles are common in the shallower areas, while mantas often cruise just off the wall. The sandy bottom is more densely covered with corals here, and the wall becomes much steeper at around 15m or so.

You'll see lots of triggerfish—remember, they can be territorial and have been known to bite divers during the mating season (which varies by species and location), so keep your distance if they act aggressively.

Countless species are well represented east of the northern lagoon, which is a great dive for photographers and a good site for experienced snorkelers who can deal with an often-high swell as well as sometimes-strong currents.

To the southeast and southwest it's more of the same. Some interesting formations line the southwest wall, where the crevices attract diverse marine life, though some portions of the upper reef have been damaged by blast fishing.

Look for the remains of a small tugboat in the shallows on the west side, a reasonable snorkeling spot.

Amos Rock, on the extreme southern tip of the northern lagoon, is a popular night dive. Lots of sea pens, sea squirts, sea whips, branching corals and a good variety of soft corals are interspersed with sandy areas on a gradually sloping seafloor, home to anemones and plenty of mollusks, including the occasional Triton's trumpet.

STEVE ROSENBERG

Giant gorgonians grow along this gently sloping wall.

90 Tubbataha South

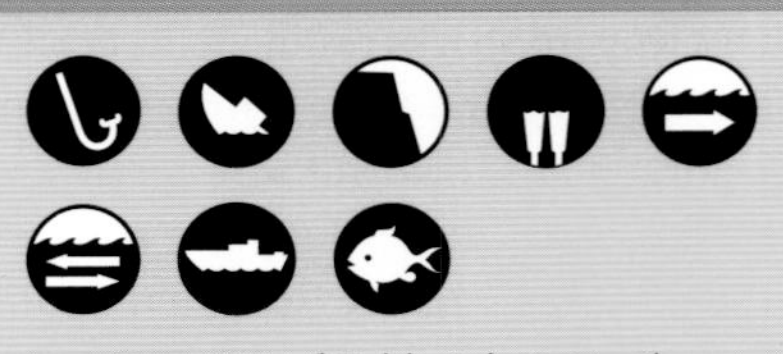

Location: SW of Tubbataha's North Islet

Depth Range: Surface-40m+ (130ft+)

Access: Live-aboard

Expertise Rating: Intermediate

Although this reef is smaller than North Islet, you can visit even more dive sites here. The lighthouse is worth a visit for the views it affords, and seagrass beds lie just offshore (this is a good snorkeling point and a place you can expect to find turtles feeding). The shallow reeftop is quite extensive but has some blast-fishing damage throughout. Currents can wash either way and can get quite strong, so if you have a specific destination in mind, check which way they are running before you enter the water, and prepare to be carried the other way if they change.

To the east, the wreck of the ***Delsan***, a good landmark, sits half out of the water and is close to the wall. The reeftop is a variegated rolling panorama of coral heads and bommies, thickly carpeted in places with corals and sponges, but damaged by blast fishing in some areas. Tropical reef fish are abundant. Look for rays in the sand and lobsters under the coral and rocks.

TIM ROCK

Visit the lighthouse for the view it affords.

The wall, which starts at around 16m, is quite steep and runs for about 12km north to south. Lots of gorgonians, tube sponges and soft corals thrive here, and you'll find a good array of fish life all along the wall. Green and hawksbill turtles are not uncommon, and you should expect to see lots of Moorish idols, triggerfish and surgeons, as well as whitetip and blacktip sharks. Mantas are frequently seen, as are tuna, jacks, rainbow runners and a variety of other pelagics.

The northern end of the lagoon has a well-developed, gently sloping reeftop that is healthier than the southern areas. The north wall is not as steep as the eastern side. It boasts some impressive gorgonians and barrel sponges, as well as some rich soft corals. The most commonly used landmark is **Black Rock**, where most divers enter the water. Turtles are common, and the pelagic action is wild. Barracuda, several species of sharks, tuna, manta and eagle rays, mackerel and rainbow runners are all likely to show up, especially when a current is running.

The western side of the lagoon has a more pronounced drop-off with outstanding soft corals, whose rich reds, purples and pinks resonate, even at depth. Sea fans, sea whips and plenty of soft and hard corals complete the canvas, while tuna, sharks, rainbow runners and barracuda pass by in the current just off the wall. The upper reef and the wall are home to many tropical reef fish, including puffers, angelfish, butterflyfish, wrasses, anthias, gobies, snappers, groupers, soldierfish and tangs.

91 Basterra North Reef

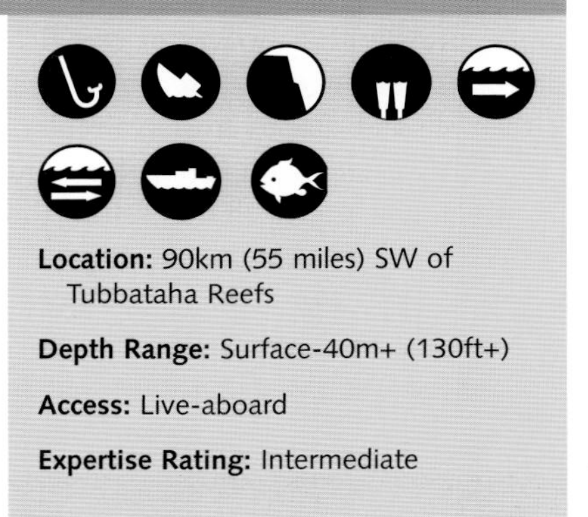

Location: 90km (55 miles) SW of Tubbataha Reefs

Depth Range: Surface-40m+ (130ft+)

Access: Live-aboard

Expertise Rating: Intermediate

Basterra is a sand-capped seamount that rises to the surface from more than 1,000 fathoms below—you don't want to see the bottom here. Indeed, you'll have no need to go deep at this site because there's so much to see in the first 30m. Visibility is usually well over 30m, but currents are unpredictable, often fierce, and can push an unwary diver down the wall, so watch your buoyancy.

Basterra, which encompasses several dive sites, is not particularly large, but it's renowned for having more and larger fish than either Jessie Beazley or Tubbataha. Though it's impossible to take it all in on one dive, when the current is running you can cover a lot of the reef. Most divers prefer to spend several days here, weather permitting.

The wreck of the ***Tristar B*** lies at the north end of the reef. One of the engines sits apart from the wreck at 13m, close to a triggerfish nesting site. The coral immediately around the wreck has been damaged by blast fishing and storms, but plenty of fish still hang around, especially in the wreck itself—wrasses, spadefish, chromis and sergeant majors, groupers, snappers, sweetlips, parrotfish and a shoal of bigeye trevallies are among what you might see. A couple of whitetip sharks usually lurk here as well.

The wreck itself is worth a look around, but if the current permits, head north a bit to where the coral cover is much healthier, with sea whips, sponges and plenty of hard corals such as table, brain and boulder. Another wreck, the ***Oceanic II***, pokes out of the water at this end of the reef.

The reef drops away to form an impressive wall, where the corals are particularly good. You may see pelagics cruising by. Mantas and turtles are not uncommon. Tuna, jacks, barracuda and grey reef sharks frequent this site, as well as Napoleon wrasses, all kinds of angelfish, goatfish, coral trout and triggerfish. If you can take your eyes off the big fish, the cracks and crevices along the wall shelter octopuses, lobsters, blue triggerfish, tangs, unicornfish and surgeonfish.

92 Basterra South Wall

Location: 90km (55 miles) SW of Tubbataha Reefs

Depth Range: Surface-40m+ (130ft+)

Access: Live-aboard

Expertise Rating: Intermediate

More of the same here—the reef slopes gently away from the surface to around 15m and then drops away to infinity. The visibility is usually phenomenal, but the currents swirl unpredictably, so you need to keep on your toes.

You'll see lots of life on the shallower parts of the reef: murex and other shells and rays hiding in the sand; lettuce and table corals with a variety of reef fish darting in and out of their folds; morays, garden eels and various crustaceans playing hide and seek with each other; and a couple of whitetip sharks cruise the periphery to keep things interesting.

The wall boasts a huge colony of brown coral and an assortment of hard and soft corals and sponges, as well as some large gorgonians. In this area divers often see massive shoals of barracuda, as well as whitetip, grey, hammerhead and blacktip sharks. Other species that thrive here include mantas, tuna, snappers, fusiliers, butterflyfish, squirrelfish, Moorish idols, a huge school of sweetlips, jacks, pennant butterflyfish and surgeons. Keep an eye open for lobsters, which live in the many cracks and crevices. No, you can't have one for dinner—everything in the Sulu Sea is protected and cannot be removed. Also watch out for discarded fishing lines, which have etched themselves into the reef.

If the current allows, head north to where the wall sports unusual dents in it—a close inspection may reveal a rare leaffish. Moving right along (and you usually have little choice in the matter), at around 13m huge boulder corals poke out of the wall. Once you arrive here, expect the unexpected. The current can speed up radically, and you may find yourself flying along, and sometimes down, the wall, swimming with an assortment of sharks, mantas, tuna and other pelagics. The reeftop is only 3m deep.

TIM ROCK

Inspect the wall here for rare and unusual leaffish.

Palawan Dive Sites

Palawan is a fertile island province that offers outstanding tropical scenery, both onshore and off. While getting to most of the diving areas can be done relatively simply and directly from Manila, traveling from one place to another is often a bit of a hassle, requiring long, sometimes arduous and uncomfortable jeepney journeys over rough, dusty or muddy (depending on the time of year) roads, or on banca boats across potentially rough stretches of water. That said, the diving almost always makes it worth the effort. Northern Palawan encompasses some of the best diving around—from the wrecks of Coron to the impressive coral reefs and walls of El Nido.

Dugongs (large, seagrass-eating mammals that are relatives of Florida's manatee) inhabit the Busuanga area north of Coron—if you're lucky, you might meet one of these shy, peculiar animals.

Coron

Coron Bay is a large, sheltered body of water that has become the wreck-diving capital of the Philippines. In September 1944, Admiral "Bull" Halsey's fleet was heading north toward Luzon. Having no accurate charts of the area, he sent reconnaissance planes ahead to map out a route. As they flew over Coron Bay, they discovered an auxiliary Japanese fleet at anchor in the bay. He immediately ordered an air attack, and several waves of fighter bombers sunk many of the vessels. To date, nine of these wrecks have been discovered and are regularly visited by divers, but according to U.S. naval records, several more were destroyed and await discovery.

Diving is possible year-round in Coron's sheltered waters, but visibility isn't perfect—on a good day you might get up to 25m, but be prepared for less. You'll have a number of dive centers to choose from, but select carefully—competitive pricing might outweigh equipment safety at some shops. Tech diving is very popular here: It's well worth considering taking a IANTD, PADI or

SCOTT TUASON

You can explore Coron Island's saltwater lakes by kayak.

ANDI course, as the area lends itself perfectly to both the training and practice of technical diving.

Other attractions in the area are the islands' impressive limestone cliffs, most notably those surrounding Coron Island, which also has some stunningly beautiful saltwater lakes that are best explored by kayak—a great and easily arranged option for a nondiving day.

North of Coron you'll find Apo Reef and Hunter's Rock, two seamounts with plentiful marine life. Divers often access Apo and Hunter's by live-aboard and from Mindoro's west coast.

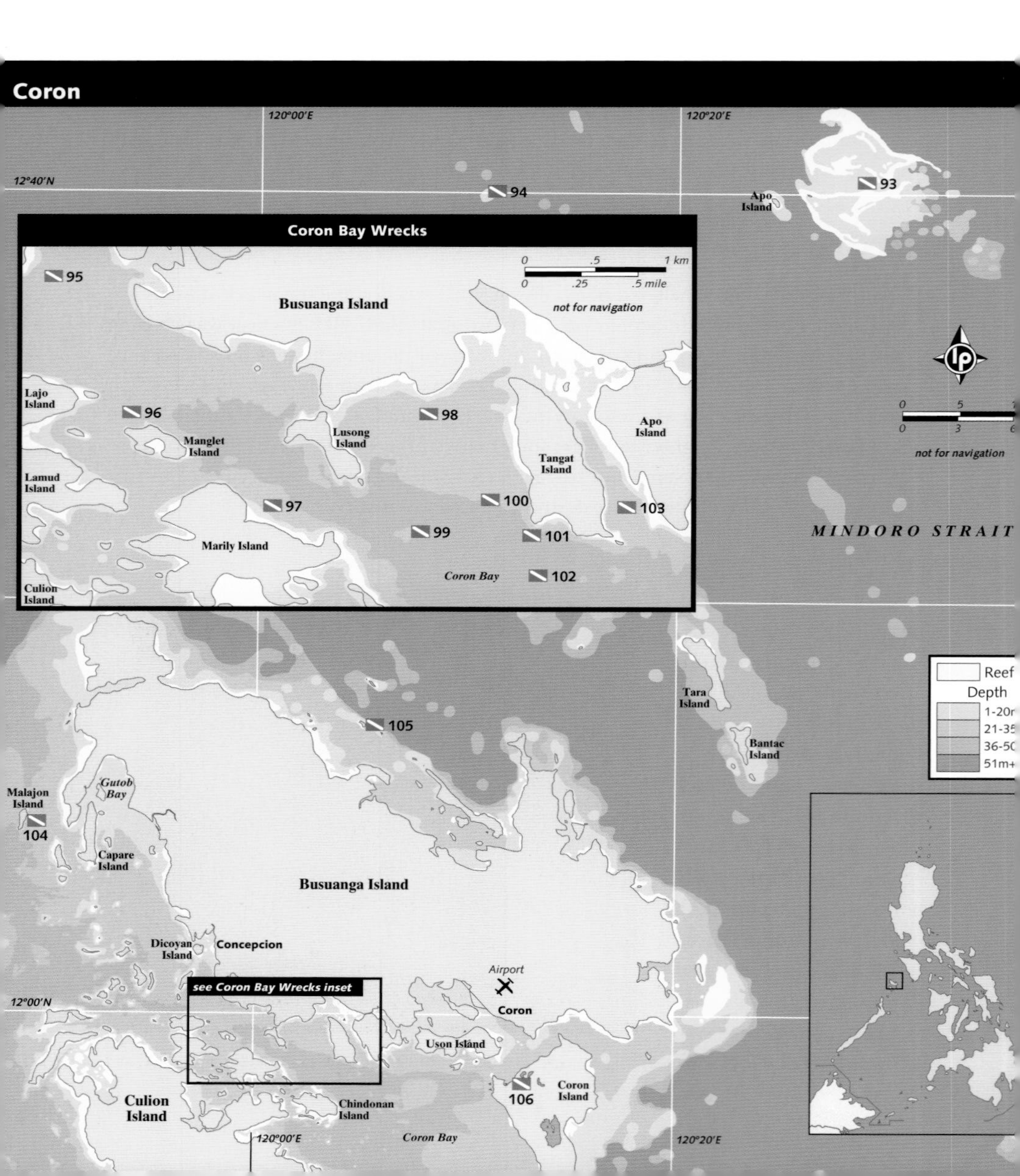

Coron Dive Sites

Site	Good Snorkeling	Novice	Intermediate	Advanced
93 Apo Reef	●		●	
94 Hunter's Rock				●
95 *Tae Maru* (Concepcion Wreck)				●
96 *Akitsushima* (Flying Boat Tender)				●
97 Lusong Gunboat	●	●		
98 *Olympia Maru*	●			●
99 *Mamiya Maru*				●
100 *Kogyu Maru*				●
101 Tangat Wreck			●	
102 *Irako*				●
103 Tangat Gunboat	●	●		
104 Black Island Wreck				●
105 Dimakya Island	●	●		
106 Barracuda Lake	●	●		

93 Apo Reef

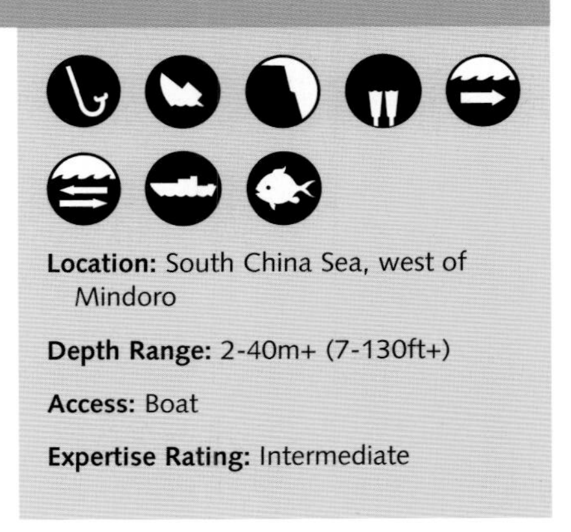

Location: South China Sea, west of Mindoro

Depth Range: 2-40m+ (7-130ft+)

Access: Boat

Expertise Rating: Intermediate

About 32km from Mindoro and not far from the port town of San Jose, Apo Reef has been a popular live-aboard destination for many years. Its numerous dive sites are now frequently accessed by large banca boats from Panadan Island's dive resort, as well as from Puerto Galera. Dives such as **Shark Ridge**, **Binangaan Drop-Off** and **North Wall** are some of the many attractions on Apo Reef.

Apo has enjoyed on-again, off-again status as a marine reserve over the years. Unfortunately, policing it has proven to be a difficult task for the authorities, with the result that much of the shallower portions of the reef have been devastated by intermittent dynamite fishing. At the time of writing, its protected status has been reestablished, and visiting divers are charged a small fee to help finance a basic environmental protection program.

The reef is a 340m-wide dual-lagoon system divided by a narrow channel that runs west to east. It is accessible from January to June. The rest of the year, high seas and swells make it a difficult trip to undertake.

More than 380 species of fish are known to reside around Apo. These include various sharks (including whitetip, blacktip, hammerhead and whale sharks), stingrays, mantas, jacks and snappers, many different types of tuna, wahoos, Spanish mackerel, Napoleon wrasses, surgeons, bumphead parrotfish, triggerfish, lionfish, pufferfish, soldierfish and so on. In addition, researchers have identified almost 500 different species of corals here.

Despite the damage done to the reef-top, the walls surrounding the reef are pretty much intact and are as impressive as the list of marine denizens would suggest. You'll find an abundant supply of gorgonian sea fans and prolific large fish almost anywhere you descend along the drop-offs.

Three wrecks dot the reef—an old steamer in shallow water at the northern end and two steel-hulled fishing boats, one in 10m on the southwest portion of the southern reef (the masts stick out of the water at low tide), the other on the west side of the same reef.

94 Hunter's Rock

Location: West of Apo Reef

Depth Range: 5-40m (15-130ft+)

Access: Boat

Expertise Rating: Advanced

Twenty-one kilometers due west of Apo Reef lies the seamount Hunter's Rock. Hunter's is best known for its sea snakes, which literally carpet the ocean's surface during their breeding season (June to July). At other times of the year, they are less noticeable—and less excitable as a consequence.

Hunter's Rock can be quite capricious: Sometimes the reef is teeming with sea life, while at other times it's relatively quiet. However, the corals covering the walls are impressive (especially the gorgonians), and the many cracks and crevices are an enticing attraction. Night diving at Hunter's Rock is a thrill, but not for the squeamish or nervous—remember, sea snakes prefer to hunt at night.

SAMMY ANG

At times, Hunter's Rock is teaming with life.

95 *Tae Maru* (Concepcion Wreck)

Location: SW of Concepcion

Depth Range: 10-26m (33-85ft)

Access: Boat

Expertise Rating: Advanced

The *Tae Maru*, a 168m-long oil tanker that was sunk during a 1944 air raid, has a smashed bow and lies at 26m, listing slightly to port. If properly trained, you can enter the wreck, which is also a popular technical-diving training site.

Visibility is often less than 10m. Currents can be particularly nasty here—to prevent getting swept away, try to stay on the leeward side of the vessel when the current is running. Use a shot line to descend and remember where you left it to ensure a safe ascent. Also, leave enough air in your tank for a safety stop.

The strong currents encourage the wreck's coral and sponge growth, which includes a profusion of healthy cabbage corals, a variety of sponges, and hard and soft corals of all sorts. A shoal of barracuda often circles divers, and you're likely to encounter sweetlips, groupers, batfish, lionfish, surgeons, several varieties of wrasses, tangs, snappers and soldierfish.

SAMMY ANG

Batfish cruise through the *Tae Maru* wreck.

96 *Akitsushima* (Flying Boat Tender)

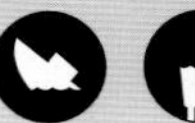  

Location: Due east of Lajo Island

Depth Range: 18-40m (60-130ft)

Access: Boat

Expertise Rating: Advanced

Although this is one of the deepest wrecks in the area, you'll see plenty without descending past 25m. Though the flying boat hasn't been found yet, an impressive crane twists off to the port side of the tender, its tip buried in the sand at 38m. Tuna, barracuda and yellowfins frequently patrol the wreck, and groupers, batfish, sweetlips and snappers hide inside it.

The wreck is penetrable through a huge crack amidships, but enter only if you're properly trained and guided.

The 150m-long *Akitsushima* is another popular technical dive. Again, descend along a shot line, tied preferably to the bridge (if the boatman can find it) to make it easier for you to locate it when you're ready to ascend. Be sure to save enough air in your tank for a safety stop.

97 Lusong Gunboat

Location: South of Lusong Island

Depth Range: Surface-10m (33ft)

Access: Boat

Expertise Rating: Novice

Both the wreck and the reef adjacent to this small gunboat are an easy dive and an excellent snorkeling site. This is a perfect introductory wreck dive and, because of its shallow depth, is a good choice for a second or third dive of the day.

Lots of soft corals and sponges dot the site, while many pufferfish, angelfish, batfish and butterflyfish flit about. Not much of the wreck remains, but this is a good site for photographers, as there is usually little current and lots of light illuminating the variety of subjects.

98 *Olympia Maru*

Location: Between Lusong and Tangat Islands

Depth Range: 12-25m (40-82ft)

Access: Boat

Expertise Rating: Advanced

Lying on its starboard side, this wreck features black coral, finger sponges and a variety of soft and hard corals encrusted along its 135m-long hull. You'll find lots of anemones and clownfish, as well as resident batfish, a couple of large groupers and many smaller ones, goatfish and fusiliers. Scorpionfish hide in crevices throughout the boat, so be careful!

The engine room and cargo holds are easily penetrated. Sometimes the current can be a factor on this dive. This is also a popular training site for advanced and wreck diving classes.

99 *Mamiya Maru*

Location: West of Tangat Island

Depth Range: 23-34m (75-112ft)

Access: Boat

Expertise Rating: Advanced

This 160m-long freighter still has some of its cargo (construction materials) intact in the holds. Lying on its starboard side, the wreck is encrusted with lots of hard and soft corals. Barracuda (see photo) regularly patrol it, as do sweepers and fusiliers. Batfish are common, as are anemones and clownfish. Snappers, some large groupers, wrasses and surgeons call this home. Watch out for lionfish, which seem to hide everywhere. Currents are usually mild, but can occasionally be strong.

STEVE ROSENBERG

100 *Kogyu Maru*

Corals grow thickly along *Kogyu Maru's* hull.

Location: South of Olympia Maru

Depth Range: 20-34m (65-112ft)

Access: Boat

Expertise Rating: Advanced

Kogyu Maru is a deep wreck lying on its starboard side. The port hull of this 160m-long cargo ship lies at 22m. Her hold still contains construction materials and a bulldozer, and you can see anti-aircraft guns along the deck.

It has some pretty hard and soft corals on its port hull. As usual, lionfish thrive here, and you'll likely see a shoal of barracuda and a reasonable assortment of tropical reef fish.

The wreck is deep, and bottom time is limited, so it's not a suitable dive site for most scuba divers. But technical divers enjoy this dive, and it is a good technical training dive.

101 Tangat Wreck

Location: Off SW point of Tangat Island

Depth Range: 18-30m (60-100ft)

Access: Boat

Expertise Rating: Intermediate

Another good site for underwater photographers, Tangat Wreck (also known as Sangat Wreck) is covered with lots of soft corals, sponges and some hard corals. Several large, friendly pufferfish make for accommodating photo subjects. Again, watch out for lionfish and scorpionfish. The currents are usually quite light, but can occasionally pick up—check with your dive guide before entering.

The wreck lies more or less upright. The cargo holds, which are easily accessible, are home to angelfish, snappers and batfish, among others. This is a good training wreck but is also popular with experienced wreck divers.

102 *Irako*

Location: South of Tangat Island

Depth Range: 28-40m+ (92-130ft+)

Access: Boat

Expertise Rating: Advanced

A deep wreck with its deck sloping from 28 to 33m, the *Irako* was a refrigeration ship. It is a good penetrable wreck, but because of its depth and size (about 150m long), safe penetration requires specialized training and an experienced guide.

Some big groupers call this home now, and you may also see shoals of barracuda and yellowfin tuna circling the site. Look for batfish, snappers, some wrasses and lots of lionfish and scorpionfish around the wreck. The hull and deck are well covered in a variety of soft corals and sponges. The current can get quite strong here, so plan your dive accordingly.

103 Tangat Gunboat

Location: East of Tangat Island

Depth Range: 2-18m (7-60ft)

Access: Boat

Expertise Rating: Novice

Tangat Gunboat is another great place to snorkel, as the bow is very close to the surface. This 35m-long vessel lies a few meters off the rocky east coast of Tangat Island. It's easy to find, as you can see the wreck clearly from the surface. This is a popular site with kayakers, as well as snorkelers and divers.

Not a lot of coral grows on the wreck, but some lettuce sponges and a few small reef fish call this home. Because of the light currents and bright conditions, this is another good spot for photography.

The Gunboat at Tangat

JUSTIN MARLER

104 Black Island Wreck

Location: NW of Busuanga, east of Malajon Island

Depth Range: 12-32m (40-105ft)

Access: Boat

Expertise Rating: Advanced

Not far offshore from Malajon Island, Black Island Wreck sits upright on the sloping sandy bottom, its stern at 20m and its bow at 32m. Look for another beached wreck close to shore and you should be able to find this one nearby. Little is known about this wreck, the most northerly of Coron's wrecks. Unlike most of the region's wrecks, this one wasn't sunk during the September 1944 air raid and may not even be of Japanese origin.

Although the sea journey here is long and rough (it's not within the sheltered confines of Coron Bay), it's still a favorite training ground for wreck diving and is popular with photographers. Because Black Island Wreck is quite shallow, there is lots to see on it. Named for the black rocks of adjacent Malajon Island, the wreck is home to lots of sweepers, shoals of snappers, fusiliers, several different species of angelfish, groupers and (surprise) scorpionfish and lionfish. It's also a good night dive—look for lobsters, cuttlefish and other nocturnal hunters.

TIM ROCK

Don't touch the lionfish's venomous spines.

105 Dimakya Island

Location: NE of Busuanga

Depth Range: 5-17m (16-56ft)

Access: Shore or Boat

Expertise Rating: Novice

Dimakya Island is home to some of the area's better coral dives. You may even spot one of Coron's reclusive dugongs here, as they feed on the abundant fields of seagrass that flourish near shore. Even if you aren't that lucky (and frankly, you probably won't be), there are some good dive sites, and the snorkeling is great.

The west side of the island has a house reef where the fish are accustomed to divers and usually expect some food to arrive with you. (The fish seem to like bananas, which are much easier to carry around than bread.) The coral gardens at the shallower portion of the reef give way to a sloping drop-off that descends to 17m. Parrotfish and other tropical reef eaters nibble away at the corals. Lots of tunicates reside here, as do some groupers.

At the end of the wall the impressive growth of staghorn corals is frequently visited by barracuda, rainbow runners and goatfish. Turtles are occasionally seen here, and one or two mantas have been spotted, although these are more common north of Dimakya.

106 Barracuda Lake

Location: Coron Island

Depth Range: Surface-40m+ (130ft+)

Access: Boat and hike

Expertise Rating: Novice

One of the most unusual diving and snorkeling sites in the Philippines, Barracuda Lake, officially called Cayangan Lake, is an inland body of water fed by a freshwater hot spring, by seawater intruding from deep subterranean cracks and by freshwater from rain and springs. As a result, at different depths you'll find extremes in temperature (thermoclines) and salinity (haloclines). Temperatures can range from 30 to 40°C and can change several degrees over just a few centimeters' depth. You can see the shimmering layers of different temperatures and salinity as you descend.

SCOTT TUASON

Divers must hike with their gear to this lake.

There's not a lot of marine life, but a curious mix of shrimp, crustaceans, rabbitfish and a few snappers, among others, call this home. The water is really clear, and as it is a lake, there is no current.

Getting to the site is a bit of a challenge—you hike with your gear from the beach through a gap in the cliff and then along the winding track up and over sharp limestone. Wear strong-soled booties to avoid slipping and cutting your feet.

Take your camera! The scenery is magnificent, the lake is turquoise blue and, if you're lucky, the lake's star attraction, a 1.5m barracuda, may make an appearance, look for a handout and even escort you around the lake.

El Nido

Towering marble cliffs dominate the seascape of El Nido (The Nest), named in honor of the indigenous birds—swiftlets, or *balinsasayaw*—that make the nests used in bird's nest soup. A quiet, unprepossessing provincial town, El Nido's main attractions are underwater.

Accommodation choices are fairly limited. You can opt for the budget inns, pension houses and beach cottages or for high-end luxury resorts, but there's not

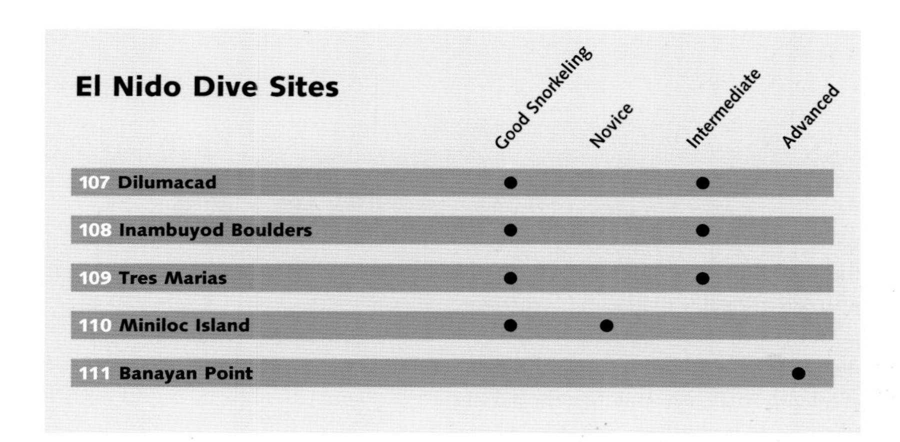

El Nido Dive Sites

	Good Snorkeling	Novice	Intermediate	Advanced
107 Dilumacad	●		●	
108 Inambuyod Boulders	●		●	
109 Tres Marias	●		●	
110 Miniloc Island	●	●		
111 Banayan Point				●

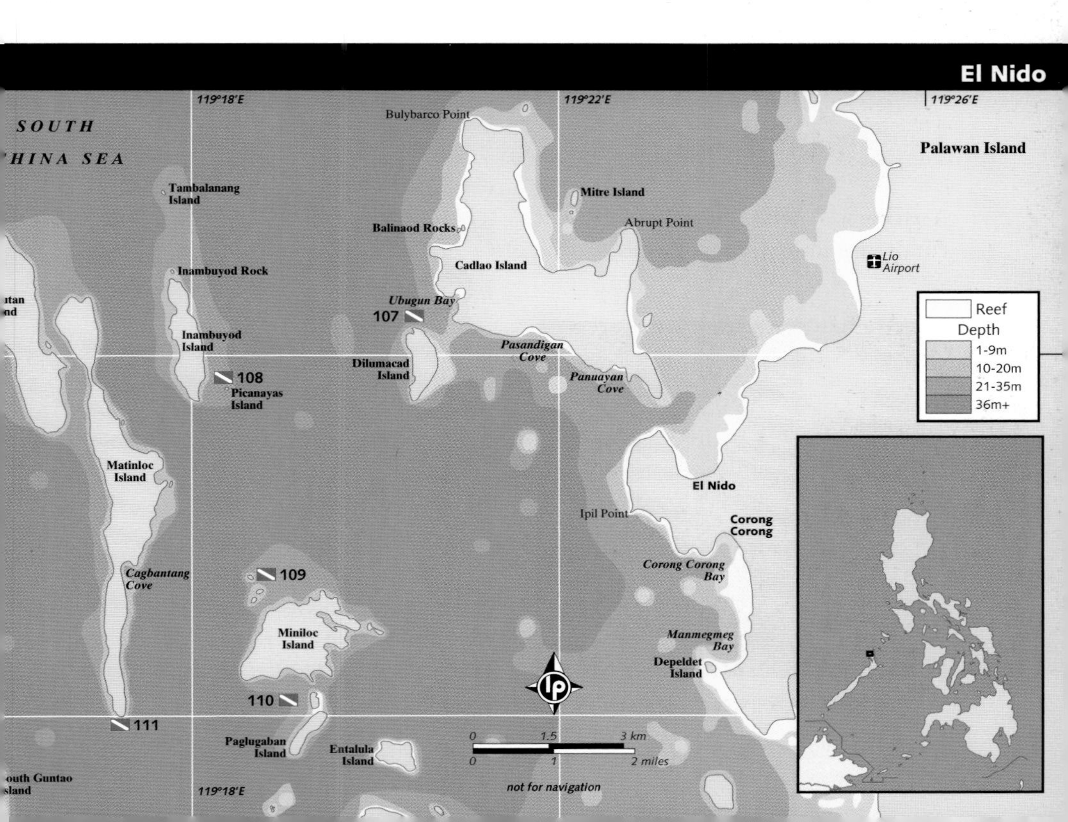

much in between. Soriano Air flies daily to El Nido's small airport from its Manila terminal. In season (from February to June) there are often two flights a day. El Nido is also a jumping-off point for several inland excursions, such as the St. Paul subterranean river, and is a pleasant place to relax and unwind if you're not looking for sophisticated resources.

The three dive centers in town, as well as the luxury resorts (which are all on privately owned islands several kilometers away from the town proper), have good facilities. El Nido is good place to learn to dive and is an excellent destination for snorkelers, as it's easy to explore many of the coral reefs. But you may see significant damage due to illegal fishing, such as dynamiting, in many areas.

107 Dilumacad

Featuring a cave entrance at 12m that's wide enough for two divers to pass through, this year-round site is El Nido's nearest reasonable diving and is therefore popular with local dive centers. The cave descends to a sandy bottom, home to crabs and small fish, and then the passage narrows to an exit at 22m. Some large rocks sit nearby, and you'll likely see some large fish, such as Spanish mackerel and jacks, that hang around here.

Location: Northern tip of Dilumacad Island

Depth Range: 10-25m (33-82ft)

Access: Boat

Expertise Rating: Intermediate

108 Inambuyod Boulders

A steep wall with some lovely green corals and impressive gorgonians, this dive's main attraction is the chance to encounter large pelagics. The current, which can be quite strong, encourages them to cruise the wall.

Location: Off SE point of Inambuyod Island

Depth Range: 5-35m (16-115ft)

Access: Boat

Expertise Rating: Intermediate

TIM ROCK
Green coral decorate the boulders.

109 Tres Marias

Location: Tagbao Island, NW of Miniloc Island

Depth Range: 5-28m (16-92ft)

Access: Boat

Expertise Rating: Intermediate

Tres Marias is a rewarding dive and a good snorkeling site with lots of reef fish and colorful corals. The huge rocks to the southwest offer plenty to see in their nooks. Keep an eye open for the telltale antennae of the painted crays that live here. Also of interest is the endemic *Pomacanthus annularis*, an angelfish with an extra stripe, found only here and at nearby Inambuyod Boulders.

A painted cray retreats into the reef's recesses.

110 Miniloc Island

Location: SW Bacuit Bay

Depth Range: 13-21m (42-70ft)

Access: Boat

Expertise Rating: Novice

Miniloc Island offers two sites, **South Miniloc** and **Twin Rocks**, both of which are relatively calm and sheltered year-round. Both sites are good training grounds for novice divers and can also be appreciated by experienced snorkelers.

South Miniloc features lettuce corals and sponges. The site's large colony of blue eels presents a bizarre sight as they poke their heads out of the sandy bottom, waving in the usually negligible current, at first glance appearing like a bed of blue seagrass. Squid and cuttlefish like this area, as do jacks and barracuda. Look for angelfish and parrotfish here as well.

Twin Rocks, which is north of Miniloc, offers lots of sea whips, table and other hard corals, as well as sponges and a good variety of tunicates. Look for angelfish plying the waters here and small stingrays nestled in along the sandy seafloor.

TIM ROCK

A blue ribbon eel pokes out of the bottom.

111 Banayan Point

Location: Southern point of Matinloc Island

Depth Range: Surface-30m+ (100ft+)

Access: Boat

Expertise Rating: Advanced

This is not a dive for the fainthearted, as the current can rip though these waters. But it's the current that attracts schools of large pelagics, such as tuna, jacks, trevally and mackerel.

The diving is better on the west side of the point, where there is more coral on the steep rocky wall. But this side is less protected and at times can be difficult if not impossible to reach or dive safely. March through June are the best times to try. The eastern side is diveable year-round, but it too is subject to some mighty currents.

SAMMY ANG

Schools of trevally congregate in the current-swept waters off Banayan Point.

Port Barton

On the west coast of Palawan, Port Barton is a small fishing village with a fine silica-sand beach. About 150km (90 miles) north of Puerto Princesa (the capital of Palawan), the town takes about 4 hours to reach by private jeepney (about US$100 one way), or 5 to 6 hours by public jeepney (for around US$3 per person). Transportation can be arranged through Trattoria Hotel in Puerto Princesa, ☎ (63-48) 433 6101.

Port Barton has some great coral diving for beginners and advanced divers alike, as well as some good snorkeling. The dozen or so most popular dive sites are about half an hour out to sea and comprise the fringing reefs around the offshore islands and seamounts. You won't see much pelagic action, but the shallow reefs and drop-offs are enjoyable and are also ideal for snorkelers. March to August is the best time to visit, but sea conditions are often surprisingly good at other times of the year. El Busero at the San Isidro Beach Resort (Puerto Princesa booking office, ☎ (63-48) 433 6101) is currently the only dive center in town and offers ADSI and CMAS courses for all levels.

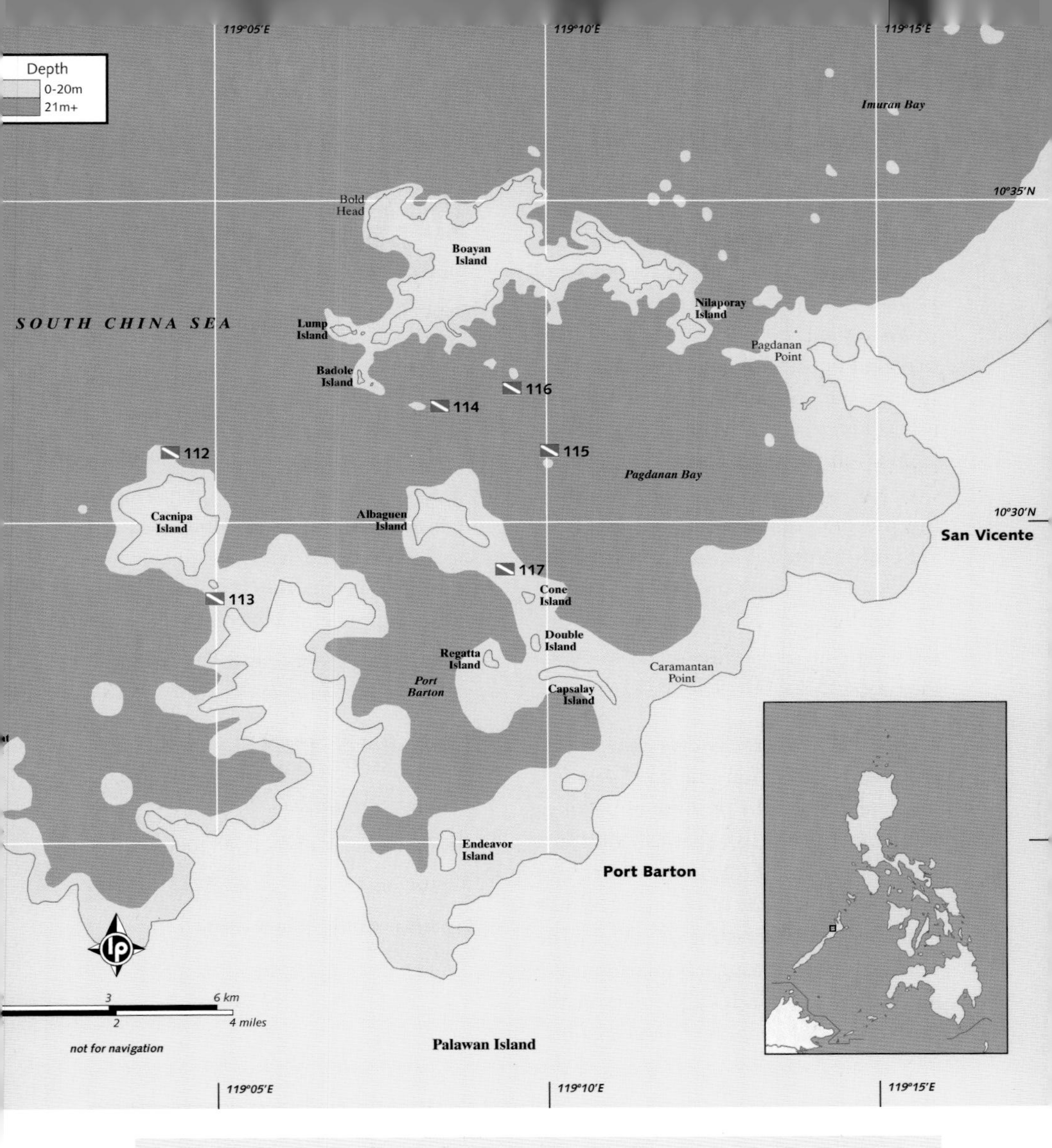

Port Barton Dive Sites

	Good Snorkeling	Novice	Intermediate	Advanced
112 Shark Point			●	
113 Middle Rock	●		●	
114 Royalist Shoal	●		●	
115 Ten Fathoms	●			●
116 Wilson Head	●		●	
117 Black Coral	●		●	

112 Shark Point

Location: 40 min. from Port Barton

Depth Range: Surface-33m (108ft)

Access: Boat

Expertise Rating: Intermediate

You can circle this large rock in a single dive. Lots of soft corals carpet the reef, and some large hard corals are clustered in places. You can poke around several small caves and a cavern where you may find lobsters (painted crays), several species of crabs and lots of tropical reef fish lurking about. Divers occasionally see whitetip and blacktip sharks as well. From time to time, whale sharks are spotted at this site, but odds of seeing one are slim.

South China Sea swells can make the journey a bit bumpy and make suiting up a bit challenging. You can minimize your chances of getting seasick by preparing as much of your gear as possible ahead of time and by being ready to quickly slip into it. Despite the rough water, there is usually not much of a current.

113 Middle Rock

Location: East of Shark Point

Depth Range: Surface-31m (100ft)

Access: Boat

Expertise Rating: Intermediate

Middle Rock is a rocky dive site covered with hard corals. You might see Spanish mackerel cruising by or some of the huge bumphead parrotfish that call this area home—shoals of 20 or more are not uncommon. Clouds of tropical reef fish round out this interesting site. Again, the water can be a bit rough, but currents are not usually a factor. It's also a reasonable snorkel site if the sea conditions are OK.

TIM ROCK

Topical reef fish dart amid this site's corals and anemones.

114 Royalist Shoal

The steep walls of this seamount boast some of Port Barton's best hard and soft corals. At this site, divers can see all kinds of tropical reef fish—angelfish, pufferfish, lionfish, soldierfish, tangs, gobies, squirrelfish and more. Watch your depth and bottom time, as it's easy to get engrossed with the enormous variety of marine life clustered on this reef. Don't lose track of your dive profile.

Location: West of Port Barton

Depth Range: 12-40m+ (40-130ft+)

Access: Boat

Expertise Rating: Intermediate

115 Ten Fathoms

Ten Fathoms is another seamount, but is a little deeper than Royalist Shoal and, therefore, is more suitable for advanced divers. You may see hammerheads cruising through the open water, and leopard and nurse sharks occasionally pass by. Hard corals grow prolifically, especially star, brain and pillar corals. Look also for a variety of colorful fish living amid the plentiful anemones' tentacles.

Location: West of Port Barton

Depth Range: 18-34m (60-112ft)

Access: Boat

Expertise Rating: Advanced

STEVE ROSENBERG

Look for colorful fish living amid the tentacles of anemones.

116 Wilson Head

Location: West of Port Barton

Depth Range: 3-35m (10-115ft)

Access: Boat

Expertise Rating: Intermediate

Wilson Head rarely has a current to bother with, and the shallow reeftop makes this a good snorkeling venue. The hard corals here are the region's best, the most impressive being some huge brain corals with crabs, painted crays and a variety of other crustaceans living in their folds.

Plenty of soft corals, sea fans, sea whips, anemones, tunicates and sponges carpet the reef. Lots of tropical reef fish round out this excellent dive. Bring a camera with a wide-angle lens and be ready to shoot a whole roll of film.

117 Black Coral

Location: West of Port Barton

Depth Range: 5-25m (16-82ft)

Access: Boat

Expertise Rating: Intermediate

This reef is like a big city's central square—it attracts a large number of diverse visitors. Expect to see lots of large groupers darting in and out of the hard and soft corals.

STEVE ROSENBERG

Fish congregate around black coral.

Also look for a cavern that has lots of shrimp, glassfish and several cleaning stations inside it, further evidence that this reef is like an underwater fish metropolis. Farther down the wall, at 18m, you'll find several huge clumps of black coral, each the size of a small room—a rare and fascinating group of these unusual corals.

Puerto Princesa & Environs

On maps, Puerto Princesa looks like a huge city, spanning from coast to coast. Puerto is in fact a small, friendly and unassuming city with a market, an airport served daily by several flights form Manila, a port with a ferry terminal, and a crossroads (literally) for land transportation north, south and west.

The town has several dive operators, most along Rizal Avenue. Honda Bay offers the best and closest dive sites, but operators also run trips to other nearby regions. A few hours north is pretty Taytay Bay, with gorgeous coastlines but only

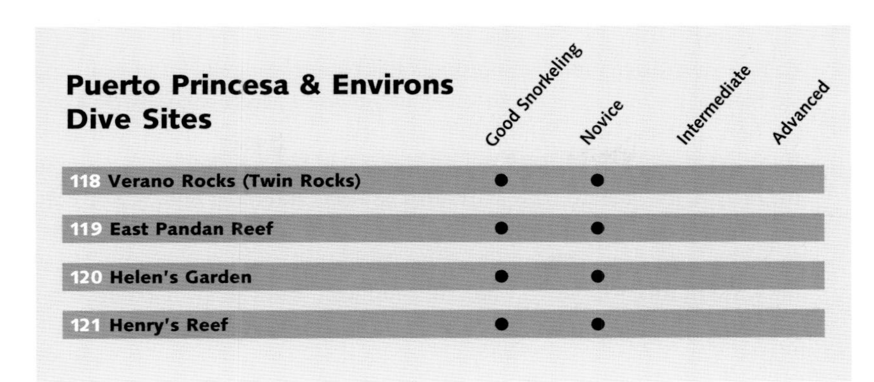

Puerto Princesa & Environs Dive Sites

	Good Snorkeling	Novice	Intermediate	Advanced
118 Verano Rocks (Twin Rocks)	●	●		
119 East Pandan Reef	●	●		
120 Helen's Garden	●	●		
121 Henry's Reef	●	●		

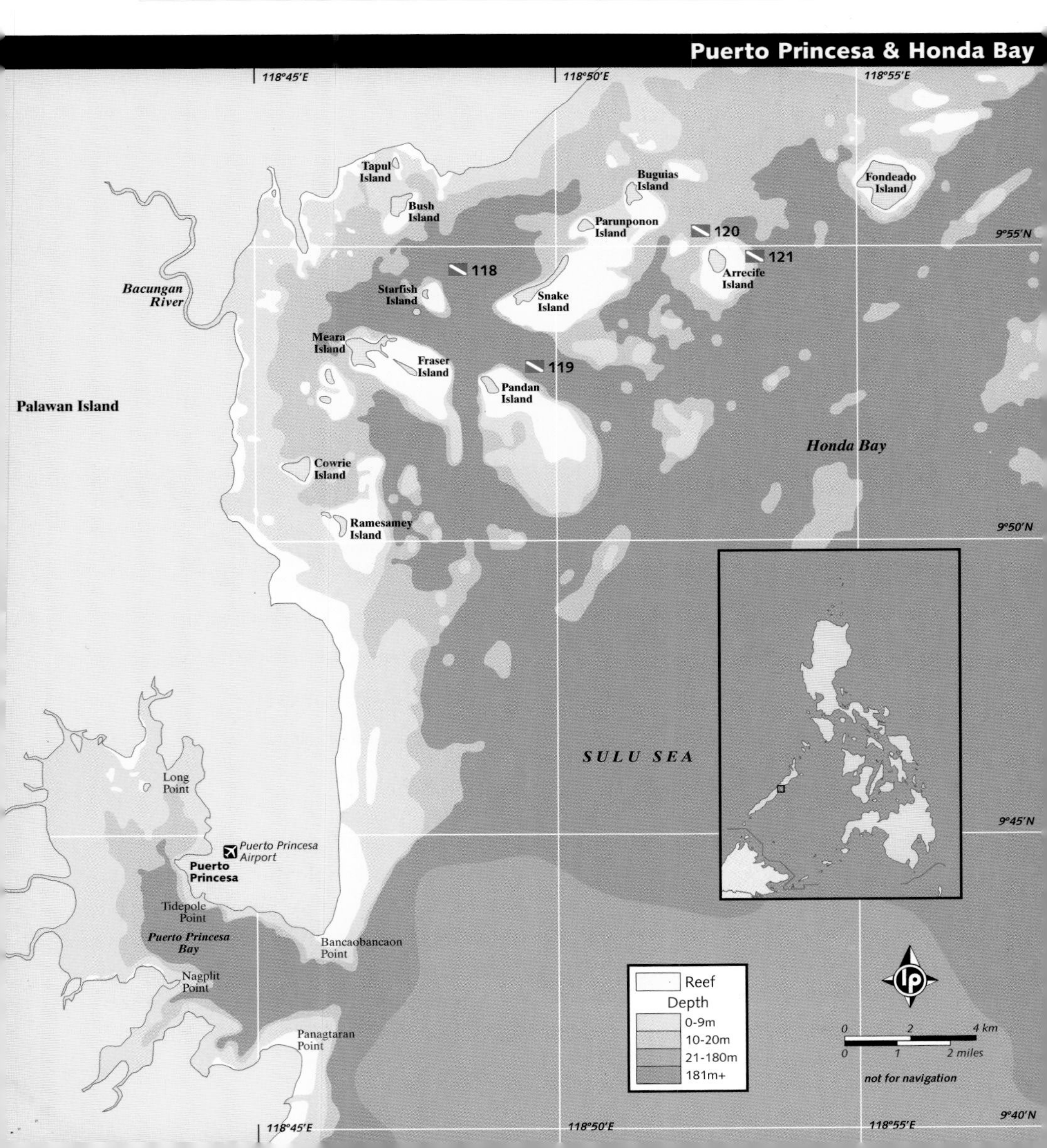

fair diving. Offshore, Constancia reef has suffered some fairly serious reeftop damage due to dynamite fishing, but is still a worthwhile site for its walls and varied marine life. Adjacent Apulit Island boasts some excellent corals, on a par with the best in the country, and Nabat and Malatamban Islands, as well as Noah's Rock, are also worth a visit. Puerto Princesa is also the embarkation point for the majority of live-aboard trips to Tubbataha Reefs and other Sulu Sea dive sites.

Honda Bay is affected by the *amihan* winds from July to January. These blow from the northeast and can kick up the surge and waves significantly. The rest of the year (February to June), when the southwest winds (known as *hagabat*) blow, you can hope for 10 to 20m (33 to 70ft) visibility, depending on the site.

118 Verano Rocks (Twin Rocks)

Location: NE of Starfish Island

Depth Range: 10-18m (33-60ft)

Access: Boat

Expertise Rating: Novice

A year-round site protected from all but the worst weather conditions, Verano Rocks is actually two reef systems just off Starfish Island. The reeftops slope away to 18m and are well covered in a variety of hard and soft corals.

The most striking feature is a jungle of black coral that bridges the two reefs. You're likely to find snappers, fusiliers, anemonefish and pufferfish at this site.

This is also a fair site for experienced snorkelers.

119 East Pandan Reef

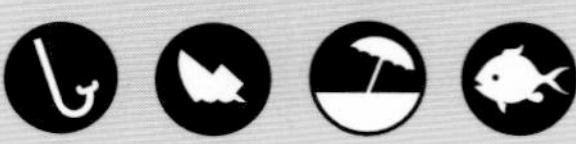

Location: East of Pandan Island

Depth Range: 10-17m (33-56ft)

Access: Shore or boat

Expertise Rating: Novice

TIM ROCK

Colorful nudibranchs live throughout Honda Bay.

This site along Pandan's fringing reef is usually inaccessible during the amihan months. You'll find some interesting corals on the steep slope that drops to the sandy seafloor at 18m. Stingrays are common, and you'll likely encounter gobies, blennies, parrotfish and triggerfish.

120 Helen's Garden

Location: NW of Dos Palmas Resort

Depth Range: 5-15m (16-50ft)

Access: Shore or boat

Expertise Rating: Novice

Helen's Garden is easy to access (except when the sea is rough) because the management of Dos Palmas has installed a diving platform over the site. With usually clear water, this is a great training site, an excellent snorkeling site and for more experienced divers a good introduction to Honda Bay diving. It's also an easy and rewarding night dive.

The reef itself is small and circular, encrusted with table and black corals and lots of soft corals. Several giant clams also reside here. Local divers have set up a fish-feeding station, and the reef's denizens are quick to look for a handout from visiting divers and snorkelers. Among the hungry takers are sergeant majors and snappers. Juvenile blacktip sharks are quite common around Dos Palmas, and you may get lucky and chance on one or two at this site.

Just off the reef lie the remains of an old Taiwanese boat, home to lionfish, snappers and stingrays.

STEVE ROSENBERG

Unusual colors and patterns decorate a giant clam's mantle.

121 Henry's Reef

Location: East of Dos Palmas Resort

Depth Range: 5-18m (16-60ft)

Access: Boat

Expertise Rating: Novice

Running the entire length of the eastern side of Arreceffi Island, this fringing reef is characterized by a small wall that drops off from 5 to 10m. The wall is pocked with lots of caves and crevices, so bring a flashlight to discover some of the more interesting residents. These include lionfish, snappers, sweetlips, cardinalfish and lots of nudibranchs.

This is a good site for underwater photographers, and snorkelers will also enjoy cruising over the extensive reef system. Its relatively shallow depth makes it an easy free-dive even for inexperienced snorkelers, and it's another good place to go on a night dive.

Note that this site is usually inaccessible during the amihan, but is a popular site during the hagabat season.

TIM ROCK

Marine Life

Divers will find an incredible diversity of marine life within the Philippines' waters. New species of fish and invertebrates are constantly being discovered at dive sites throughout the country. Even at sites that by local standards are relatively unpopulated, patient divers with a keen eye for detail are sure to find plenty of marine life to hold their interest. This section identifies some of the common species divers see here.

Common names are used freely by most divers but are often inconsistent. The two-part scientific name, usually shown in italics, is more precise. This system is known as binomial nomenclature. It consists of a genus name followed by a species name. A genus is a group of closely related species that share common features. A species is a recognizable group within a genus whose members are capable of interbreeding. Where the species is unknown or not yet named, the genus name is followed by *sp.* Where the species or genus is unknown, the naming reverts to the next known level: family (F), order (O), class (C) or phylum (Ph).

Common Vertebrates

SCOTT TUASON

whale shark
Rhincodon typus

STEVE ROSENBERG

reef whitetip shark
Triaenodon obesus

ROBERT YIN

thresher shark
Alopias vulpinus

ROBERT YIN

hammerhead shark
Sphyrna zygaena

TIM ROCK

manta ray
Manta birostris

STEVE ROSENBERG

striped barracuda
Sphyraena obtusata

SAMMY ANG

bluefin trevally
Caranx melampygus

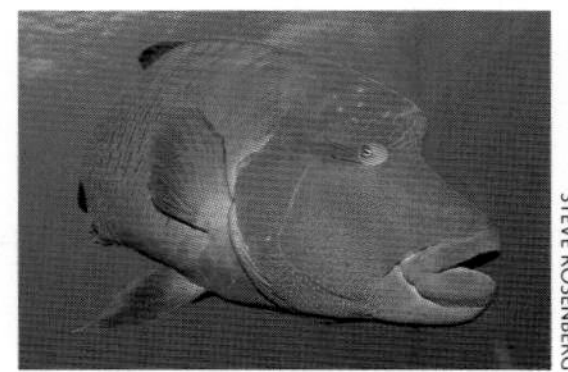
STEVE ROSENBERG

Napoleon wrasse
Cheilinus undulatus

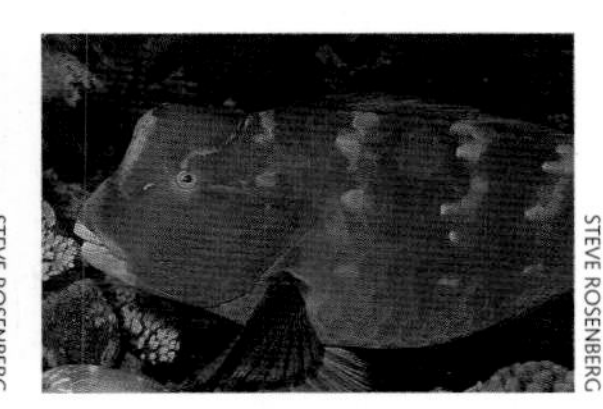
STEVE ROSENBERG

bumphead parrotfish
Bolbometopon muricatum

TIM ROCK

spotted coral cod
Plectropomus maculatus

STEVE ROSENBERG

oblique-banded sweetlips
Plectorhinchus lineatus

STEVE ROSENBERG

spotted sweetlips
Plectorhinchus picus

STEVE ROSENBERG

long-jawed squirrelfish
Sargocentron spiniferum

STEVE ROSENBERG

bigeye
Priacanthus hamrur

ROBERT YIN

emperor angelfish (juvenile)
Pomacanthus imperator

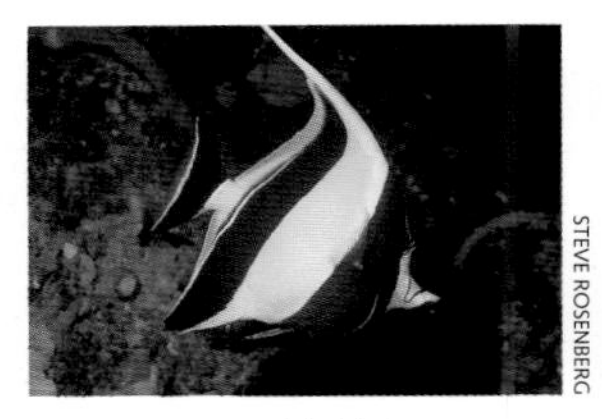
STEVE ROSENBERG

moorish idol
Zanclus cornutus

STEVE ROSENBERG

Pacific double-saddle butterflyfish
Chaetodon ulietensis

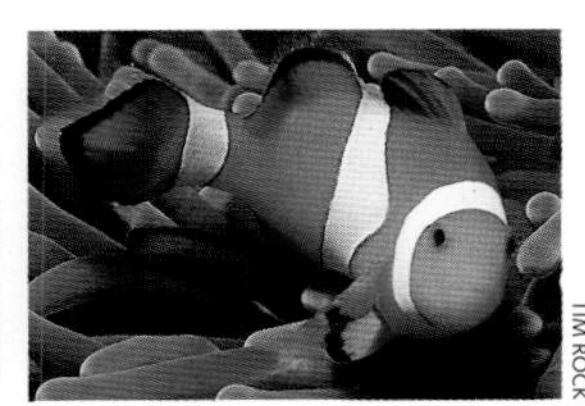
TIM ROCK

common clownfish
Amphiprion ocellaris

STEVE ROSENBERG

clown triggerfish
Balistoides conspicillum

TIM ROCK

lionfish
Pterois volitans

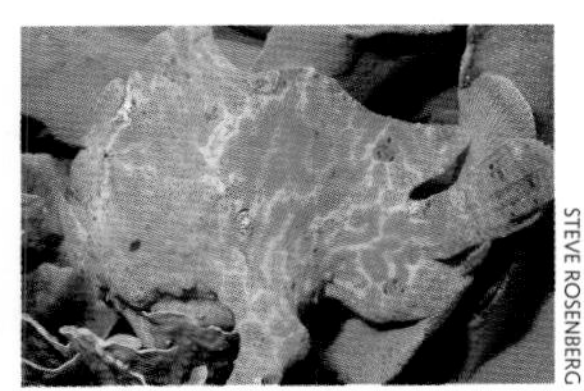
STEVE ROSENBERG

frogfish
Antennarius sp.

Common Invertebrates

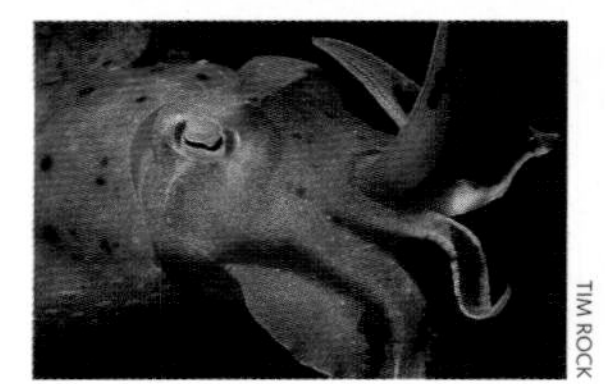
TIM ROCK

cuttlefish
Sepia sp.

STEVE ROSENBERG

octopus
Octopus sp.

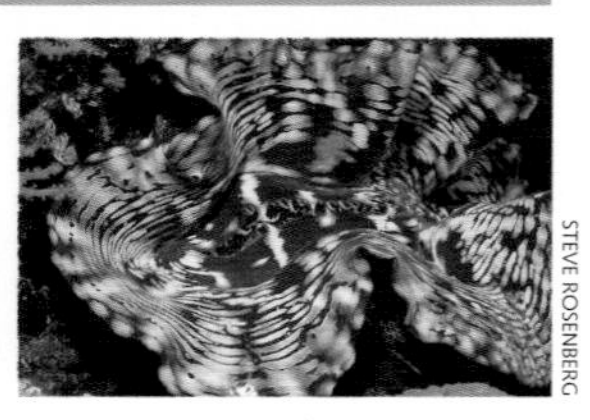
STEVE ROSENBERG

giant clam
Tridacna sp.

STEVE ROSENBERG

blue dorid nudibranch
Hypselodoris bullockii

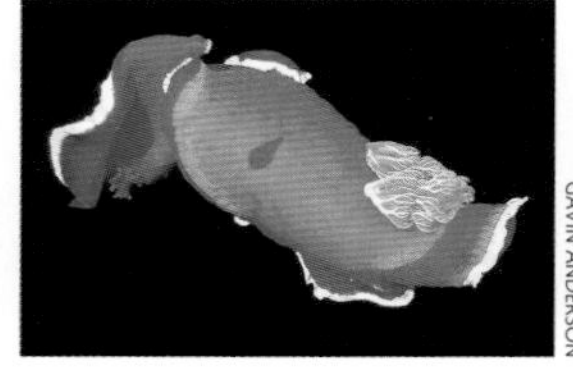
GAVIN ANDERSON

Spanish dancer nudibranch
Hexabranchus sanguineus

TIM ROCK

sea cucumber
Bohadschia argus

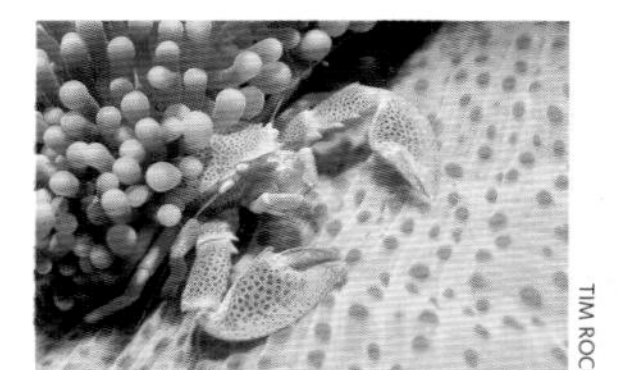
TIM ROCK

anemone crab
Neopetrolisthes maculata

STEVE ROSENBERG

mantis shrimp
Odontodactylus scyallarus

STEVE ROSENBERG

barrel sponge
Xestospongia testudinaria

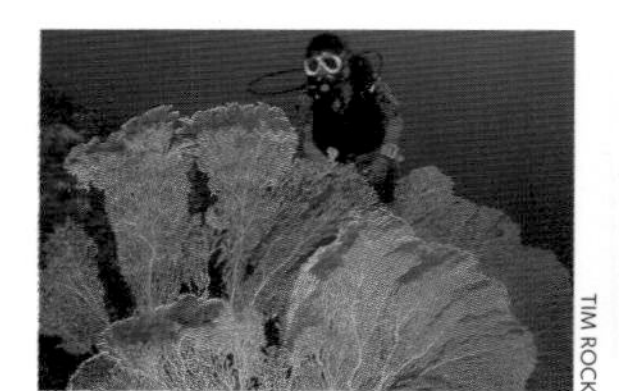
TIM ROCK

gorgonian fan
Subergorgia mollis

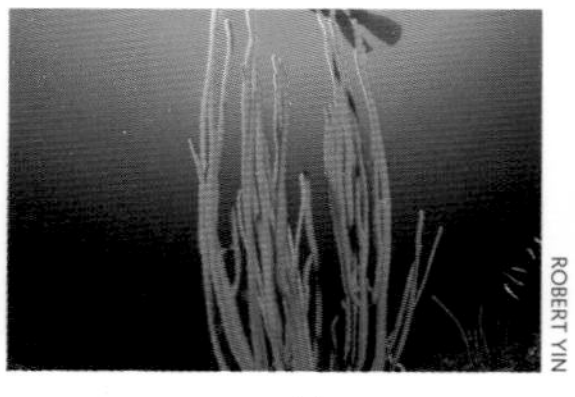
ROBERT YIN

sea whip
Junceella sp.

TIM ROCK

Christmas tree worm
Spirobranchus giganteus

TIM ROCK

crinoid
Comantheria sp.

TIM ROCK

tube anemone
Pachycerianthus sp.

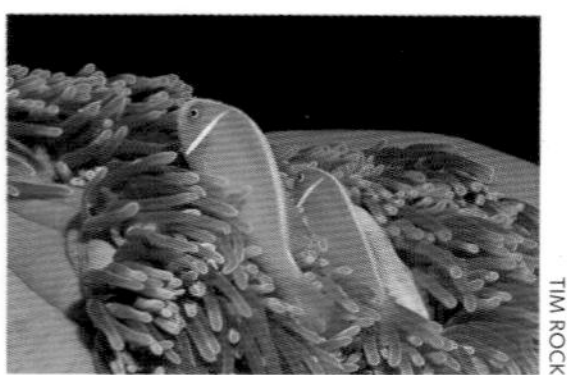
TIM ROCK

magnificent anemone
Heteractis magnifica

Hazardous Marine Life

Marine animals almost never attack divers, but many have defensive and offensive weaponry that can be triggered if they feel threatened or annoyed. The ability to recognize hazardous creatures is a valuable asset in avoiding injury. Following are some of the potentially hazardous creatures most commonly found in the Philippines.

STEVE ROSENBERG

Sharks

Whitetip reef sharks are often found resting in caves and channels on the reef. The grey reef shark is less common but still found at several locations throughout the Philippines.

Although rarely a threat to divers or swimmers, if a shark feels threatened it may display aggressive behavior. Be sure to allow enough space for the shark to escape if you chance upon one in a confined space. Sharks will generally not attack unless provoked, so don't taunt, tease or feed them. Avoid spearfishing and carrying fish baits and your likelihood of being attacked will greatly diminish. Face and quietly watch any shark that is acting aggressively and be prepared to push it away with a camera, knife or tank. If someone is bitten by a shark, stop the bleeding, reassure the patient, treat for shock and seek immediate medical aid.

Jellyfish

ROBERT YIN

Several species of jellyfish are commonly found throughout the islands. Some cluster off the beaches in shallow, warm water (typically from March to May), and can be a nuisance for swimmers and snorkelers. Though only one species of box jellyfish is found in Philippine waters, it is not as poisonous as the Australian variety.

The fast spinning props of banca boats can mince the jellyfish into fine, invisible particles, each of which can still sting. Stings are often irritating and not painful, but should be treated immediately with a decontaminant such as vinegar, rubbing alcohol, baking soda, papain or dilute household ammonia. If none of these are immediately available, then gasoline or even Coca Cola can do the trick. Beware that some people may have a stronger reaction than others, in which case you should prepare to resuscitate and seek medical aid.

Stonefish

Hard to spot and prevalent throughout the islands, it is a wonder that more people are not seriously injured through contact with the chameleon-like stonefish.

SAMMY ANG

Able to inject venom through dorsal spines that can penetrate booties, wetsuits and leather gloves, the stonefish prefers to remain motionless amid the rocks while awaiting its prey. To treat a puncture, wash the wound and immerse it in nonscalding hot water for 30 to 90 minutes.

Triggerfish

STEVE ROSENBERG

Triggerfish are common throughout the Philippines. There are several species, all with the characteristic "trigger" along their back that they use to anchor themselves in crevices in the coral to stabilize themselves when feeding. Although not a threat to divers or swimmers most of the year, when they are breeding they can become extremely aggressive, and a bite from a triggerfish can be very nasty. Breeding seasons differ from region to region, so be sure to check with local divers before diving. Treat bites with antiseptics, anti-tetanus and antibiotics.

TIM ROCK

Seaweed Anemone

Like its more colorfully tentacled cousins, seaweed anemones deliver a poisonous sting to any unwary fish—or human—that brushes against it. Control your buoyancy and look carefully before placing your hands anywhere. If you do make contact with it, you will notice a burning, itchy sensation, and quite probably develop a slight rash in the area. Treat stings immediately with a decontaminant such as vinegar, rubbing alcohol, baking soda, papain or dilute household ammonia.

Sea Snakes

Often seen by divers but rarely a threat, banded sea snakes can be quite territorial, especially in the breeding season (most species breed between May and August). Sea snakes are air breathers and have to return to the surface to breathe. If you get between a snake and the surface, it could become agitated and bite. To treat a sea snake bite, use a pressure bandage and immobilize the victim. Try to identify the snake, be prepared to administer CPR and seek urgent medical aid.

ROBERT YIN

Diving Conservation & Awareness

SAMMY ANG

The Philippines was, until a few decades ago, rich in marine and timber resources. Unrestricted logging and overfishing—in many cases using illegal techniques such as dynamite, cyanide, *muro-ami* and drift netting—have seriously depleted forest, coastal and offshore resources. Coral bleaching resulting from the increased water temperatures of El Niño storm years has also stressed the marine ecosystem, although most reefs seem to have bounced back quickly from the effects.

Coastal waters are also stressed by the depletion of forests through extensive—and again, often illegal—logging, which causes the topsoil to wash away into the rivers and then onto the reefs, smothering them. Add to this water pollution, lack of education about sustainable fishing practices and a growing population hungry for seafood and you'll begin to understand why the Philippines has a long way to go before it can start redressing the destruction.

There is no shortage of regulations to protect the reefs and fisheries of the Philippines. Spearfishing by scuba divers was declared illegal some years ago, but the law has been relaxed to allow it in some designated areas. Fortunately, most dive operators have outlawed the practice at popular dive sites, having realized that one live fish is worth far more over its natural life span than the same fish dead on a dinner plate.

Dynamite fishing and muro-ami, fish collection using cyanide and the hunting of marine mammals and whale sharks are all banned, but still occur in many parts

Muro-Ami: Circle of Destruction

Perhaps the most distressing form of illegal fishing still practiced in the Philippines is *muro-ami*. Fishermen encircle a reef with nets, then bounce rocks attached to fishing lines across the reef, thereby scaring the fish into the nets. Throughout this process, young children free-dive over the reef, corralling the fish into the nets and then tying the nets together to trap the fish. The technique completely destroys the reef and spares none of the resident fish, whether edible or not.

In many parts of the country, muro-ami fishing has destroyed the majority of offshore reefs. Both environmentalists and child protection groups condemn this disgraceful practice. Unfortunately, the fleets of grimy stinkpots practicing this appalling technique continue to ply their unsavory trade, apparently protected by powerful politicians and unscrupulous businessmen.

TIM ROCK
Destroyed reefs can't support fish life.

of the country. Likewise, coral and shell collection is illegal, but tell that to the thousands of shell vendors lining the beaches and tourist traps of the Philippines—and to the subsistence fishermen who supply them.

The problem is manifold. On the one hand, many fishers don't understand that bombing a reef for fish to feed their families today will ensure that they go hungry tomorrow. On the other hand, businessmen and politicians who profit from the sale of fish and other marine products can buy or extort the protection they need to ensure that destructive fishing continues.

ERIC L WHEATER

Use of sustainable fishing practices will help preserve the reefs' vitality.

In between are the police and the military. These enforcement officials lack sufficient vessels to patrol the fishing grounds, don't have the mandate to educate fishers and lack the resources to chase after the big-shot bad guys. In all probability, some of these officers *are* the bad guys who supply the explosives used to blast the reefs to smithereens.

Various environmental groups and government agencies are now teaching communities about sustainable fishing practices and are establishing marine reserves so fish stocks can replenish. Divers with a love of the environment and a desire for pristine, protected reefs can also have a positive effect by supporting tourism industries as an alternative source of income for the locals. With this comes the impetus for locals to work with the dive centers to establish sanctuaries, to discourage fishing, to develop a healthier attitude about the environment and to pass this on to their children.

It's a long battle, and the odds seem stacked against the local environmentalists, but the more people that actively work to create a sustainable marine ecosystem, the greater the chances of turning the tide in favor of the planet, the oceans and ultimately the Filipino people themselves.

Responsible Diving

Dive sites are often located where the reefs and walls display the most beautiful corals and sponges. It only takes a moment—an inadvertently placed hand or knee, or a careless brush or kick with a fin—to destroy this fragile, living part of our delicate ecosystem. By following certain basic guidelines while diving, you can help preserve the ecology and beauty of the reefs:

1. Never drop boat anchors onto a coral reef and take care not to ground boats on coral. Encourage dive operators and regulatory bodies in their efforts to establish permanent moorings at appropriate dive sites.

2. Practice and maintain proper buoyancy control and avoid overweighting. Be aware that buoyancy can change over the period of an extended trip. Initially you may breathe harder and need more weighting; a few days later you may breathe more easily and need less weight. Tip: Use your weight belt and tank position to maintain a horizontal position—raise them to elevate your feet, lower them to elevate your upper body. Also be careful about buoyancy loss: As you go deeper, your wetsuit compresses, as does the air in your BC.

3. Avoid touching living marine organisms with your body and equipment. Polyps can be damaged by even the gentlest contact. Never stand on or touch living coral. The use of gloves is no longer recommended: Gloves make it too easy to hold on to the reef. The abrasion caused by gloves may be even more damaging to the reef than your hands are. If you must hold on to the reef, touch only exposed rock or dead coral.

4. Take great care in underwater caves. Spend as little time within them as possible, as your air bubbles can damage fragile organisms. Divers should take turns inspecting the interiors of small caves or under ledges to lessen the chances of damaging contact.

5. Be conscious of your fins. Even without contact, the surge from heavy fin strokes near the reef can do damage. Avoid full-leg kicks when diving close to the bottom and when leaving a photo scene. When you inadvertently kick something, stop kicking! It seems obvious, but some divers either panic or are totally oblivious when they bump something. When treading water in shallow reef areas, take care not to kick up clouds of sand. Settling sand can smother the delicate reef organisms.

6. Secure gauges, computer consoles and the octopus regulator so they're not dangling—they are like miniature wrecking balls to a reef.

7. When swimming in strong currents, be extra careful about leg kicks and handholds.

8. Photographers should take extra precautions, as cameras and equipment affect buoyancy. Changing f-stops, framing a subject and maintaining position for a photo often conspire to thwart the ideal "no-touch" approach on a reef. When you must use "holdfasts," choose them intelligently (e.g., use one finger only for leverage off an area of dead coral).

9. Resist the temptation to collect or buy coral or shells. Aside from the ecological damage, collection of marine souvenirs depletes the beauty of a site and spoils other divers' enjoyment.

10. Ensure that you take home all your trash and any litter you may find as well. Plastics in particular pose a serious threat to marine life.

11. Resist the temptation to feed fish. You may disturb their normal eating habits, encourage aggressive behavior or feed them food that is detrimental to their health.

12. Minimize your disturbance of marine animals. Don't ride on the backs of turtles or manta rays, as this can cause them great anxiety.

Listings

Telephone Calls

Though the Philippine telephone system was once notoriously unreliable, it has improved with the addition of cell phone technology. More islands are becoming connected each year. To call the Philippines from another country, dial the international access code of the country you are calling from + 63 (the Philippines' country code) + the local number (including the city code or cell phone prefix, listed below in parentheses). From within the Philippines, dial 0 + the local number (including the prefix).

Diving Services

The Philippine Commission on Sports Scuba Diving (www.pcssd.com.ph) registers and accredits dive establishments throughout the country. You can expect these dive shops to provide well-maintained and safe equipment, airfills and facilities. Most dive stores offer quality rental gear, though the selection may be limited on the smaller islands. Excellent certification programs (most often PADI) and competent, friendly, professional personnel are standard at most shops. Most operators offer Open Water referral courses, so you can complete the book and pool work at home and do the checkout dives in the Philippines.

Luzon

Aquatropical Sports
Barrio Ligaya, Mabini,
Anilao, Batangas
☎ (2) 522 2536

Aquaventure Philippines – Makati
7805 St. Paul, P.O. Box 758
Makati City, Metro Manila
☎ (2) 899 2831
fax: (2) 899 2551
aqua@aquaventure.com
www.aquaventure.com

Aquaventure Philippines – Pasig
Unit 6M, 8137 Plaza
Amber Dr., Ortigas Center
Pasig City, Metro Manila
☎ (2) 637 4317
fax: (2) 637 4340
aqua@aquaventure.com
www.aquaventure.com

Aquaventure Reef Club
Barrio Bagalangit,
Mabini, Anilao, Batangas
☎ (912) 254 7140
aqua@aquaventure.com
www.aquaventure.com

Blue Reef Adventure
149-H Aurora Blvd.
San Juan, Metro Manila
☎ (2) 726 4646 or 725 1521

Bonito Island
2/F LPL Mansions,
122 Alfaro St.
Salcedo Village,
Makati City, Metro Manila
☎ (2) 812 2292 or 812 2294

Coral Beach Dive Center
Matabungkay, Batangas
☎ (918) 903 5867

Dive Buddies Philippines
G/F Robelle Mansion Bldg.,
877 J.P. Rizal St.
Makati City, Metro Manila
☎ (2) 899 7388
fax: (2) 899 7393
divebuddies@divephil.com
www.divephil.com

Dive Republic
8 Divino Amore Bldg.,
Holy Spirit Dr.
Don Antonio Heights,
Quezon City, Metro Manila
☎ (2) 951 4760

Dive Shoppe
71-B Constancia Bldg.,
Timog Ave.
Quezon City, Metro Manila
☎ (2) 921 2020
fax: (2) 413 6737
dveshop@skyinet.net

Luzon (continued)

Divenet Philippines
2468 Bobcock St.
San Isidro, Makati City,
Metro Manila
☎ (2) 843 9359
fax: (2) 843 9326
divenet@pworld.net.ph

Dugong Dive Center
Euro-Pacific Resort
Taguig, Metro Manila
☎ (2) 838 4956
fax: (2) 838 4462

Eagle Point Resort
Mabini, Anilao, Batangas
☎ (918) 222 8466
fax: (43) 986 0177 to 0178
eaglept@i-manila.com.ph
www.eaglepoint.com.ph

Eureka Dive
Power Plant Mall, Store 316,
Rockwell Center
Makati City, Metro Manila
☎ (2) 756 0170
fax: (2) 756 0149
moteyza@eurekadive.com
www.eurekadive.com

Johan's Adventure & Wreck Dive Centre
Baloy Long Beach,
Bario Barretto
Onlongapo, Subic Bay
☎ (47) 224 8915 or
(45) 892 6852
sportad@mozcom.com

Nautilus Dive & Sport Center
839 A. Arnaiz St. (Pasay Rd.)
Midland Mansion, Unit I
Makati City, Metro Manila
☎ (2) 812 2848 or
(917) 792 8074
nautilusdive@surfshop.net.ph

Ocean Deep Diver Training Center
P.O. Box 180, San Fernando,
La Union
☎ (72) 888 4440
oceandp@sflu.com
www.oceandeep.ws

Oceancolors
G/F Cancio Bldg.,
1047 Metropolitan Ave.
Makati City, Metro Manila
☎ (2) 890 1785
fax: (2) 890 7765
bo@oceancolors.com

Pacific Blue
G/F #8 Asian Mansion II,
Dela Rosa St.
Legaspi Village, Makati City,
Metro Manila
☎ (2) 888 4521

Scuba World
1181 Vito Cruz Extension
Makati City, Metro Manila
☎ (2) 890 7805
fax: (2) 890 8982
info@scubaworld.com.ph

Subic Bay Aqua Sports
Bldg. 249, Waterfront Rd.
SBMA, Olongapo City,
Subic Bay
☎ (47) 252 7343 or 252 3005
fax: (47) 252 6084
sbas@svisp.com

Sunbeam Marine Sports Shop
Traders Hotel,
3001 Roxas Blvd., Manila
☎ (2) 729 4900

Sunbeam Marine Sports Shop
Balangit, Anilao, Batangas
☎ (2) 831 1328
fax: (2) 729 4900
sunbeam@broline.com

Undersea Scuba Adventures
Velasquez Bldg., Rizal Ave.,
Batangas City
☎ (43) 7230 367 or
(918) 902 1108

Philpan Diving Resort
Ligaya, Mabini, Anilao,
Batangas

Verde Island Resort
Pastor Ave., New Market Site,
Batangas City
☎ (43) 980 6149, 300 1924 or
723 2411
fax: (43) 980 5988
mukha@pworld.net.ph

Whitetip Divers
Joncor II Bldg., Units 206-210,
1362 A. Mabini St., Ermita,
Metro Manila
☎ (2) 521 0433
fax: (2) 522 1165
whitetip@mnl.sequel.net
www.whitetip.com

Mindoro

Action Divers
Small La Laguna Beach,
Puerto Galera
☎ (973) 751 968
fax: (973) 776 704
info@actiondivers.com
www.actiondivers.com

Asia Divers
El Galleon Beach Resort
Sabang Beach, Puerto Galera
☎ (973) 782 094
admin@asiadivers.com or
manila@asiadivers.com
www.asiadivers.com

Atlantis Resort Hotel & Dive Center
Sabang Beach, Puerto Galera
☎ (97) 349 7503, 723 9160,
(912) 308 0672 or
(973) 497 503
georg@atlantishotel.com
www.atlantishotel.com

Big Apple Beach Resort
Sabang Beach, Puerto Galera
☎ (912) 308 1120 or
899 6852 to 54
info@big-apple.com.ph or
big-apple@qinet.net
www.dive-bigapple.com

Capt'n Gregg's Dive Resort
Sabang Beach, Puerto Galera
☎ (973) 496 691
fax: (917) 754 5919
info@captngreggs.com.ph
www.captngreggs.ph

Mindoro (continued)

Cocktail Divers
Sabang Beach, Puerto Galera
☎ (912) 353 4177
cdiver@vasia.com
www.vasia.com/cdiver

Coral Cove Resort
Sabang Beach, Puerto Galera
coral-cove@asiagate.net
www.coral-cove.com/

Diver's Cove
Puerto Galera
☎ (917) 533 2985
fax: (917) 876 5902
diverco@globe.com.ph

Frontier Scuba
Sabang Beach, Puerto Galera
☎ (973) 490 095
fdivers@mozcom.com

La Laguna Beach Club
Big La Laguna Beach,
Puerto Galera
☎ (973) 878 409 or 855 545
lalaguna@llbc.com.ph
www.llbc.com.ph

Octopus Diver
P.O. Box 30413, Puerto Galera
☎ (917) 562 0160
info@octopusdivers.org
www.octopusdivers.org

Pacific Divers
White Beach, Puerto Galera
☎ (912) 270 9663

Philippine Divers Corp.
Cocobeach Island Resort,
Puerto Galera
☎ (912) 918 7994
tauchtom@batangas.i-next.net

Sabang Inn Beach Resort
Sabang Beach, Puerto Galera
☎ (912) 311 4335
sab-inn@mozcom.com

Scuba Triton
P.O. Box 36555, Hondura,
Puerto Galera
☎ (43) 442 0150
s.triton@dalcan.com
www.dalcan.com/triton/

Scubaplus
Small La Laguna Beach,
Puerto Galera
☎ (912) 388 4831
martin@scubaplus.com
www.scubaplus.com

Sea Explorers
Villa Estellita Beach,
Puerto Galera
☎ (917) 911 1442 or 911 3117
cebu@seaexplorersscuba.com or
seaexplorers@hotmail.com
www.seaexplorersscuba.com

Seoul Beach Club
Santo Nino, Puerto Galera
☎ (912) 367 6899 or
(919) 557 7677

South Sea Divers
Sabang Beach, Puerto Galera
☎ (912) 347 6993
dive@southseadivers.com
www.southseadivers.com

Triton Divers
Sabang Beach, Puerto Galera
☎ (917) 400 7616
tritondivers@mindoro.net

Whitetip Pandan
Pandan Island, Sablayan
info@pandan.com
www.whitetip.com

The Visayas

Alice in Wonderland Beach Resort
Manggayad, Boracay Island
☎ (36) 288 3278 or
(918) 750 0015
☎/fax: (36) 288 3330
alice@mediawars.ne.jp
www.aliceinwonderland.com.ph

Alona Divers
Alona Beach, Panglao, Bohol
☎ (38) 502 9043

Apo Island Diving Center
Dumaguete, Negros Oriental
☎ (35) 424 0388
apo@date.mozcom.com

Aqua Life Divers Academy
Manggayad, Boracay Island
☎ (36) 288 3276
fax: (36) 288 3414
aqualife@boracay.i-next.net

Aquarius Scuba Diving
Boracay Island
☎ (36) 288 3132
fax: (36) 288 3189
aquarius@boracay.i-next.net

Balicasag Island Dive Resort
Balicasag Island
Panglao, Bohol
☎ (912) 516 2675
sales@philtourism.com
www.philtourism.com

Beach Life Club
Boracay Island
☎ (36) 288 5211
fax: (36) 288 3495
blive@boracay.i-next.net

Big Dive Philippines Co.
Townhouse Unit 1,
S. Osmena St.
Gun-ob, Lapu-Lapu,
Mactan Island
☎ (32) 231 5061 or 340 7784

Bituon Beach Resort
Basdio Guindulman, Bohol
☎ (918) 600 0408
bituon@wtal.de

Blue Coral
c/o White Sands,
Maribago Beach
Maribago, Mactan Island
☎ (32) 341 0247
fax: (32)495 8063
alvin@bluecoraldive.com

Blue Coral Scuba Diving School
South Sea Resort, Bantayan
Dumaguette, Negros Oriental
☎ (32) 341 0247
alvin@bluecoraldive.com

The Visayas (continued)

Blue Coral Scuba Diving School & Tours
Bohol Tropics Hotel
Tagbilaran City, Bohol
☎ (32) 341 0247
alvin@bluecoraldive.com

Blue Depth Dive Resort
Cantutang, Padre Burgos,
Southern Leyte

Bohol Beach Club
Alona Beach, Panglao, Bohol
☎ (32) 340 5936,
(38) 411 5222 to 5225 or (912) 516 3866
fax: (38) 411 5226
bbclub@mozcom.com or
salesdirector@tambuli.com
www.tambuli.com

Bohol Divers Lodge
Alona Beach, Panglao, Bohol
☎ (38) 502 9050
fax: (38) 502 9048
dive@phildivers.com
www.boholdivers.com

Calypso Diving
Boracay Island
☎ (36) 288 3206
fax: (36) 288 3478
calypso@boracay.i-next.net
www.calypsodiving.ph

Captain Nemo's Nautilus Diving
Tawala, Panglao, Bohol
☎/fax: (38) 501 8991

Cebu el Acuario Divers – Dumaguete
Tapon Norte Wuthering Heights
Beach Resort
San Jose, Negros Oriental
☎ (35) 417 0440
hpitokyo@tky3.3web.ne.jp

Cebu el Acuario Divers – Mactan
c/o CMMC Cebu Seaside Beach
Resort, Looc, Maribago
Lapu-Lapu, Mactan Island
☎ (32) 495 8060 or 495 8061

Cocktail Divers
c/o Yhalasan Beach
Mangnao, Dumaguete,
Negros Oriental
☎ (912) 891 2006
cdiver@vasia.com
www.vasia.com/cdiver

Coral Point Dive House
Buyong Beach, Lapu-Lapu,
Mactan Island
☎ (32) 411 4436 or
(912) 501 3149

Coral Point Dive House
Bilisan, Panglao, Bohol
☎ (38) 411 3915 or 411 2958
fax: (38) 411 3433

Crispina Aquatics
Costabella Tropical Beach Resort
Buyong Beach, Lapu-Lapu,
Mactan Island
☎ (917) 925 5473
fax: (917) 875 6249
dannyalmaden@eircom.net

Davliz Scuba Center
Cantutang, Padre Burgos,
Southern Leyte

Emerald Green Diving
P.O. Box 29
Lapu-Lapu, Mactan Island
☎ (918) 773 0833
fax: (32) 495 7864

Far East Scuba Institute
Barrio Balabag, Boracay Island
☎ (36) 288 3223
fesi@iloilo.net

Fisheye Divers Corp.
Balabag, Boracay Island
☎ (36) 288 6090
fax: (36) 288 6082
info@fisheyedivers.com

Get Crackin'
SuperCat Terminal Pier 4,
Reclamation Area
Cebu City, Cebu
☎ (32) 232 6669
fax: (32) 412 9715
getcrackincebu@bizlinks.net.ph

Guard-Dive Shop
Buyong Beach, Lapu-Lapu,
Mactan Island

IDC Boracay
Boracay Island
☎ (919) 554 9800
georgewegmann@hotmail.com
or dsafari@boracay.i-next.net
www.diving.itgo.com

Kawayan Marine Dive Shop
Santo Nino, Malabuyoc, Cebu
☎ (918) 773 8624
fax: (32) 261 6367

Kiwi Dive Resort
Sandugan Beach
Larena, Siquijor
☎ (912) 504 0596
fax: (35) 424 0534
kiwi@fil.net

Kon-Tiki Resort
Maribago Beach
Cebu City, Cebu
☎ (36) 288 3337
fax: (36) 288 3531
info@kontikispa.com
www.kontikispa.com

Malapascua – Exotic Island Dive Resort
P.O. Box 1200
Malapascua Island, Cebu
☎ (918) 774 0484
info@malapascua.net
www.malapascua.net

Malapascua Island Dive Center
Logon, Malapscua Island, Cebu
☎ (38) 502 9050
fax: (38) 502 9048
stay@boholdivers.com
www.boholdivers.com

Marine Village Dive Shop
Lower Liloan, Cebu
☎ (35) 225 2426 or
(918) 740 0785

Neptune Diving Unlimited
Panagsama Beach
Moalboal, Cebu
☎/fax: (32) 474 0087
info@neptunediving.com
www.neptunediving.com

Ocean Field Diving College
101-AB EGI Bldg., Maribago
Lapu-Lapu, Mactan Island
☎ (32) 411 4441
fax: (32) 340 8115
info@ofjam.com
www.ofjam.com

The Visayas (continued)

Ocean Field International Dive Center
P.O. Box 119 (beside Tamburi), Maribago
Lapu-Lapu, Mactan Island
☎ (32) 492 3900
fax: (32) 231 5098

Ocean Safari Philippines II
Panagsama Beach
Moalboal, Cebu
☎ (918) 772 1873
panagsama@hotmail.com

Paradive Scuba Diving Resort
Buot Punta Engano
Lapu-Lapu, Mactan Island
☎ (32) 340 9234
fax: (32) 340 0234
paradive@dateinternet.com

P.C. Divers
c/o Pacific Cebu Resort, Subabasbas
Lapu-Lapu, Mactan Island
☎ (32) 340 5982 or 340 5984
pcri@cebu.iqnet.net

Peter's Dive Resort
Lungsodaan, Padre Burgos, Southern Leyte
☎ (919) 585 3891
scuberph@yahoo.com
www.whaleofadive.com

Polaris Dive Center
Pantudian
Cabilao Island, Bohol
☎ (918) 773 77681
fax: (32) 253 0265
info@atpolarisdive.com

Prosafari Diving & Education
Alona Beach, Panglao, Bohol
☎/fax: (38) 502 9122
info@prosafari.com
www.prosafari.com

PSQ Divers
c/o Cebu Beach Club
Buyong Beach, Maribago
Lapu-Lapu, Mactan Island
☎ (915) 203 2525 or (32) 340 8034
psq@skyinet.net

Pulchra
P&I Resort, San Isidro
San Fernando, La Union
☎ (32) 232 0823 to 25
fax: (32) 232 0816

Punta Cruz Diving Club
Punta Cruz, Maribojoc, Bohol
☎ (38) 411 2338 or 255 4114

Ryo Marine Diving Center
Buyong Beach, Maribago
Lapu-Lapu, Mactan Island
☎ (32) 495 8100 or (912) 895 9757

Sampaguita Resort & Diving Center
11 Somiso d'Oriente, Tonggo Point
Moalboal, Cebu
☎ (32) 474 0066
fax: (32) 474 0065

Savedra Dive Center
Panagsama Beach
Moalboal, Cebu
(32) 474 0014 or 474 0011
moalboal@savedra.com
www.savedra.com

Sazanami Marine Sports
c/o Hadsan Beach Resort, Agus
Lapu-Lapu, Mactan Island
☎ (32) 254 0568 or 261 2349
fax: (32) 254 0745

Scotty's Dive Center
Shangri-La's Mactan Island Resort
Punta Engana Rd.
Lapu-Lapu, Mactan Island
☎ (32) 231 0288
dive@divescotty.com
www.divescotty.com

Scuba World – Boracay
Barangay Balabag, near Boat Station 1, Boracay Island
☎/fax: (36) 288 3310
boracay@scubaworld.com.ph
www.scubaworld.com.ph

Scuba World – Cebu City
800 Maria Cristina St., Capitol Site, Cebu City, Cebu
☎ (32) 254 9554
fax: (32) 254 9591
swi-cebu@skyinet.net
www.scubaworld.com.ph

Scuba World – Dumaluan
c/o Dumaluan Beach Resort
Panglao Island, Bohol
☎/fax: (32) 254 9591
cebu@scubaworld.com.ph
www.scubaworld.com.ph

Scuba World – Mactan Island
Hadsan Cove Resort, Agus
Lapu-Lapu, Mactan Island
☎ (32) 340 5938
fax: (32) 231 6009
swi-cebu@skyinet.net
www.scubaworld.com.ph

Scuba World – Plantation Bay
c/o Plantation Bay – Mactan Marigondon
Mactan Island
☎ (32) 340 5900
fax: (32) 340 5988
swi-cebu@skyinet.net
www.scubaworld.com.ph

Sea Explorers
Alona Tropical Beach Resort
Alona Beach, Panglao Island, Bohol
☎/fax: (38) 502 9035
cebu@seaexplorersscuba.com
www.seaexplorersscuba.com

Sea Explorers
Cabilao Beach Resort
Cabilao Island, Bohol
☎ (918) 740 0033
cebu@seaexplorersscuba.com
www.seaexplorersscuba.com

Sea Explorers
Dauin, Negros Oriental
☎ (35) 424 0238 or (918) 740 0033
fax: (35) 225 7725
cebu@seaexplorersscuba.com
www.seaexplorersscuba.com

Sea Explorers
Love's Lodge, Panagsama Beach
Moalboal, Cebu
☎ (918) 740 0033
cebu@seaexplorersscuba.com
www.seaexplorersscuba.com

Sea Explorers
Tubod, San Juan, Siquijor
☎ (918) 740 0033
cebu@seaexplorersscuba.com
www.seaexploreresscuba.com

The Visayas (continued)

Sea Gaia
Boat Station 1
Balabag, Boracay Island
☎ (36) 288 3661
fax: (36) 288 3662
funny@soeinet.or.jp
www.nkansai.ne.jp/org/pro-ject7/seagaia/seagaia.htm

Sea World Dive Center
Balabag, Boracay Island
☎ (36) 288 3033
fax: (36) 288 3032
seaworld@boracay.i-next.net

Seaquest Dive Center
Alona Beach
Panglao Island, Bohol
☎ (32) 346 9629
fax: (32) 346 0592
seaquest@sequestdivecenter.com
www.seaquestdivecenter.com

Seaquest Dive Center
Panagsama Beach
Moalboal, Cebu
☎ (32) 349 9629
fax: (32) 346 0592
seaquest@sequestdivecenter.com
www.seaquestdivecenter.com

Sierra Madre Divers
c/o Bohol Tropics
Tagbilaran, Bohol
☎ (915) 707 0669
fax: (912) 720 0078

Splash – the Dive Center
c/o Coco Grove Beach Resort
Tubod, San Juan
☎ (918) 740 4092

Tambuli Beach Club & Villa
Buyong Beach, Mactan Island
☎ (32) 340 5936, 232 4811 or 253 7901 fax: (32) 253 1545 or 495 7718
☎/fax: (32) 232 4913
tambuli@mozcom.com or cbclub@mozcom.com
www.tambuli.com

Tharsis Marine Dive Shop
Bagumbayan, Maribago
Lapu-Lapu, Mactan Island
☎ (32) 495 7698

Triple "S" Divers
Buyong Beach
Lapu-Lapu, Mactan Island
☎ (32) 492 0111

Tropical Island Adventure Dive Shop
(L&M Ross) Buyong Beach
Lapu-Lapu, Mactan Island
☎ (36) 231 0501 or 340 1845
fax: (32) 340 5909

Tropical Island Divers
Buyong Beach, Maribago
Lapu-Lapu, Mactan Island
☎ (32) 340 1845 or 340 6909
tiacebu@skyinet.net

Victory Divers
Boracay Island
☎/fax: (36) 288 3209
boracay@victory-divers.de
www.victory-divers.de

Visaya Divers
Panagsama Beach
Moalboal, Cebu
☎ (32) 474 0018 or (918) 771 1853
☎/fax: (32) 474 0019
quavadisb.r@skinet.net
www.moalboal.com

Whitetip Divers – Dumaguete
Harold's Mansion,
205 Hibbard Ave.
Tubod, Dumaguete,
Negros Oriental
☎ (35) 225 2381
whitetip@mozcom.com

Mindanao

Amphibian
Stall IA, VAL Learning Village
Ruby St.,
Marfoni Heights Subdivision
Davao
☎ (82) 227 2049

City Shack Corp.
PPA Bldg.
Santa Ana Wharf, Davao City
☎ (82) 227 6175

Genesis Divers
Caves Resort
Agoho, Camiguin Island
☎/fax: (88) 387 9063
genesisc@cebu.weblinq.com
www.genesisdivers.com

Mantangale Alibuag Dive Center
Lapasan Highway
Cagayan de Oro
☎ (8822) 722 591
fax: (88) 856 2324
mantadive@col.com.ph

Tuna City Scuba Center
Lautengco Bldg., Quirino Ave.
General Santos City
☎ (83) 554 5681 or (917) 330 1237
divegensan@gslink.net

Whitetip Divers – Davao
PPA Bldg., Santa Ana Wharf
Davao City
☎ (82) 222 1721 or 227 6175
ctshack@dv.weblinq.com
www.whitetip.com

Palawan

Aquaventure in Pamalican
Pamalican Island
☎ (2) 759 4040 or 899 2551
aqua@aquaventure.com
www.aquaventure.com

Bacuit Diver Services
El Nido Town Proper

Club Noah Isabelle
Apulit Island
Taytay, Puerto Princesa City
☎ (48) 433 5756 to 5757 or 810 7291 fax: (48) 433 5755
clubnoah@i-manila.com.ph
www.clubnoah.com.ph

Palawan (continued)

Discovery Divers
Barangay 5
Coron City, Busuanga,
Northern Palawan
☎ (2) 912 4868
ddivers@vasia.com
www.vasia.com/ddivers

Dive & Let Live
Moana Hotel
Rizal Ave., Puerto Princesa City
☎ (48) 433 4892
ponnetpeter@hotmail.com

Dive Right – Coron
LM Pe Lodge, Barangay 3
Coron City, Busuanga,
Northern Palawan
☎ (45) 892 0332
diving@mozcom.com

Diving El Busero
P.O. Box 18
Puerto Princesa City
☎/fax: (48) 433 6101

Sangat Island Reserve
Sangat (Tangat) Island,
Northern Palawan
☎ (873) 763 0024 (satellite)
info@sangat.com.ph
www.sangat.com.ph

Scuba Venture
Barangay 3
Coron City, Busuanga,
Northern Palawan
sventure@mozcom.com

Sea Dive Center
Sea Breeze Lodge
Coron City, Busuanga,
Northern Palawan
seadive@starnet.net.ph

Live-Aboards

A wide range of vessels serves divers in search of pristine diving around remote reefs and atolls. You'll find luxurious custom dive boats, local fishing boats converted into no-frills dive boats and even oversized banca boats plying Philippine waters year-round, carrying divers on two- to 10-day live-aboard trips.

MV *Eagle 5*
P.O. Box 1587, Manila
☎ (2) 715 2124 fax: (2) 713 8882
eagle@diver.com.ph
www.eagleoffshore.com.ph
Home Port: Subic
Description: 32m (107ft)
Destinations: Sulu Sea, Palawan, Visayas, Sibuyan Sea
Accommodations: 6 air-conditioned and 3 fan cooled twin-share cabins, 3 heads and showers with hot and cold water
Other: Custom trips, O_2, diving & fishing equipment, deck crane, shark cat chase boat

Island Explorer
Scuba World
1181 Vito Cruz Extension
Makati City, Metro Manila
☎ (2) 895 3551, 890 7805 or 890 7807
fax: (2) 890 8982
Mailing Address: MCPO Box 2815, Makati City, Metro Manila
info@scubaworld.com.ph
www.scubaworld.com.ph
Home Port: Batangas
Description: 36m (116ft) steel monohull
Destinations: March-June, Tubbataha and Sulu Sea; July-Feb., Mindoro, Visayas and Sibuyan Sea
Accommodations: Fully air-conditioned interiors, 8 twin-share cabins with private toilet & bath, 5 twin-share cabins with common toilet & bath, 4 open rinse showers on deck
Other: 7-day trips, custom trips, E6 processing, diving equipment, library

MY *Jinn Sulu*
Queen Anne Palawan, c/o Trattoria Terrace
353 Rizal Ave., Puerto Princesa City, Palawan
☎ (48) 433 9344
www.queenannedivers.com
Home Port: Puerto Princesa
Description: 17m (55ft)
Destinations: April-June, Tubbataha Reefs; Aug.-March, Northern Palawan (Honda Bay and Turtle Bay)
Accommodations: 4 twin-share cabins
Other: Custom trips, diving equipment

Oceanic Explorer
Scuba World, 1181 Vito Cruz Extension
Makati City, Metro Manila
☎ (32) 895 3551, 890 7805 or 890 7807
fax: (32) 890 8982
Mailing Address: MCPO Box 2815, Makati City, Metro Manila
info@scubaworld.com.ph
www.scubaworld.com.ph
Home Port: Manila
Description: 38m (127ft) steel monohull
Destinations: March-June, Tubbataha and Sulu Sea; July-Feb., Mindoro, Visayas and Sibuyan Sea

Live-Aboards (continued)

Accommodations: Fully air-conditioned interiors, 12 twin-share cabins with private toilet & bath, 5 twin-share cabins with common toilet & bath, 4 open rinse showers on deck
Other: 7-day trips, custom trips, E6 processing, diving equipment, library

MY *Southern Cruise*
c/o Shemberg Marketing Corp.
Paknaan, Mandaue, Cebu City
☎ (32) 345 1040 or 346 0789
fax: (32) 346 0863
shemberg@bizlinks.net.ph
www.philexport.org/dacay/cruise.htm
Home Port: Cebu Yacht Club
Description: 50m (165ft) steel hull
Destination: March-June, Sulu Sea and Puerto Princessa; July-Feb., Visayan Triangle (Moalboal, Dumaguete, Negros, Leyte, Cebu and Bohol)
Accommodations: All rooms fully air-conditioned. 1 master's cabin and 2 twin-share cabins with private bath, 1 quad-share cabin and 6 eight-berth cabins with shared baths
Others: 3-day trips, custom trips, diving equipment

MY *Svetlana*
c/o Dakak Park Beach Resort
Taguilon, Dapitan City, Mindanao
☎ (918) 595 0714 or 595 0716
www.divephil.com/liveabs/svetlana/
Home Port: Zamboanga
Description: 34m (110ft) steel hull
Destinations: March-June, Tubbataha Reefs, Jessie Beazly and Basterra; June-Nov., Aliguay, Silinog, Apo, Pescador, Panglao, Sumilon and Balicasag; the Spratly Islands (a.k.a. Kalayaan Islands, South China Sea) and Turtle Islands (south of Palawan) upon request
Accommodations: 6 air-conditioned twin-share cabins with individual bath
Others: Custom trips

MY *Tabibuga*
14 Dona Juana Rodriguez St.
New Manila, Quezon City
☎ (36) 288 5041 or (919) 554 9800
georgewegmann@hotmail.com
www.divegurus.com
Home Port: Boracay
Description: 22m (72ft)
Destinations: Sulu Sea and Palawan
Accommodations: 4 fan-cooled twin-share cabins, 2 toilets & 1 shower with hot and cold water
Other: Custom trips, diving equipment, library

MY *Tristar*
UG 48 Cityland Pasong Tamo Cond.
6264 Estacion St., Barangay Pio del Pilar
Makati City, Metro Manila
☎ (2) 752 2552, 844 7054, 844 5159
info@divetristar.com
www.divetristar.com
Home Port: Manila
Description: 33m (108ft) steel hull
Destinations: March-June, Tubbataha Reefs; June-Feb., Batangas, Mindoro, Sulu Sea and Palawan; special cruises to Apo Reef, Coron, Visayas and Donsol
Accommodations: 6 twin-share and 2 five-berth cabins, 1 stateroom with private bath
Other: Custom trips, diving equipment

Tourist Ofices

The Philippine Department of Tourism (DOT) is the official division of Philippine tourism. The main DOT center in Manila has helpful staff, but you don't need to load up with brochures and handouts there—regional outlets usually have anything the head office has, and the information may be more up-to-date.

You can find regional offices in Bacolod, Baguio, Boracay, Butuan, Cagayan de Oro, Cebu City, Cotobato, Davao, Iloilo City, Laoag, Legaspi City, San Fernando (La Union), San Fernando (Pampanga), Tacloban, Tuguegarao and Zamboanga. The DOT website lists the addresses of regional and international offices.

Philippine Department of Tourism Main Office
DOT Bldg., T.M. Kalaw St., Ermita, Metro Manila
☎ (32) 524 2345 or 525 6114 fax: (32) 524 8321 or 521 1088
ncr@tourism.gov.ph
www.tourism.gov.ph

Index

dive sites covered in this book appear in **bold** type

A

accommodations 22
Agutaya Reef 117
air travel 16, 18-19, 33
***Akitsushima* 141**
Alona Beach 14
Amadora's 128
Amos Rock 133
Angeles City 25
Anilao 51-58
Apo Island 103
Apo Reef 14, 139-140
Aquarium, The 118
Arco Point 110

B

Bajura 55
Balicasag 108-109
Baluarte 113
Banayan Point 150
banca boats 35
Banton Big Rock Coral Garden 74
Banton Northwest Wall 74-75
Banton Southeast Wall 75
Barracuda Lake 146
Barracuda Point 128
Basterra North Reef 135
Basterra South Wall 136
Beatrice Rock 54-55
Big La Laguna Beach 65
Binangaan Drop-Off 139
Black Buoy 44
Black Coral 154
Black Forest 109
Black Island Wreck 145
Black Rock 134-135
Bohol 27-28, 104-111
Boracay 26, 76-83
business hours 22
Busuanga *see* Coron

C

Caban Cove 57
Cabilao Island 14, 105-107
Cabuan Point 119
Calamian Group *see* Coron
Calong Calong 102
Camiguin 29, 116-128
Canyons 69-70
Capitancillo Island 89
Cathedral Cave 78
Cathedral Rock 53-54
Cathedral, The 97
Caves, The 45-46
cave dives 44, 45, 56, 57, 67, 69, 78, 86, 96, 100, 110, 114, 123, 148, 154, 157
Cebu 26, 89-93
Centers for Disease Control 31
certification 36
Cervera Shoal 111
Chocolate Hills 28
climate 15
Concepcion Wreck 141
conservation 163-165
Constancia Reef 120
Copton Point 95
Coral Gardens 65
Coron 14, 29, 137-146
Corregidor 24
Crocodile Island 80-81

D

DAN 33
Davao 29, 121-126
deep diving 79
***Delsan* wreck 134**
Dilumacad 148
Dimakya Island 145-146
dining 22-23
Diver's Alert Network *see* DAN
diving services 35, 166-172
Dog Drift 83
Donsol 14, 59
***Doña Marilyn* wreck 85**
drift diving 43
Dumaguete 27, 98-103

E, F, G

East Pandan 156
***El Capitan* 50**
El Nido 14, 30, 147-150
electricity 20
emergency facilities *see* health
entry 19
environmental concerns 34, 163-165
Ernie's Cave 67
Fagg Reef 42
Fishbowl, The 43-44
Flying Boat Tender 141
food 22-23
Friday's Rock 80
Gato Island 86-87
General Santos 29, 127-129
geography 9, 13

H

Hammerhead Point 105-107
Happy Wall 110
hazardous marine life 161-162
health 31-33
Helen's Garden 156
Hell Ship, The 48
Henry's Reef 157
Hill, The 65
history 11-13
Hole in the Wall (Bohol) **110**
Hole in the Wall (Mindoro) **68**
Hole, The 88
Honda Bay 30
Hot Springs 58
House Reef 95-96
Hunter's Rock 140

I, J, K

icons 37
Inambuyod Boulders 148
Irako 144
jellyfish 161
Jessie Beazley 132
Jigdup Shoal 118
Kalipayan 110
Kogyu Maru 143
Kon Tiki House Reef 92-93

L

La Union 40-46
language 15-16
Laurel Island 81-82
Lau-Tengco Point 128
Leyte 28
Ligid Caves 123
Liloan 101
Linosutan Coral Gardens 126
Lionfish Cave 97
listings 166-173
live-aboards 36-37, 172-173
Lusong Gunboat 142
Luzon 24, 40-59

M

Mactan Island 89-93
Maestre de Campo Island 73-74
Maharlika Beach Resort 128
Mainit 57
Malapascua Island 84-89
Malipano Japanese Wrecks 126
Mamiya Maru 142
Manila 16, 24
Manila Channel 64
maps
- Anilao dive sites 52
- Bohol dive sites 104
- Boracay dive sites 76
- Camiguin dive sites 116
- Coron dive sites 138
- Davao dive sites 122
- Dumaguete dive sites 99
- El Nido dive sites 147
- General Santos dive sites 127
- Highlights 14
- Index 39
- La Union dive sites 41
- Locator 9
- Mactan Island & Cebu City dive sites 90
- Malapascua dive sites 84
- Mindoro dive sites 61
- Moalboal dive sites 94
- Port Barton dive sites 152
- Puerto Princesa & Honda Bay dive sites 155
- Sibuyan Sea dive sites 72
- Southern Leyte dive sites 112
- Subic Bay dive sites 47
- Sulu Sea dive sites 131

Mapating 56
Marigondon Cave 93
marine life 158-160
Marissa 1, 2 & 3 125
Max Climax Wall 113
measurement system 20
medical facilities *see* health
Medina Underwater Springs 118
Middle Rock 152
Mindanao 29, 115-129
Mindoro 25-26, 60-71
Miniloc Island 149
Moalboal 93-98
Monad Shoal 87-88
money 19
Monkey Beach 66-67
muro-ami 163
Mushroom Rock 125
MV *Mactan* 14, 73-74

N

Napaling 107
Napantaw Fish Sanctuary 114
Nasog Point 83
Negros 27
North Wall 139
Northwest Channel 64
Nuñez Shoal 89

O

***Oceanic II* wreck** 135
Olympia Maru 142
Ormoc Shoal 89
Oryoku Maru 48

P

Palawan 29-30, 137-157

Pamilacan Island 111
Panagsama Beach 95-96
Paradise Canyon 118
People's Park in the Sky 25
Pescador Island 14, 96-97
Peter's Mound 114
photography 21-22
Pindawon Wall 124
Pink Wall 69-70
Pinnacle Point 124
population 11
Port Barton 150-154
Puerto Galera 25-26, 60-71
Puerto Princesa 30, 154-157
Punta Bonga 1 & 2 79-80
Punta Diwata 119

R

recompression facilities 33
Red Buoy 43-44
religion 11
Research Reef 45-46
responsible diving 164-165
Rio's Wall 114
Royalist Shoal 153
Rudy's Rock 109

S

safety 11, 17, 31-33, 38
Sangat *see* Tangat
***San Quintin* 51**
sea snakes 162
seaweed anemone 162
Sepok Wall 56
Shark Cave 69
Shark Point (Port Barton) **152**
Shark Point (Capitancillo Island) **88**
Shark Ridge 139
sharks 161
shopping 23, 24
shore dives 57, 65, 80, 91-93, 95, 97, 107, 113, 114, 128, 144-146, 156, 157
Sibuyan Sea 72-75
Sinandigan Wall 70
Sipaka Point 120
snorkeling 35-36
Sombrero Island 54-55
South Miniloc 149
Southern Leyte 112-114
Southwest Cabilao 106-107
St. Paul's Subterranean River 30
stonefish 161-162
Subic Bay 14, 25, 46-51
Sulu Sea 130-136
Sumilon Island 100
Sunken Island 98
sunken treasure 64
supplies 20-21, 31-32

T

Taal Lake 25
Tacot 101-102
***Tae Maru* 141**
Tagaytay Ridge 25
Talipanan Reef 63
Tambuli Fish-Feeding Station 91
Tampuan 128
Tangat Gunboat 144
Tangat Wreck 143
Tangkaan Point 113-114
Tangnan Wall 107
technical diving 36
telephone calls 166
Ten Fathoms 153
thresher sharks 88
time 20
Tinoto Wall 128
Tongo Point 97-98
Toshi's Wall 114
tourist offices 173
training 36
transportation 16-19, 35
travel *see* transportation
travel advisories 11
Tres Marias 149
triggerfish 162
***Tristar B* wreck 135**
Tubbataha North 132-133
Tubbataha Reefs 14, 132-135
Tubbataha South 134-135
Twin Rocks (El Nido) **149**
Twin Rocks (Puerto Princesa) **156**
typhoons 15

U, V

underwater photography 21-22
USS *New York* 49-50
Verano Rocks 156
Verde Island Wall 14, 71
Visayas, The 26-28, 76-114
VOA Reef 45

W

Washing Machine 70-71
water temperature 34
weather *see* climate
West Escarceo 67
whale sharks 14, 59
Wilson Head 154
wreck diving 48
wreck dives 42, 48-51, 64, 66, 73, 85, 91, 126, 132, 134, 135, 139, 141-145, 156
Wreck of the *Doña Marilyn* 85

Y

Yapak 78-79